From Tragedy to Triumph

*The Politics Behind the Rescue
of Ethiopian Jewry*

MITCHELL G. BARD

 PRAEGER

Westport, Connecticut
London

Library of Congress Cataloging-in-Publication Data

Bard, Mitchell Geoffrey, 1959–
    From tragedy to triumph : the politics behind the rescue of Ethiopian Jewry /
  Mitchell G. Bard
        p. cm.
    Includes bibliographical references (p.) and index.
    ISBN 0–275–97000–0 (alk. paper)
    1. Jews—Ethiopia—History. 2. Jews—Ethiopia—Migrations. 3. Operation Moses,
  1984–1985. 4. Operation Solomon, 1991. 5. Ethiopia—Emigration and immigration.
  6. Israel—Emigration and immigration. 7. Israel—Ethnic relations. I. Title.
  DS135.E75B37 2002
  963′.00924—dc21   2001057736

British Library Cataloguing in Publication Data is available.

Library of Congress Catalog Card Number: 2001057736
ISBN: 0–275–97000–0

First published in 2002

Praeger Publishers, 88 Post Road West, Westport, CT 06881
An imprint of Greenwood Publishing Group, Inc.
www.praeger.com

Printed in the United States of America

∞™

The paper used in this book complies with the
Permanent Paper Standard issued by the National
Information Standards Organization (Z39.48–1984).

10 9 8 7 6 5 4 3 2 1

This book is dedicated to the Ethiopian Jews who remained committed to their faith and the return to Zion for centuries, the American activists who worked tirelessly and selflessly on their behalf, and the courageous Israelis who rescued them.

Contents

Acknowledgments   ix

Introduction   xi

CHAPTER 1   Who Are the Ethiopian Jews?   1

CHAPTER 2   The Big Picture: Ethiopia in Israel's
             Foreign Policy   25

CHAPTER 3   A New Opening in Ethiopia   39

CHAPTER 4   Early Rescue Efforts   59

CHAPTER 5   Escape to the Sudan   83

CHAPTER 6   American Pressure   105

CHAPTER 7   A Trickle of Jews   125

CHAPTER 8   Operation Moses   143

CHAPTER 9   Operations Sheba and Solomon   161

CHAPTER 10   The Holocaust Analogy   177

CHAPTER 11   The Situation Today   189

Selected Bibliography   207

Index   209

Acknowledgments

I am particularly grateful to Howard Lenhoff for his invaluable contribution to this project. He allowed me unfettered use of his extensive archive of material on the Ethiopian Jews, provided insight and guidance, as well as his own personal knowledge of events. In particular, I want to thank him for his inspiration to pursue the topic, his unswerving devotion to the cause of the Ethiopian Jews, to telling the truth about the politics behind their rescue, and for setting an example for the scholarly investigation of the subject.

I would also like to thank the AAEJ for the grant to Howard that made it possible for me to conduct much of the research contained in this book and to travel to Washington and Israel to conduct interviews with many of the key players. The AAEJ did not attach any conditions to the grant and placed no restrictions on the research. It also did not review or have any role in the preparation of the manuscript.

I also want to acknowledge the University of California at Irvine, which employed me as a postdoctoral fellow and provided office space during which time I conducted much of the research for this book.

I also want to thank the Irving Louis Horowitz Foundation for Social Policy for its generous support of this project.

Unless otherwise noted, private correspondence cited in the book was obtained from the Lenhoff archive and used with his permission.

Introduction

In many corners distant from the centers of Judaism, tens of thousands of our brothers have remained isolated from Judaism for hundreds of years where their numbers have diminished, many have become assimilated among those in whose midst they dwelt, and those who remain are exposed to assimilation and disappearance for the lack of new forces to infuse them with a stream of Jewish life.

One of these remote corners is Abyssinia, far from the center of Jewish life, where, for more than 2,000 years, tens of thousands of Jews have lived, who, despite the trials and tribulations they endured, have remained faithful to their faith and people. But in the course of time, all ties with the large Jewish world have been cut off, so that their numbers are growing ever small, conversion to Christianity endangers them, and even those who remain Jews are in a deteriorated physical and spiritual state, and many sections of the Torah have been forgotten and the crisis of physical and spiritual extinction threatens.

Brethren, please rescue our brothers, the Falashas, from extinction. Please help restore to us these cast-off brothers of ours, so that a tribe of Israel may not disappear. Rescue 50,000 souls of the house of Israel, and thus strengthen our people. The Rock of Israel will come to Israel's aid and will gather our dispersed from the four corners of the earth, that they may come with song to the heights of Zion and bow before the Lord in the holy mountain in Jerusalem.

—Israeli Chief Rabbi Isaac Kook[1]

In 1984, 1985, and 1991, Israel dramatically rescued thousands of Ethiopian Jews in large-scale, secret airlifts. Thousands more were brought to Israel in other ways including government-run covert operations, exchanges for arms, and open immigration. These operations represent the triumph in the story of the politics behind the rescue of Ethiopian Jews and illustrate what Israel can do when Jewish lives are at stake. While other countries turned a blind eye to the suffering of the thousands of refugees in the Sudan, Israel took action. Mossad agents, and Ethiopian Jews from Israel working for them, risked their lives to save other Jews in the tradition of *pikuach nefesh*. As the Talmud says, to save one life is as if one saved the entire human race. The exploits of the agents involved in the rescue were truly heroic. The U.S. government also played an important role, especially in Operation Sheba, after public disclosures undermined the Israeli operations. It was an instance in which an American administration placed humanitarian concerns above national interests.

Israel's effort to bring an ancient Jewish community to its homeland also reinvigorated the *raison d'être* of Zionism that Golda Meir expressed when she said, "There is no Zionism except the rescue of Jews."[2] Jews in Israel and around the world expected the response. As Yehuda Dominitz, head of the immigration department of the Jewish Agency related, "If someone told Ugandan refugees a plane was going to pick them up, they wouldn't believe it. . . . The Ethiopian Jews did believe it."[3] The Ethiopian Jews, and Jews around the world, knew that Israel would answer the call made by Rabbi Kook.

The tragedy of this story, however, is that Rabbi Kook warned of the extinction of the Ethiopian Jews in 1921, yet it took nearly half a century for world Jewry and the leaders of Israel to take action to save this ancient branch of the Jewish people. The number of Ethiopian Jews, estimated to be as high as two hundred thousand late in the nineteenth century had dwindled to twenty-eight thousand by the time of the 1976 census.[4] A handful of activists, primarily in the United States, helped prod the Israeli government to act by demonstrating that mere "amateurs" could rescue Jews through the constant lobbying of both the Israeli and U.S. governments and by the sometimes shameless propaganda and unwarranted attacks on Israel's motives. While these advocates tirelessly advanced the cause, the American Jewish establishment stayed mostly silent, satisfied with Israeli assurances that everything that could be done was being done.

Tragically, the Beta Israel, a proud people, who had maintained their religion for millennia, had its Jewishness questioned for years and nearly disappeared before the eyes of a generation that had watched helplessly as the Holocaust unfolded. Did we fail to learn our lesson from that event? If not, why did it take so long to act on behalf of the Ethiopian Jews and what were the factors that brought about the ultimate decision to prevent the community from being relegated to an encyclopedia entry, or a museum exhibit of lost Jewish communities? The remainder of this book will explore the answers to these questions and explain the politics behind the rescue of the Jews of Ethiopia.

NOTES

1. Israel Goldstein, *Israel at Home and Abroad* (Israel: Rubin Mass Press, 1973), pp. 364–365.

2. Marie Syrkin, *Golda Meir: Israel's Leader* (NY: Putnam, 1969), p. 118.

3. Interview with Yehuda Dominitz.

4. Estimates of the number of Ethiopian Jews have consistently proven inaccurate. As we will see later, no one is even sure today of the actual figure. The Ethiopian Jewish population in Israel is nearly three times the total found in the 1976 census.

CHAPTER 1

Who Are the Ethiopian Jews?

Once they were kings. A half million strong, they matched their faith with fervor and out-matched the Moslem and Christian tribesmen around them to rule the mountain highlands around Lake Tana. They called themselves Beta Israel—the house of Israel—and used the Torah to guide their prayers and memories of the heights of Jerusalem as they lived in their thatched huts in Ethiopia.

But their neighbors called them Falashas—the alien ones, the invaders. And even three hundred years of rule, even the black features that matched those of all the people around them did not make the Jews of Ethiopia secure governors of their destiny in Africa.[1]

For centuries, most of the world was unaware that a community of black Jews existed in Ethiopia. Even after contacts had been made between European Jews, and later Israeli Jews, knowledge of the Ethiopian Jews was scant. It was not until the early 1980s, and the famine in North Africa that drove many Jews to seek an escape route through the Sudan, that the Beta Israel became widely known. At the same time, the Ethiopian Jews were equally unaware that Jews lived anywhere else and were at least as shocked to learn of the existence of white Jews as the Europeans were to discover black Jews.

As noted in the beginning quotation, the Ethiopian Jews were generally referred to as Falashas by their neighbors. This is a pejorative term meaning "strangers" or "immigrants" that was nevertheless widely used by outsiders as well. Throughout this book, references are made to the Falashas, usually without negative connotation. I have not changed the usage of others but restricted my own references to the neutral term "Ethiopian Jews" or the community's preferred designation, Beta Israel.

ORIGINS

Little is known about the early origins of the Beta Israel beyond the fact that they represent one of the oldest diaspora communities. The Bible refers to Jews living in the region now known as Ethiopia. The prophet Isaiah, for example, spoke of the return of the Jews who had been exiled to a variety of lands, including Cush, which is now part of Ethiopia and the Sudan. Isaiah chapter 18 is devoted to a description of Cush and the people living there.[2]

The ninth century traveler Eldad ha-Dani maintained that the tribe of Dan chose to leave the holy land rather than join the fight between Rehoboam and Jeroboam when the kingdom of David split. The tribe went to the land of Cush. It is probably from this account that the idea arose that the Ethiopian Jews were descendants of the tribe of Dan, a view held by the Beta Israel themselves. A more modern theory is that the Beta Israel are related to the Agau tribes and adopted Judaism from Jews who came to the area from southern Arabia.[3] A number of other theories concerning the origin of the Ethiopian Jews have been offered, but none are convincing or verifiable. However they originated, the Beta Israel have consistently viewed themselves as Jews and maintained a distinguishable culture as such.

JEWISH INFLUENCE IN ETHIOPIA

Ethiopian culture has been influenced by Judaism. The Ethiopian Church, for example, adopted customs associated with Judaism, such as circumcision, dietary laws, and the observance of the Sabbath. Ethiopians also believe that the founder of the royal dynasty, whose last ruler was Haile Selassie, was the son of King Solomon and the Queen of Sheba. According to legend, their son, Menelik, settled in Ethiopia and brought with him members of the Israelite tribes. He also smuggled the Ark of the Covenant out of Jerusalem and brought it to Aksum, the capital of ancient Abyssinia. The Beta Israel, however, do not accept this story. Moreover, the Beta Israel stress their differences with the Christians, rejecting the New Testament, Jesus, Mary, and the saints. Besides religious differences and their confinement to mostly menial jobs, little distinguishes the Beta Israel from their neighbors. They look and dress the same, live in similar types of homes and conduct their lives in much the same manner as the non-Jews.

BETA ISRAEL CUSTOMS AND TRADITION

Ethiopian Jews reside in simple villages where most families live together in a small round house made of branches and grass, coated with mud, called a *tukul*. Families are patriarchal, with women primarily involved in child-rearing and homemaking. The men engage in a number of activities, including agriculture, weaving, pottery, and iron works. It is their work as blacksmiths and goldsmiths, in particular, that led their non-Jewish neighbors to call them *buda* (possessors of the evil eye). Though the pejorative term was not applied only to Jews, the association of the Jews with manual crafts made them more commonly viewed as sorcerers with magical powers and thus carriers of the evil eye. This notion has remained a contemporary problem for Ethiopian Jews.[4]

The Ethiopian Jews have continued to practice Judaism for centuries, despite persecution and isolation. Because of their isolation, however, the brand of Judaism they adhere to differs from that practiced elsewhere. The most significant difference, from a Jewish theological perspective, is that the Ethiopian Jews base their beliefs on the Written Law (the Torah) and some oral traditions passed from generation to generation. The rest of the Jewish world bases its practices on both the Written Law and the Oral Law, which is the interpretation of the Written Law by rabbis that was largely codified by the year 400 C.E. in the Talmud.

Orthodox Jews believe that most of the oral traditions date back to God's revelation to Moses on Mount Sinai. Conservative and Reform Jews acknowledge that some commentary was needed to make the Torah comprehensible and workable, but they do not believe that it is unchangeable or that it was part of a revelation on Sinai. Since the Ethiopian Jews were unaware of the Oral Law, they were not familiar with any of the practices, rituals, and interpretations developed over the centuries by the rabbis. The Ethiopian Jews also had their own interpretations of the Written Law and did not fulfill many of the biblical commandments, such as the wearing of prayer shawls (*tzitzit*), posting of *mezuzot* on doorposts, or sounding the shofar on Rosh Hashanah.

Unlike Jews elsewhere, the Ethiopians did not speak or write Hebrew. Most, in fact, were illiterate. The language of most Ethiopian Jews is Amharic, the official language of Ethiopia. Jews living in the region of Tigre speak Tigrinya. Their holy books are written in Geez, a language considered holy and used also by Ethiopian Christians. Their Torah is handwritten on parchment as a book, rather than as a scroll. The Beta Israel share with other Jews the belief in one God who chose them to receive His law at Mount Sinai. Most of the Ethiopian Jews know little about their faith. Their priests (*kessim*) are usually the only ones who have an intimate knowledge of the Jewish tradition, and they do not generally teach others what they know. The knowledge is handed down principally among the priestly caste.

Religious life in Ethiopian Jewish villages revolves around the synagogue, which is typically a distinctive hut. Only priests wear head coverings, while all worshipers remove their shoes when entering the synagogue. As in traditional Orthodox synagogues, women sit separately from the men, either in a special area or behind a partition. Prayers are directed toward Jerusalem and recited with song, dance, and music. Since the prayers are in Geez, which is not commonly spoken, most of the participants either have memorized the passages or simply say "amen" at their completion. Some of the Beta Israel rituals are similar to those practiced in the days of the Temple in Jerusalem. Many of these were discarded over the centuries by the rabbis or were deemed unnecessary or inappropriate in the absence of the Temple. One rite discarded in modern times is that of animal sacrifice; however, the Beta Israel still offer a sacrifice on the fourteenth of the Hebrew month of Nisan as part of the Passover celebration.

The Beta Israel observe Jewish festivals prescribed in the Bible, but not those that were developed later, such as Chanukah. The Ethiopian Jews strictly observe the Sabbath and the laws of *kashrut* (dietary laws). They also have stringent rules regarding ritual purity; for example, non-Jews are considered impure and the Beta Israel do not touch them, eat their food, or allow them into their homes. During menstruation, women are also considered impure and are sent to a special hut where they remain for seven days. Marriages are typically arranged by the fathers. Divorce is rare but not unknown.

This is a very cursory description of the religious traditions of the Beta Israel but it is necessary to understand the religious and political decisions that affected their status in the eyes of Israelis and other Jews who would ultimately decide whether they should be helped to immigrate to Israel.

THE JEWISH EMPIRE

It is remarkable that the Ethiopian Jews remained isolated for centuries. It is perhaps even more surprising, especially given Jewish history elsewhere, that this community became a powerful force in society rather than a persecuted minority. In fact, the Ethiopian Jews had a great deal of power for several centuries, though little first-hand documentation exists of their society.[5] The Beta Israel never wrote down their own history, and their ancestors did not leave behind any artifacts. Most of what we know about them comes from first and second-hand accounts by non-Jewish visitors who provided subjective observations.

The known history of the Beta Israel begins around the tenth century when they rebelled against the kings of Abyssinia. Their leader was a queen known as Judith who led a Jewish crusade to eradicate Christianity from the country, burning churches and monasteries and slaughtering monks and priests. Although this story is part of Beta Israel folklore, many scholars question whether such a queen existed or if she did, whether she even was a Jew. The Menelik Dynasty that Judith fought against returned to power in the thirteenth century and prosecuted a war against the Jews that lasted for nearly four hundred years. In 1332, Emperor Amda Siyon (1314–1344) put down a Jewish rebellion, and his great grandson, Negus Ishak (1414–1429), continued the fight against the Beta Israel and built churches on the ruins of their synagogues. Though the Ethiopian ruler Zarra Yakob (1434–1468) was given the appellation "Exterminator of the Jews," he did not succeed in eliminating the Beta Israel as a threat. His son, Baeda Maryam (1468–1478), massacred many Jews and forced others to convert to Christianity.

Warfare and persecution sporadically continued. In the sixteenth century, Muslim forces conquered large areas of Ethiopia, including regions where the Jews lived. Negus Claudius (1540–1559) succeeded in driving the Muslims out and then took revenge against the Jews for aiding his enemies. The Beta Israel king, Yoram, was executed. Yoram's successors continued to fight against the Ethiopian rulers, and it was left to Negus Susenyos (1607–1632) to finally end the revolt by slaughtering Jewish men, women, and children, including their king, and forcing many of the survivors to convert to Christianity and/or to become slaves. This put an end to Jewish independence in Ethiopia.

Jewish life became largely confined to the Gondar region of Ethiopia. In 1862, a group of Jews followed a messianic leader in search of the Promised Land. Most died of starvation along the route. Some of the survivors returned to their homes in Gondar; others established a small community in the province of Tigre. The two communities subsequently became the principal settlements of the Beta Israel but had little contact with each other and spoke different languages. Over the years, the larger Gondar community also received more assistance from abroad and consequently enjoyed better health, education, and welfare benefits than the Jews of Tigre.[6] At the height of its power, the Beta Israel community may have numbered as many as half a million. By the nineteenth century, though, the population was at most half that, devastated by drought, disease, and warfare with the invading Muslim Dervishes from the Sudan. The Jews' right to own land was taken away and the Beta Israel became a persecuted minority.

DISCOVERING BLACK JEWS

While the Ethiopian Jews may have had some influence on their non-Jewish neighbors, the impact of European Christian missionaries on the Beta Israel was far greater. The missionaries began to arrive in the seventeenth century and persisted for the next three hundred years in their efforts to convert the Jews. The missionaries also began to relate stories about the exotic Jews of Ethiopia, thereby stimulating the interest of other missionaries, curiosity seekers, and, eventually, other Jews.

The first modern contact with the Beta Israel occurred in 1769, when Scottish explorer James Bruce stumbled upon them while searching for the source of the Nile River. He found them impoverished, heavily taxed, and oppressed. His estimates at the time placed their population at 100,000. A Jew who converted to Christianity, Henry Stern, offered a detailed description of the condition of the Ethiopian Jews in the middle of the nineteenth century. As a representative for the London Society for Promoting Christianity Amongst the Jews, his views were largely colored by his objective to convert the Jews that he found. Stern found Jews with "rigid notions as to the sanctity of the Sabbath" who told him, "We believe that Jerusalem will again be rebuilt." Stern described the Jews as "exemplary in their morals, cleanly in their habits and devout in their belief." Still, he became convinced that "numbers of Falashas are fully persuaded of the truth of the Gospel, and anxious to be baptized."[7]

World Jewry began to hear about the Jews of Ethiopia in part through communications sent by the Beta Israel to rabbis in Jerusalem and, in part, through the reports of the missionaries. European and Palestinian Jews began to take a greater interest in the Ethiopians if for no other reason than to help them combat the missionaries. The German rabbi Azriel Hildesheimer became one of the earliest champions of the Ethiopian Jews and sent the following appeal to "fellow believers":

> For several years a most melancholy account has made tremble the heart of every Jew who feels for the weal of his nation. It is the sad news that two hundred and fifty thousand of our believers live in Abyssinia, who have lost during their long exile the knowledge of Jewish doctrines, and only manifest their noble extraction by the sacred volume, which they have preserved as a precious good, and by the observance of the Sabbaths and holidays. That these hundreds of thousands who are dispersed among other people, separated from those who profess the same faith, certainly have the strongest claim possible on our sympathies, cannot be denied . . . and I believe that all my fellow believers whose hearts still beat warmly for our faith, will feel with me the profound grief which must possess the hearts of all Jews, wherever they live and to whatever party they may belong . . . it is the duty of the whole of Judaism to grant assistance to our poor brethren who are exposed to the imminent danger of being swallowed up in the abyss, not only of religious but also of moral corruption. . . . We must exert ourselves to prove the oneness of all Israel.[8]

Rabbi Hildesheimer did not doubt the Beta Israel's status as Jews and called on world Jewry to donate money, books, and religious articles to send with a delegation to the Ethiopian Jews.

As interest grew in the Ethiopian Jews along with concern about the activities of missionaries, the European Jewish philanthropic organization L'Alliance Israélite Universelle (AIU) decided to send an emissary to make contact with the Beta Israel. In 1867, Joseph Halevy was dispatched and became the first outside Jew to visit the Beta Israel. Ironically, when Halevy reached the Jews in Wolkait, they did not want to have anything to do with him. They did not believe that he could be Jewish and feared he was a missionary trying to trick them.

> I assured them that all the Falashas of Jerusalem, and in other parts of the world, were white; and that they could not be distinguished from the other inhabitants of their respective countries. The name of Jerusalem, which I had accidentally mentioned, changed as if by magic the attitude of the most incredulous. A burning curiosity seemed all at once to have seized the whole company. "Oh, do you come from Jerusalem, the blessed city? Have you beheld with your own eyes Mount Zion, and the House of the Lord of Israel, the holy Temple? Are you also acquainted with the burying-place of our mother Rachel? With glorious Bethlehem, and the town of (Kiebron) Hebron, where our holy patriarchs are buried?" They were never weary of asking me questions of this nature; and they eagerly listened to my replies. I must confess I was deeply moved on seeing those black faces light up at the memory of our glorious history.[9]

Upon his return, Halevy appealed to the alliance and the rest of world Jewry to aid the Ethiopian Jews. The alliance did not consider Halevy's reports reliable and decided not to help; the 150,000–200,000 Jews Halevy estimated to be in Ethiopia were soon forgotten.

THE COMING OF FAITLOVITCH

By the end of the nineteenth century, the Beta Israel community had significantly declined because of the invasion of Muslim raiders from the Sudan, epidemics, famines, and the persistence of missionaries. It was not until 1904 that one of Halevy's students in Paris, Jacques Faitlovitch, took enough of an interest in the Ethiopian Jews to make the long, difficult journey to their villages. When he reached them, he estimated that no more than sixty thousand remained. Like his mentor, Faitlovitch was convinced of the authenticity of the Beta Israel and urged the AIU to establish schools in Ethiopia, but the request was again denied.

Faitlovitch established the American Pro-Falasha Committee to raise money for the education and welfare of the Beta Israel. He opened a school in Addis Ababa, the Ethiopian capital, in 1923. He also helped forty[10] young Ethiopian Jews enroll in school in Italy, France, Switzerland, Germany, and Jerusalem. Faitlovitch hoped these students would return to their villages to teach them about Judaism and what they had learned in the outside world.

To his regret, few of the students fulfilled his goal. While in Ethiopia, Faitlovitch's intent was to introduce European Jewish traditions and discourage some of the more archaic practices of the Beta Israel. Thus, for example, he taught the Ethiopian Jews about the modern calendar, the lighting of Sabbath candles, and the observance of post-biblical holidays and tried to persuade them to stop animal sacrifices and isolating menstruating women. It was not Faitlovitch's intention to encourage the Beta Israel to immigrate.

In the 1920s, Faitlovitch's Pro-Falasha committees raised money for the Ethiopian Jews' educational, religious, and material needs and between 1919 and 1932, the American Joint Distribution Committee (AJDC) distributed $25,000 to $30,000 for education. According to Diane Winston, the National Council of Jewish Women, the Central Conference of American Rabbis, and the United Synagogue of America also contributed, but the aid was sporadic. From 1930 to 1934, virtually no aid was forthcoming.

THE ITALIAN INVASION

In 1935, the Italians overran Ethiopia. Emperor Haile Selassie fled the country and took refuge in Jerusalem. During the Italian occupation, the small Jewish communities of Addis Ababa and Diredawa, which were made up of European and Yemenite Jews, were disbanded. Faitlovitch's school in Addis Ababa was also closed, and he was forced to leave the country. Some of his students fled to Gondar. Although anti-Semitic legislation was ultimately adopted in Ethiopia, the Beta Israel were largely unaffected because the laws were not enforced against them.

Between 1936 and 1938, the AJDC provided $3,000, and another $6,000 in 1938, but all assistance was subsequently curtailed until the Jewish Agency, the Israeli organization responsible for helping overseas Jewish communities, began its program in Ethiopia in 1954. In 1941, Haile Selassie returned to power, and life for the Beta Israel returned to the way it had been before the war. By that time, the Jewish population was thought to be no more than 50,000.

THE ESTABLISHMENT OF ISRAEL

In May 1948, the state of Israel declared its independence and immediately became embroiled in a war for its survival against its Arab neighbors. Israel prevailed and made a priority of state-building and promoting the immigration of Jews to the new state. According to former Minister of the Interior Yosef Burg, "the first priority was to rescue the Jews in the displaced persons camps in Europe and then the Jews in Muslim countries."[11] Few Israeli officials were familiar with the Jewish community in Ethiopia and little attention was paid to it. Unlike places such as Iraq, and later Morocco and Yemen, the Jews in Ethiopia were not believed to be facing imminent danger, so there was no reason to push for rescuing them. Furthermore, serious doubts remained at that time as to whether the Ethiopians were in fact Jews. Images of the Ethiopian Jews were also hampered by stereotypes that, at best, bordered on racism. This attitude was typified by an article written in the 1956 issue of *The Jewish Horizon* by the World Zionist Organization's Malkah Raymist. She wrote:

> There is much spadework to be done [in training Falashas in Ethiopia] . . . before a thought could be given to bringing them to Israel. The reasons are single and weighty. On one hand, they are well off where they are, while their development and mental outlook is that of children; they could fall an easy prey of exploitation, if brought here without any preparation. On the other hand, being a backward element, they would be unproductive and it would take several years before they could be educated towards a minimum of progressive thinking. And, as experience has shown time and time again, the fully grown-up and the elderly people would never change at all.[12]

Thus, no *shlichim* (messengers to encourage emigration) were sent to Ethiopia. In addition, unlike the Arab countries that were Israel's enemies, Ethiopia was viewed by Israel as a potential friend. The government would not risk alienating the Ethiopian emperor by the type of secret airlift used in May 1949 to rescue 50,000 Yemenite Jews in "Operation Magic Carpet." The point was moot anyway, because Israel had no interest in bringing the Ethiopian Jews to Israel at that time and the Jews in Ethiopia had not given any indication that they were anxious to come. Of course, no one asked them. Still, even before the Israel-Ethiopia political relationship was solidified and, despite questions regarding their Jewishness, Israel did begin to provide aid to the Ethiopian Jews. Israel had no special policy toward the Ethiopian Jews, according to Israel's former ambassador to Ethiopia, Chanan Aynor, but, he said, "A Jew helps a Jew even if he's a Falasha."[13]

Israel's efforts to help the Ethiopian Jews began after the Jewish Agency sent Alexander Rosenfeld to Ethiopia in 1950 and 1951. Rosenfeld reported back that the Ethiopian Jews needed education. It took another three years before Isaeli president Yitzhak Ben-Zvi insisted that the Torah Department of the Jewish Agency open schools for religious instruction in Ethiopia. Ben-Zvi had a scholarly interest in looking for the lost tribes of Israel, but his concern for the Ethiopian Jews was an exception at the time; few other Israelis knew or cared about them. This disinterest was typified by vice-speaker of the Knesset, Yisrael Yeshayahu, who visited Ethiopia and observed that "the Ethiopian government is supported mainly by the Christian community, and apparently any part of the population that is not Moslem (i.e., the Falashas) is likely to strengthen this support. Perhaps it is for this reason that there is much pressure brought to bear on the Falashas—not by the government, but by the Christian community—to convert to Christianity and to cease being different."[14] Yeshayahu's solution was for the Ethiopian Jews to convert. That report reinforced the negative attitudes toward helping the Ethiopian Jews.

A TEST OF JUDAISM

Representing the opposite viewpoint, Daniel Friedenburg, who also visited Ethiopia, wrote in 1956 that "for those who believe in Judaism as a religion valid for all men, rather than an ethnic doctrine limited to a small group of particular descent, the test today of their thought lies in any help that can be given to the perishing Falasha remnant in Ethiopia."[15]

These conflicting opinions were held by people within the Jewish Agency and therefore led to the inconsistency in the agency's Ethiopian policy. Initially, the view that the Beta Israel were Jews who needed help prevailed and the first agency school—to train teachers—was opened under the supervision of Yehuda Sivan in Asmara in January 1954. That school was attended by fifty-seven students, men and women, and included seven *kohanim* (priests). The following year, twenty-seven boys and girls were sent to Kfar Batya in Israel for the purpose of being trained to be teachers who would then be sent back to Ethiopia to help educate their people.

During a visit to Israel, an American social worker named Graenum Berger toured Kfar Batya and met the Ethiopian youngsters. Though it made little impression on him at the time, the introduction to the Jews would ultimately provoke Berger to spend most of the remainder of his life campaigning on their behalf. Coincidentally, Faitlovitch died in Israel in 1955 while on a vacation tour. According to Berger, at that time only twenty-three Ethiopian Jews were living in Israel, all women married to Yemenites.[16] Before his death, Faitlovitch had changed his attitude about Ethiopian Jewish policy and had begun to advocate *aliyah*. In 1950, he wrote:

> It is naturally hard to foretell what the future has in store for the Falashas in Abyssinia, their existence there as ethnic and religious minority in this abnormal period of crude nationality feelings and radical social upheaval depends greatly upon the economic and spiritual development of the country in general but as conditions are prevalent there at present, however, and if left to their own fate, the danger is very great that they will be in a few decades completely wiped out as Jews and absorbed by their surroundings.[17]

After studying in Israel, some of the Jews who returned to Ethiopia assimilated. The result, according to Yehuda Dominitz, was that "some people saw the Kfar Batya group as a failure, others became more convinced afterward of the need for *aliyah*."[18]

By 1958, the Jewish Agency helped to establish a total of twenty-seven schools employing thirty-six teachers who were trained either in Kfar Batya, Addis Ababa, or Asmara. At the teacher's seminary in Asmara, thirty students were given instruction in basic Judaism, Hebrew, and general subjects in three to four month cycles. The schools were spread over a wide area from Semien in the north, to Gojjam in the south, and Kwara to the west of Lake Tana. With the exception of the school in Ambober, the level of education was elementary; nevertheless, the Ethiopian Jews enthusiastically welcomed the opportunity to study and to be exposed to modern Judaism.

The first supervisor of the schools in Addis Ababa, Rabbi Samuel Beeri, a teacher from Safad, Israel, brought with him the traditional Hebrew calendar, which was accepted in a ceremony held on the eve of Passover in 1954. This seemingly innocuous innovation actually typified the difficulties created by the Jewish Agency's inconsistency. The regular Ethiopian calendar has twelve months and a short "leap month" that is out of sync with the Jewish calendar; therefore, Jewish holidays occurred at different times in Ethiopia. By printing the calendar in Amharic, Beeri hoped to bring the Ethiopian Jews closer to Jews in Israel. A great argument erupted among the *kohanim* before they decided to accept the calendars. Then, a year later, according to Moshe Bar-Yehuda, an employee for the Jewish Agency in Ethiopia, someone in Jerusalem decided that no money was available to print calendars. "They didn't have money," he said, "because of their ambivalent attitude toward the Ethiopian Jews." The impact of that decision was to demoralize and confuse the Ethiopian Jews. Bar-Yehuda wrote to the Jewish Agency several times telling his superiors about the damage they were doing and that they were ruining the good feelings created in Ethiopia, but his warnings went unheeded.[19]

Rabbi Beeri's assistant, a former student of Faitlovitch's named Yona Bogale, translated a book of Jewish festivals into Amharic and distributed it to the Beta Israel villages, along with cards with the Hebrew alphabet, so that by the time Aryeh Newman visited Ethiopia in 1957 about 80 percent of the Ethiopian Jews were familiar with the *alef-bet*, the *Shema* and several other basic Hebrew prayers. Newman also reported that the community suffered from a lack of funds and he lamented that world Jewry had neglected the Ethiopian Jews.[20]

In 1957, Moshe Bar-Yehuda, a former paratrooper and yeshiva student who had been uninvolved in Jewish Agency activities, was recruited by Rabbi Chaim Gavariyahu to work for the agency in Ethiopia. According to Bar-Yehuda, Gavariyahu had been a driving force behind the effort to educate the Jews. He had decided the schools had not reached their goals and the agency had to reach the Ethiopian Jews in the villages instead of bringing them to the city. Gavariyahu wanted an educated person who could live in the jungle and Bar-Yehuda met both criteria.

Bar-Yehuda did not know anything about Ethiopian Jews at the time, but he saw the proposition as an opportunity for adventure. "It was romantic to go to Ethiopia," he said. Before accepting the position, however, he said that he would have to confer with three rabbis because, as an observant Jew, he did not want to violate any Jewish laws. He went to see Ashkenazic Chief

Rabbi Yitzhak Herzog, who told him: "If I were as healthy as you, I would go to Ethiopia myself." The rabbi did not want to bring the Ethiopian Jews to Israel, but he did want to help them. He said it was a *mitzvah* (religious obligation). The Sephardic Chief Rabbi, Yitzhak Nissim, was less understanding. When Bar-Yehuda asked for permission to go to Ethiopia, Rabbi Nissim replied, "Who needs these blacks?" and left the room angrily. Bar-Yehuda also spoke to the head of his yeshiva, the son of Chief Rabbi Kook, who was cited at the beginning of this book. Rabbi Kook showed Bar-Yehuda his father's letter and blessed him. With the approval of two out of three rabbis, Bar-Yehuda decided to go to Ethiopia. Before leaving, however, Bar-Yehuda discovered the Jewish Agency's ambivalent attitude toward the project. While Gavariyahu was enthusiastic, his boss, Tsfi Asael was not. The latter had been to Ethiopia and said, "If it was up to me, I wouldn't send anyone to Ethiopia."[21]

At the end of 1957, Bar-Yehuda went to Ethiopia and stayed for four months. He received a salary of $200 a month, a fortune in Ethiopia. When he visited Asmara, he met Sivan and discovered there was no longer a school there. He then realized, for the first time, that his job was not going to be as easy as he originally thought. Bar-Yehuda also learned shortly after he arrived that Gavariyahu had left the Jewish Agency. The agency's policy then changed, and he did not receive any money for five months, nor did the nine teachers who had arrived just before him from Kfar Batya. Bar-Yehuda had sent the Jewish Agency a budget based on a survey he did of the Ethiopian Jews' needs, but he did not receive any of the money that he requested. He sent many letters to Jerusalem because, he said, he had nothing else to do, but received no reply. "The serious problem was of the eight men and one woman," he added, referring to the teachers, "who had been taken out of impoverished tukuls, taken to Israel where they got used to a different standard of living and then were sent back to the Ethiopian 'cesspool.'" Bar-Yehuda called it a personal tragedy for them. Bar-Yehuda had a two-year contract, but he returned after one year and sued the Jewish Agency for breach of contract. He won a settlement in arbitration, but, he said, no damages were awarded to the Ethiopian Jews who had returned from Kfar Batya.

The amount of attention the Jewish Agency did provide through the schools had stimulated great interest among the Ethiopian Jews in *aliyah* and Israel. The education Israel was providing was seen as the preparation Raymist spoke of as a prelude to bringing them to Israel; however, the agency abruptly ended its support. Actually, there had been an indication that the agency's commitment was wavering when they stopped sending children to Kfar Batya. In fact, no one was sent to Israel after Faitlovitch died in October 1955, largely because he had been the only one vigorously pushing the government to help the Ethiopian Jews.

Two years later, in January 1958, the school in Asmara was closed, but the Ethiopian Jews opened a new school with seventy students in Wuzuba, in the mountains near Gondar. This school aroused the suspicions of the inhabitants, however, who feared the Jews were going to steal their land. After the dining hut and one of the then unoccupied dorms were set on fire, the school was moved again, this time to Ambober. By the end of 1958, the Jewish Agency, claiming it could not afford to pay the teachers' salaries, withdrew almost all of its support from the Ethiopian Jews, closed all of the schools except the one in Ambober, and continued to pay only the Kfar Batya-trained teachers.[22]

ORT STEPS IN

In March 1959, Robin Gilbert was sent to Ethiopia on a fact-finding trip for the Organization for Rehabilitation and Training (ORT) and found it heartbreaking to hear the pleas for assistance from the Ethiopian Jews. "It would surely have been far better not to have taught them at all," Gilbert concluded, "than to have taught them and then to have abandoned them."[23]

In addition to frustrating the students, the Israeli withdrawal had the more serious consequence of stimulating assimilation by leaving the students who wanted to continue their education with little choice but to attend Ethiopian Muslim or Christian schools. The only advanced education available to most was provided by the Church of England Mission to the Jews whose director told Gilbert that "the greatest break the mission had had was the closing of the [Jewish] Agency schools."[24] When those schools opened, he said he lost all of his students, but after they closed he was inundated with more applicants than he could accept.

Gilbert also spoke with the emperor and was told the Ethiopian government looked favorably on the establishment of an ORT program. Haile Selassie offered to provide land for a school in Gondar and also suggested that ORT open a school in his native region of Harar. The emperor, Gilbert said, realized the ORT schools would be meant to benefit the Jews; nevertheless, he made it clear he considered it unwise to exclude other students for fear of arousing jealousy among the people. Gilbert replied that it was ORT's policy to provide nonsectarian aid.

At the end of his report, Gilbert concluded that since both Ethiopia and Israel officially opposed the *aliyah* of the Jews, it was wrong for Israel to be saddled with the entire burden of providing aid. "Here surely is an opportunity for world Jewry to do a great service," he said. ORT, he wrote, was "particularly suited to tackle the Falasha problem" because of "its ability to adapt itself to different situations in different countries." Although he did not report any emergency, he did say "the people are poor and anything that can be done to raise their standard of living, should be done."[25]

Unfortunately, nothing was done. According to Norman Bentwich, a prominent British Zionist who had taken an interest in the Beta Israel, the condition that aid be provided to Jews and non-Jews discouraged both ORT and the American Joint Distribution Committee (AJDC) from following through with the project Gilbert proposed to Emperor Selassie. This irritated Selassie, who was never notified that the project was abandoned and, worse yet, disappointed the Ethiopian Jews who believed they were being forsaken by world Jewry.[26]

FEUDAL SOCIETY

The Jews of Ethiopia were indeed poor, the lowest class in one of the world's most impoverished nations. Beyond their economic difficulties, however, they also suffered from oppression from their neighbors. In 1958 or 1959, two delegates for the Beta Israel, Kes Debetra Gothe Assress and Andargeh Tegabeh, presented a petition to the emperor reminding him that in response to an earlier request he had issued a decree to prevent the oppression of the Jews and expressing the hope he would do so once again. They complained that their patriotism displayed in fighting beside Christians in earlier centuries and, more recently, in fighting with the underground against the Italians, was being repaid with "grief and humiliation." The petition listed eleven Jews who were killed for being magicians and cannibals from 1946 to 1957 and another seventy-two who were killed for other reasons. In addition, they listed numerous incidents of arson and the desecration of cemeteries, as well as the efforts of landlords to expel them from their land.

The Ethiopian Jews lived in feudal servitude and were forced to pay their landlords half their harvest, a fee to use the land, a grain tax to the church, and an arbitrary amount of grain at the order of the landlord. "We, your servants of the House of Israel, have lived in this land from time immemorial, and yet are held by the Christian inhabitants as a foreign people. We, your servants, are in so grievous a state," the petition said, "that if a ladder were found reaching to heaven we should go there or go down into the earth if it opened its jaw."[27] This plea to end the oppression, however, fell on deaf ears.

After failing to obtain help from the emperor, and losing the support of the Jewish Agency, the Ethiopian Jews sent an open letter in February 1960 to Jewish organizations asking for help. The World Jewish Congress (WJC) subsequently asked Norman Bentwich, a British Zionist leader to investigate. Bentwich went to Ethiopia and submitted his report a year after the letter from the Ethiopian Jews had been received. When Bentwich spoke to the Ethiopian Jews during his trip, he was not told of any personal attacks and was informed that no murder had occurred in the last two years. Although he did not mention *aliyah*, a number of young people expressed their desire to go to Israel. Bentwich knew the Israeli Foreign Office and Ethiopian Jewish leaders like Yona Bogale were against any proposal for large-scale immigration because they believed it would antagonize the emperor. In their letter to the WJC, in fact, the Ethiopian Jews had not requested that they be brought to Israel but did ask to be resettled on empty state land in Ethiopia where they could create a communal economy. Bentwich concluded this was impractical because of the resentment it would stimulate among the native Amharas and the difficulties such dissension could cause the emperor. Bentwich did present what he considered a modest proposal to the emperor to allow a group of young Ethiopian Jews to go to Israel. Haile Selassie told his English visitor that he knew some Ethiopian Jews had settled in Israel and said that he had no objection to permitting a group to go.

Haile Selassie also approved Bentwich's proposal to build two schools on state land, either in Gondar or Behardar, and expressed his hope that representatives of the Jewish organizations would come soon to arrange the details. Although Bentwich was in constant communication with the Israeli consul general in Addis, he did not suggest to Haile Selassie that Israel have any direct role in managing the Beta Israel schools because Bentwich believed the Israelis did not want to complicate their relations with the Ethiopians by intervening in a local problem. Moshe Bar-Yehuda claimed that Bentwich also made a deal with the emperor to buy Jews for $50 per person, but the Jewish Agency did not want them. Chaim Aynor denied that any such deal was made.[28] Regardless, Bentwich maintained that Israel did not consider the Ethiopian Jews a persecuted branch of the Jewish people requiring their action.[29] Still, when Bentwich reported to Israeli president Ben-Zvi, he found the president happy to learn of the emperor's willingness to allow some Ethiopian Jews to emigrate. Ben-Zvi suggested that a settlement in the Negev should be started with about one hundred people.[30]

Again, nothing came of this proposal to settle Ethiopian Jews in the Negev. In 1965, four years after Bentwich had proposed the idea, the Ethiopian government and the colonization department of the Jewish Agency approved the settlement of fifty families in Israel; however, the plan required the approval of the religious authorities and that proved to be an obstacle.[31] Because some influential secular scholars (notably Ethiopia expert Edward Ullendorf) and many *halachic* (Jewish law) authorities doubted the Beta Israel were Jews, this enabled the Israeli government to justify discouraging immigration from Ethiopia. Furthermore, this skepticism made it difficult to convince Jewish charitable organizations to contribute to the welfare of the Ethiopian Jews.[32]

Despite the reluctance of many organizations to become involved in assisting the Ethiopian Jews, Bentwich did succeed in obtaining some support. After returning from his visit to Ethiopia, Bentwich became chairperson of the Committee for Assistance to the Falasha Population of Ethiopia, and he enlisted the British OSE Society, whose purpose was to provide medical aid to Jewish communities abroad, and the Jewish Colonization Association (JCA), which encouraged agricultural settlements, to help the Ethiopian Jews. In addition, the JCA provided enough money to increase the number of schools under the supervision of Yona Bogale to seven. Eventually the number increased to eighteen with forty-nine teachers.[33]

A medical unit headed by an Israeli doctor named Dan Harel was sent to Ethiopia in the early 1960s with the assistance of the Israeli Ministry of Health and the Foreign Office. His two-year mission was successful, but he was never replaced. According to journalist Louis Rapoport, Israeli medical teams were often in Ethiopia but did not provide aid specifically for the Ethiopian Jews. The Jews had to rely on English missionaries for medical care and were, consequently, placed in a position where they were susceptible to inducements to convert.[34]

By the middle of the decade, the threat of assimilation and missionary activity had reached the point where a trio of *kohanim* (priests) sounded an alarm and pleaded for help in saving the Ethiopian Jews from extinction. The only solution they believed was *aliyah*:

> Despite the good counsel of the late Dr. Faitlovitch and the rebirth of the State of Israel, our worries have not ceased. Again, we repeat to you, as the elders of the community, whose forefathers came to Ethiopia, that to this day we have not forsaken the religion of our fathers, no matter what difficulties we have encountered. Slowly these unhappy conditions are influencing our children, and in the course of time, they are likely to become *goyim*. We are distressed and shed bitter tears that after this generation has passed there will be no new Jewish generation to follow. As it is said, "If you do not sow seeds, you will reap no crops."[35]

The letter ended with an appeal to Graenum Berger to help the Ethiopian Jews return to Israel. "We long for Her day and night and trust that in our names you will request world Jewry to take all of us. If that is not immediately feasible, save at least a small number of our people as a remnant." Three years later, Yona Bogale made a similar appeal:

> I am an old man. Since no one will help, and we are doomed to disappear, I ask only one favor. Let Israel take 50 of our young people so that our history will go on, so that future generations will know that for 3,000 years there were black Jews who swore allegiance to God and followed the precepts of the Torah in the land of their forefathers.[36]

The response of world Jewry and the Israeli government continued to be reluctance to initiate any *aliyah*. Aynor said he would not give the letter from the *kessim* (priest) much credence. In general, the *kessim* were "stumbling blocks to modern Zionism," he asserted. Aynor believed that someone probably bribed them to write the letter. He also said the *kessim* hated Bogale because he introduced factors, such as doctors and tractors, which were not under their control and thereby diluted their power. Aynor conceded that there were always individuals who wanted to go to Israel, but he insisted they numbered no more than a handful.[37] Even those few found it difficult to go to Israel, however, since the Israeli Foreign Ministry instructed the embassy in Addis Ababa not to give Ethiopian Jews visas to Israel. Ironically, Christians had no difficulty obtaining tourist visas to come to Israel.

FINDING A HOME IN ETHIOPIA

By the late 1960s and early 1970s, the consensus among American Jews and Israelis was that the best solution for the Ethiopian Jews was for them to be resettled in another part of Ethiopia, despite their deteriorating position in that country. In March 1973, the JCA issued a review of the problem of the Ethiopian Jews and a proposal for its solution. In that report, the plight of the Ethiopian Jews is documented. The average income per family was estimated to be $75, excluding the food grown for their own consumption, which was below a level of subsistence. The Ethiopian Jews had to pay from one-third to one-half of their production to their landlords and were still frequently threatened with eviction from their lands. The report predicted, moreover, that the situation would deteriorate as the landlords adopted more labor-saving agricultural equipment. "As there is no free land within the Gondar area, there is no future and hope for the Falasha population," the report concluded.

The JCA report also commented on difficulties in education created by the lack of improvements in the Beta Israel schools in the prior decade while the Ethiopian government-run schools had shown "marked development." The parents of Ethiopian Jews wanted their children to receive quality education, but this, paradoxically, was expected to contribute to assimilation because the young Ethiopian Jews were sent off to schools in the cities and then did not want to return to their villages to become primitive weavers, farmers, or blacksmiths. "Over the years," the report stated, "this drain will leave only the less educated in the villages, causing a further deterioration of the community."

The report suggested three alternatives for improving the life of the Ethiopian Jews: *aliyah*, increased aid, or resettlement in Ethiopia. "Only the resettlement program can be regarded as offering a constructive solution," the report concluded. "A group growing up under changed and improved economic and social conditions through resettlement, will also provide more suitable candidates for immigration to Israel, should this become possible at a later date." In a statement that appears in the appendix, H.G. Levy explained the psychological necessity of such a plan:

> Contact with the Israeli-trained teachers had aroused in them great hopes and aspirations for their *aliyah*. This did not materialize because of the Ethiopian government's refusal to allow their exit. Coupled with the lack of local development and inconsistent outside help, they feel let down and profoundly

disillusioned. This, in turn, is causing further communal deterioration and dis-
integration. They are now at the point, where only an actual and over all
Development Project for their entire people—with assured uninterrupted implementation—can maintain their identity within the framework of their homeland, Ethiopia.[38]

Although the JCA was a sympathetic group that already was providing aid
to the Ethiopian Jews, the report suggests the organization hoped the resettlement plan would settle the matter and implies *aliyah* would always be
limited. This was evident in the statement of Arthur Lourie, which is found
in another appendix of the JCA report:

> The Ethiopian government for its part has expressed its firm opposition to any
> project of mass emigration. This is a factor which will no doubt have to be taken
> into account in view of both the geopolitical importance of Ethiopia to Israel
> and of the sensitive nature of the relations between the two countries. As to
> the Falashas themselves, it is questionable whether pressures for mass immigra-
> tion at this stage may not do the Falasha's community in Ethiopia more harm
> than good. Granted an effective resettlement program in the years immediately
> ahead, it is perhaps realistic for a limited immigration thereafter.[39]

The primary impediment to *aliyah* cited by the Israelis was, as Lourie said,
the refusal of the emperor to permit large-scale emigration. "The Emperor
thought the Beta Israel tribe was like a finger in Ethiopia's dike—if one tribe
leaked out, all of the various peoples would clamor for independence, and
the fragile empire would collapse."[40] Aynor said that he and Foreign Minister Abba Eban raised the issue with Haile Selassie around 1968, but he was
not interested.[41] The emperor did, however, tell not only Bentwich but also
Israel Goldstein in 1969 and David Kessler in 1970 that he was willing to
let a small group go to establish a settlement in Israel, but the religious issue always seemed to stand in the way. Goldstein was convinced the religious
problem could be overcome by an agreement of some sort that the Beta
Israel undergo ritual conversion, but that was not to happen until later.[42]

One high-ranking diplomat told a reporter for the Israeli daily newspaper,
Ha'aretz that Haile Selassie's opposition was not necessarily an insurmount-
able obstacle. "Did we try to change his position on the subject?" the diplomat asked. "On other subjects which were important to us he changed his
attitude. When, in the course of time, it will be possible to open up the pro-
tected files of the Foreign Ministry concerning our relations with Ethiopia,
it will become clear how and in what circumstances the Emperor changed
his views and attitudes many times in our favor." This source cited Abba Eban
as saying the subject was not considered important and, the diplomat noted,
the Jewish Agency knew which way the winds were blowing. "They knew
that the religious ministers in the government do not see the Falashas as real
Jews, while the ministers from the secular parties saw in the Falashas primi-

tive types who would not succeed to be absorbed in a progressive, techno-logical Israel."[43]

Evidence for this interpretation was provided by Rabbi Zeev Gotthold of the Ministry of Religion, who said that Foreign Minister Golda Meir con-sistently opposed *aliyah* because she believed the Beta Israel would be mis-erable in Israel, the victims of prejudice. Another source told Rapoport that Meir once said: "Don't we have enough problems? What do we need these blacks for?"[44] Hezi Ovadia also said that Meir was "against, against, against the Ethiopian Jews." Ovadia, the head of a pro-Falasha committee, also spoke with David Ben-Gurion for an hour at Sde Boker asking for help, but the former prime minister, the man responsible for overcoming the objections of the religious authorities to bringing the Indian Jews to Israel, told Ovadia he was too busy and could not do anything.[45]

In another interview, Eban told Rapoport he did not remember if the Beta Israel had ever been brought up in a cabinet meeting. "It seems to me that there was a ministerial meeting on the matter," Eban recalled, "and the re-ligious party people were not enthusiastic." He thought that prayer books were sent to the Falashas, "but it was never considered to be an important issue. . . . It never complicated our relations [with Ethiopia] at all."[46] Others agreed that the issue did not complicate Israel's relations, but Ephraim Poran, who was later the military adviser to Menachem Begin, and responsible for the Ethiopian issue, said the issue came up regularly in the prime minister's office after 1962.[47]

As it turned out, the resettlement plan was scrapped after a small group that had moved to Humera, a flatland area near the Sudanese border, was driven off the land by the Sudanese, who believed the settlement was part of a Zionist plot.[48] Afterward, attitudes in Israel gradually changed, stimu-lated largely by the rabbinate's decision recognizing the Beta Israel as Jews, which brought about the first plans for bringing Ethiopian Jews to Israel. In the interim, however, Ethiopia was in upheaval and, in September 1974, Haile Selassie was deposed and a period of revolutionary changes began.

THE RELIGIOUS QUESTION

As the early visitors discovered, the Beta Israel viewed themselves as Jews, and their beliefs and practices were similar to those of most Jews; however, major differences also existed that led some people to question whether they were indeed Jews. Still, as early as the sixteenth century, prominent Jewish scholars and theologians recognized them as Jews. Egypt's chief rabbi, David ben Solomon ibn Avi Zimra (known as the Radbaz), was probably the first to declare that the Beta Israel were Jews according to *halacha* (Jewish law). In 1864, one of Europe's most prominent theologians, Rabbi Azriel Hildesheimer of Germany recognized the Beta Israel as Jews. Other rabbis expressed similar views. After the establishment of Israel, officials were unwilling to formally recognize the Beta Israel as Jews who were eligible for automatic citizenship under the state's Law of Return. Though the old opinions were on the record, it took a quarter of a century before any official recognition would be given to the Ethiopian Jews.

The question of whether the Beta Israel were Jews was a theological one, but it also had political overtones. In Israel, Orthodox Jews had a monopoly on political influence, so their leaders would make the determination. By definition, the Orthodox had stricter interpretations of Jewish law than Reform and Conservative Jews. Moreover, one of the theological issues that divides those movements relates to the importance attached to the Oral Law. As previously noted, the Orthodox believe this was part of God's revelation to Moses. Since the Ethiopian Jews were not familiar with the oral tradition and did not practice according to its precepts, it was difficult for Orthodox Jews to accept them as Jews. To most Orthodox Jews, the Ethiopians were more like Karaites or other sects that had Jewish roots but had adopted other practices that led them to be viewed as non-Jews.

When the Ethiopian Jews came to Kfar Batya in the mid-1950s, the chief rabbis were prompted to explore the question of their Jewishness. The rabbinical authorities in Israel were not prepared to declare outright that they were Jews, primarily because of their failure to follow the traditions of the Oral Law. Nevertheless, they did rule that if the Ethiopians went through a conversion process involving ritual immersion and a symbolic circumcision (usually a drop of blood is taken), they could be considered authentic Jews. After the initial enthusiasm stimulated by Faitlovitch to help the Ethiopian Jews, the Jewish Agency's interest waned in part because it made no sense to support the Beta Israel if there was not a presumption that they were Jewish.

The issue lay largely dormant for many years, though the general view in Israel was that the Beta Israel still were not Jews and, hence, remained ineligible to immigrate under the Law of Return. The situation did not change until one of the Ethiopian Jewish activists in Israel, Hezi Ovadia, specifically asked Rabbi Ovadia Yosef, Israel's Chief Sephardic Rabbi, for a ruling that would enable the Beta Israel to settle in Israel. On February 9, 1973, Yosef gave his reply: "I have come to the conclusion that Falashas are Jews who must be saved from absorption and assimilation. We are obliged to speed up their immigration to Israel and educate them in the spirit of the holy Torah, making them partners in the building of the Holy Land." Yosef referred to the Jews as descendants of the tribe of Dan, echoing the stories of Eldad Ha-Dani. Still, Yosef continued to insist on the symbolic circumcision to remove any doubt that the Ethiopian Jews might have intermarried with non-Jews or those not halachically converted. This is not considered a conversion; rather, it is, in Yosef's words, "an act of renewing their covenant with the Jewish people."[49]

Unfortunately for the Beta Israel, Yosef's recognition was necessary but not sufficient. In Israel, the society is divided between Ashkenazic Jews—those of European descent—and Sephardic Jews—those who descend from Jews who were expelled from Spain in 1492. Each community has its own chief rabbi and the two men do not always agree; in fact, they frequently disagree in part to demonstrate their independence. The Ashkenazic chief rabbi at that time, Shlomo Goren, initially refused to accept Yosef's opinion. It was not until 1977 that Goren told a group of Beta Israel immigrants, "You are our brothers, you are our blood and our flesh. You are true Jews." Later that same year the Israeli Interministerial Commission officially recognized the Beta Israel as Jews under Israel's Law of Return.

Given their isolation, the Ethiopian Jews had no knowledge of Zionism, the political movement to establish a Jewish homeland. Nevertheless, the Beta Israel were motivated to immigrate by a religious, messianic vision. Israel was the land promised to the Jewish people by God Almighty. The Ethiopian Jews suffered persecution and were economically disadvantaged, but this was never the principal motivation for any of them to immigrate. This distinguishes them from most other Jewish populations who made *aliyah* because of one or both of those reasons. This official recognition did not vitiate the need for the symbolic "renewal" ceremony, which the Ethiopian Jews considered an insult and a challenge to the authenticity of their Judaism. Still, recognition from the rabbinate was a crucial hurdle to clear before the Ethiopian Jews could have any chance to immigrate to Israel. Other hurdles remained.

NOTES

1. "Falashas: The Forgotten Jews," *Baltimore Jewish Times* (November 9, 1979).

2. Isaiah 11:11–12; 18:1–7.

3. "Beta Israel," *Encyclopedia Judaica*, CD-ROM edition (Israel: Judaica Multimedia, Keter Publishing House).

4. This section refers to life in Ethiopia. In Israel, Ethiopian Jews practice a conventional form of Orthodox Judaism and have adopted a modern Israeli lifestyle.

5. "Beta Israel," *Encyclopedia Judaica*, CD-ROM edition.

6. Teshome, Wagaw, *For Our Soul: Ethiopian Jews in Israel* (MI: Wayne State University Press, 1993), p. 24.

7. Henry A. Stern, *Wanderings among the Falasha in Abyssinia* (England: Frank Cass, 1862, 1968), pp. 191–193, 300.

8. *Jewish Chronicle & Hebrew Observer* (November 4, 1864), quoted in Rabbi Menahem Waldman, "World Jewry's Contact with Beta Israel" (http://www.nacoej.org).

9. Joseph Halevy, "Halevy's Travels in Abyssinia, London 1877", quoted in Rabbi Waldman, "World Jewry's Contact with Beta Israel" (http://www.nacoej.org).

10. Other sources say the number was twenty-five to twenty-seven.

11. Yosef Burg, interview with author.

12. Malkah Raymist, "The Children from Ethiopia," *The Jewish Horizon* (January 1956).

13. Chanan Aynor, interview with author.

14. Louis Rapoport, *The Lost Jews* (NY: Stein and Day, 1980), p. 196; Interview with Natalie Berger.

15. Daniel Friedenburg, "The Decline and Fall of the Falashas," *Judaism* (Summer 1956): 247.

16. Graenum Berger, *Rescue the Ethiopian Jews!* (NY: John Washburn Bleeker Hampton Publishing, 1996), p. 6.

17. Simon Messing, "Twentieth Century History of the Beta Israel in Ethiopia," in Tudor Parfitt, ed., *The Beta Israel in Ethiopia and Israel: Studies on Ethiopian Jews* (Great Britain: Curzon Press, 1998), p. 63.

18. Yehuda Dominitz, interview with author.

19. Moshe Bar-Yehuda, interview with author.

20. Aryeh Newman, "A Lost Tribe Returns," *Brooklyn Jewish Center Review* (March 1957): 6, 23.

21. Bar-Yehuda, interview.

22. David Kessler, *The Falashas* (NY: Holmes and Meier, 1982), pp. 150–151; Bogale memo, March 8, 1977.

23. Robin Gilbert, "Report on Visit to Ethiopia" (ORT, March 20, 1959), p. 4.

24. Ibid., p. 6.

25. Ibid., pp. 7–8.

26. Norman Bentwich, "Report on Falashas," February 1961.

27. Debetra Gothe Assress and Andargeh Tegabeh appeal to Emperor Lenhoff Archive.

28. Aynor, interview; Bar-Yehuda, interview.

29. Bentwich, report.

30. Report of meeting at President Ben-Zui's house, March 1, 1961.

31. Aryeh Tartakower letter to Bentob Messa (WJC), May 29, 1965.

32. Kessler, *The Falashas,* p. 154.

33. Kessler, *The Falashas,* p. 155; Bogale, memo, March 8, 1977.

34. Aryeh Tartakower, letter to British Fund for Rehabilitation and Relief, October 26, 1965; Louis Rapoport, *Redemption Song* (NY: Harcourt Brace Jovanovich, 1986), p. 48.

35. Letter from three kohanim to Graenum Berger, October 24, 1965.

36. J. I. Fishbein, "The Plight of Ethiopia's Black Jews," *Chicago Tribune Magazine* (December 1, 1968).

37. Aynor, interview.

38. "Review of the Problem of the Falashas and a Proposal for Its Solution," Jewish Colonization Association, March 1973, p. 4 [henceforth JCA 1973].

39. JCA 1973, Appendix III.

40. Rapoport, *The Lost Jews,* p. 195.

41. Aynor, interview.

42. Israel Goldstein, *Israel at Home and Abroad* (Israel: Rubin Mass Press, 1973), p. 363; Kessler, *The Falashas,* p. 157; Israel Goldstein, "Falashas: Ethiopia's Jews," *National Jewish Monthly* (December 1969), p. 15.

43. Mordechai Artzi'eli, "The Falashas: A Dying Community, The Weakness of Israel," *Ha'aretz* (December 17, 1982).

44. Rapoport, *The Lost Jews*, pp. 194–195.

45. Hezi Ovadia, interview with author.

46. Rapoport, *The Lost Jews*, p. 189.

47. General Ephraim Poran, interview with author; Yehuda Dominitz, interview; Haggai Erlich, interview with author; and Aynor, interview.

48. Louis Rapoport, "The Falashas: This Year in Jerusalem?" *Women's American ORT Reporter* (May–June 1975), 2.

49. *Jerusalem Post* (August 1977).

Chapter 2

The Big Picture: Ethiopia in Israel's Foreign Policy

W hen Golda Meir said, "There is no Zionism except the rescue of Jews,"[1] the Holocaust was in progress and there was no state of Israel. Although the *raison d'être* of the new Zionist state may still have been to save Jews, the reality was that Israel, like any other country, sometimes had to sacrifice ideology for pragmatism. The capacity and willingness of Israel's leaders to rescue the Jews of Ethiopia, therefore, cannot be understood without examining the broader foreign policy concerns of the nation.

One of the first priorities of the new Jewish state was the ingathering of the exiles, that is, the desire to bring as many Jews from the diaspora to Israel as possible. Since thousands lived in Africa, mainly north Africa, it was logical for Israel to turn its attention to that continent. Long before the state of Israel was established, the father of modern political Zionism, Theodor Herzl, had looked to Africa and recognized parallels between the black and Jewish experiences. In his book *Altneuland*, published in 1902, just five years after the Zionist conference in Basel, Switzerland, which formally initiated the drive for a Jewish state, Herzl wrote:

There is still one other question arising out of the disaster of nations which remains unsolved to this day, and whose profound tragedy, only a Jew can comprehend. This is the African question. Just call to mind all those terrible episodes of the slave trade, of human beings who, merely because they were black, were stolen like cattle, taken prisoner, captured and sold. Their children grew up in strange lands, the objects of contempt and hostility because their complexions were different. I am not ashamed to say, though I may expose myself to ridicule for saying so, that once I have witnessed the redemption of the Jews, my people, I wish also to assist in the redemption of the Africans.[2]

Almost immediately after the redemption of the Jewish people, Herzl's interest in helping the Africans was taken up by the leaders of Israel. Their idealistic and egalitarian attitude toward Africa was typified by the architect of Israel's Africa policy, Golda Meir, who believed the lessons learned by Israelis could be passed on to Africans who, particularly during the 1950s, were engaged in the same process of nation-building. "Like them," she said, "we had shaken off foreign rule; like them, we had to learn for ourselves how to reclaim the land, how to increase the yields of our crops, how to irrigate, how to raise poultry, how to live together, and how to defend ourselves." Israel could provide a better model for the newly independent African states, Meir believed, because Israelis "had been forced to find solutions to the kinds of problems that large, wealthy, powerful states had never encountered."[3]

POLITICS NOT CHARITY

While Israeli leaders have always had philanthropic attitudes toward Africa, their primary interest in the continent rested on the more tangible grounds of *realpolitik*. Just as Africa was the scene of a battle of influence among the superpowers, so too has it been a battlefield between Israel and the Arabs. This battlefield was particularly important during Israel's first two decades because the United States had not yet proven itself a reliable ally nor for that matter had the Soviet Union established itself as the guarantor of its clients in the Arab world. Thus, it was not necessarily hyperbole when Dan Avni, the deputy director of the Africa Department in Israel's Foreign Ministry, described the struggle in Africa as "a fight of life and death for us" where even small African nations such as Togo became pawns in the effort to obtain an advantage on the continent.[4]

Although Meir denied that *realpolitik* was Israel's primary motive, Israeli concern for nations such as Togo rested largely on the fact that their votes at the United Nations General Assembly counted equally with those of the United States or Russia. Since Israel already faced a large, hostile voting bloc from the Arab and Muslim states, it was important for Israel to try to win as many African votes as possible if it was to have any hope of avoiding constant censure in the General Assembly. From the perspective of the African states, however, it made less sense to side with Israel than with the Arab states because the latter bloc's votes were needed in international forums such as the United Nations to exert pressure on the major powers to protect their own interests. Israel has only one vote at the United Nations and is not represented in the Organization of African Unity (OAU), whereas the Arabs have eighteen members in the United Nations and six in the OAU.

After 1967, the Arab states also enjoyed a propaganda advantage in Africa because of Israel's control of "Arab territories," which was seen by Africans as a possible precedent for the expansion of South Africa or Rhodesia (now Zimbabwe). The Africans were also less frightened by the Arab states after the death of Egyptian president Gamal Nasser because his successor, Anwar Sadat, was far less interested in pan-Arabism—the movement to unite the Arab world—which was perceived as a threat to African independence.[5]

CARICATURE OF ISRAEL

The issue of South Africa and apartheid actually provided a good example of Israel's priorities in Africa. In denouncing apartheid for the first time in the early 1960s, despite the presence of a very large South African Jewish community, Israel risked its relations with a country that had been friendly. Israeli officials found the apartheid system morally abhorrent, but their condemnation also had political motivations, namely to attract support from the more numerous black African states. It was not until the 1970s, after the black African states severed their ties with Israel, that Israeli-South African relations became close. Even then, Israel's critics exaggerated the extent of their relationship.

No Israeli policy sufficed to offset the image that its enemies presented to the Africans: that Israel was a nation of white Europeans who had expelled more than a million people from their homeland in furtherance of imperialist efforts to retain a foothold in the Middle East. As an African state that shared the Muslim religion with much of the continent, Egypt held a major advantage in its competition with Israel prior to the 1979 peace treaty. "The people of Africa will continue to look up to us, who guard the northern gate of the continent, and who are its connecting link with the world outside," Nasser wrote. "We cannot, under any condition," he added, "relinquish our responsibility in helping, in every way possible, in diffusing the light of civilization into the farthest parts of that virgin jungle."[6] It is interesting to note that Nasser's paternalistic and racist sentiments are similar to those of the "imperialists" and reflected the mind-set that allowed the Arabs to operate a vigorous slave trade in Africa.

Egypt tried to use its geographical advantage to extract political condemnation of Israel from the African states at every opportunity, but, with the exception of the Asian-African conference at Bandung, Indonesia, in April 1955, had little success. According to political scientist Michael Brecher, the reasons for this is that, "there was no emotional disposition to favor the Arab cause: Some Africans had had no contact with neither Jew nor Arab, while those who knew the Arabs recalled the slave trade above all." Brecher adds,

"Indeed, for many Africans, Israelis were Europeans, but this was not automatically a symbol of derision, as it was for many Asians."[7]

FOREIGN AID

The Bandung conference had a tremendous impact on Israel, however. Because Israel had not even been invited indicated that after seven years the nation was still isolated in its own region. To combat this isolation, Israel sought to establish diplomatic relations with African states and to offer them aid. Unlike the aid from the superpowers, Israeli aid came without strings attached, not so much because it did not hope to obtain support in exchange, but because it was in no position to demand it. In addition, Israel feared that if it failed to give aid, then Egypt would step in and fill the vacuum. "Our aid to the new countries," Prime Minister David Ben-Gurion told the Knesset in 1960, "is not a matter of philanthropy. . . . We are no less in need of the fraternity of friendship of the new nations than they are of our assistance."[8]

The labor and socialist movements in Israel made the first contacts with the Africans, and in 1958, the Histadrut (Israel's labor federation) inaugurated Israel's formal instructional program with an international seminar in cooperation.[9] The first Israeli embassy in Africa—only its eighth overall—was opened in Accra, Ghana, in November 1956. Two years later, Golda Meir made a five-week trip to Africa and had the first high-level discussions with African leaders such as Kwame Nkrumah, William Tubman, and Felix Houphouet-Boigny, which helped to show Israeli interest in the African liberation movements as well as to stimulate African interest in Israel.

Trade with Africa has always been one-sided, since Israel's major imports, such as oil and grain, are, for the most part, not available from that continent; consequently, the aid that Israel provided its African friends was of greater value than the economic advantages it reaped. As already noted, however, Israel was more interested in political than economic advantages. One of Israel's main contributions to Africa was military aid, which was provided in the form of conventional and paramilitary training and, to a lesser extent, by the sale of arms. By 1966, ten African states had received some direct military assistance from Israel and, in each case, the aid was provided to individuals who were either influential or potentially influential; for example, Israeli trained Mobutu Sese Seko, the general of the Congolese army, who, two years later, became that nation's president and ruled for thirty-two years.[10]

The Arab League continued to pressure the Africans to expel Israeli advisers and technicians and to recognize the threat that Israel represented. "The danger lurks under the glittering surface of 'trade and aid' offered by Israel to some emerging states during the last few years," a League statement said in 1963. "Tel-Aviv's offers have been, in reality, a facade for neo-colonialism trying to sneak into Africa through a back window after the old well-known colonialism had been driven out through the front door."[11] African leaders viewed Israel's efforts differently. For example, during a 1962 visit to Israel, President David Dacko of the Central African Republic remarked: "You have not tried to create us in your image. Instead, Israel has contented itself with showing the new African nations its achievements, in helping them overcome their weaknesses, in assisting them in learning. In so doing you have conquered Black Africa."[12]

This effort to "conquer" Africa by providing trade and aid was only one facet of Israel's strategy for obtaining an advantage in its conflict with the Arabs. A second aspect of Israel's policy involved a strategically located African country—Ethiopia—which the Israelis were already cultivating for all the reasons just discussed.

A CIRCLE OF FRIENDS

In the 1950s, Israel hoped to form an alliance with the United States, but Secretary of State John Foster Dulles advised President Dwight D. Eisenhower against any formal agreement. Consequently, Israel began to look for other allies that might help encircle her enemies with a ring of friends. In late 1957 and 1958, Ben-Gurion sent agents to three non-Arab countries—Iran, Turkey, and Ethiopia—to explore possibilities for an alliance. As non-Arab states with long historical ties to the Jewish people and strategically important geographic locations, these nations were potentially valuable allies.

Located in the Horn of Africa and with a coastline along the Red Sea, Ethiopia was approached following the Suez War and after the Gulf of Aqaba had been recognized as an international waterway. Hence, Israel saw Ethiopia's port as a gateway not only to Ethiopia but to the rest of Africa. In addition, as a predominantly Christian nation, Ethiopia is, along with Israel, the only non-Muslim riparian state and therefore an obstacle to Arab efforts to make the Red Sea either an Arab or an Islamic lake. When Egypt blockaded the Straits of Tiran in 1956 to prevent Israeli shipping, it became clear to Israel's leaders that it was necessary to have a friend on the Red Sea coast to avert any future sieges. That waterway would become progressively more important as the amount of Persian Gulf oil moving to Israel from its new friend in Iran increased. It became even more significant in the 1970s after the Suez Canal reopened and traffic resumed between the Indian Ocean and the Mediterranean.

In addition to Ethiopia's strategic location, Israel believed that Ethiopia's stability was a key to the stability of the Horn of Africa, and that it was in Israel's interest to prevent Ethiopia's subversion by Egypt or Saudi Arabia. The most overt threat to Ethiopia came from Somalia, which Israel had also approached in the hope of establishing diplomatic ties, but here the Israelis were consistently rebuffed. That predominantly Muslim country, moreover, joined the Arab League, thereby convincing Israel of the need to solidify its relationship with Ethiopia.

From Ethiopia's perspective, the alliance with Israel was also advantageous because the late 1950s was the period of Nasser's greatest influence in Egypt and, hence, most threatening to Ethiopia. There were also long historical ties between Ethiopia and the Jewish people, and personal ties between Emperor Haile Selassie, and not only the Jewish people, but also Palestine.

THE LION OF JUDAH

Haile Selassie considered himself "the Lion of Judah," a direct descendant of the Jewish people. Moreover, after the Italian conquest of Ethiopia in 1936, Selassie and his family, as well as many other Ethiopians, spent part of their time in exile in Jerusalem. Six years later, when he returned to Ethiopia, the emperor established the first modern links with the Jews of Palestine.[13] The first Israeli delegation arrived in Ethiopia in 1955 for the celebration of the Emperor's Silver Jubilee. The following year, the Israeli consulate opened to handle diplomacy and the commercial relations that began after Israel built a meat-packing plant in Asmara.[14]

In 1958, Israel could not expect to obtain the cooperation of the three pro-Western nations in its periphery alliance without at least the tacit support of the United States. Consequently, Prime Minister David Ben-Gurion wrote a memo to President Eisenhower on July 24 in which he proposed:

> Our object is the creation of a group of countries, not necessarily a formal and public alliance, that will be able to stand up steadfastly against Soviet expansion through Nasser and might even be able to save the freedom of Lebanon and, perhaps, in the course of time, Syria too . . . we can carry out our mission . . . since . . . it is a vital necessity for us, as well as a source of perceptible strength to the West in this part of the world.[15]

Ben-Gurion asked the U.S. president to provide political, financial, and moral support, and to convey to Iran, Turkey, and Ethiopia that the United States backed the Israeli initiative.

Ben-Gurion's memo was neatly phrased to appeal to the primary concerns of President Eisenhower and Secretary of State Dulles; that is, the threat of Soviet expansion, rather than Israel's conflict with the Arabs. Eisenhower's initial reply came the day afterward: "I am deeply impressed by the breadth of your insight into the grave problems which the free world faces in the Middle East and elsewhere . . . you can be confident of the United States' interest in the integrity and independence of Israel."[16] This equivocal response was accompanied by a promise that Dulles would respond in more detail. When Dulles did respond, he told Ben-Gurion that the United States supported the Israeli plan and encouraged him to establish the peripheral pact.

By 1959, the trilateral alliance was informally in place, and Haile Selassie derived an almost immediate benefit when Israel helped save his reign. In December 1960, when Selassie was visiting Brazil, a coup was attempted in Ethiopia. On December 14, supporters of the emperor sent out signals to alert the Israelis. Ben-Gurion ordered a plane to pick up the emperor and transport him to Asmara where he rallied his forces and smashed the rebellion.[17]

Despite the alliance, official diplomatic relations were kept in a low profile until May 1962, when the emperor announced that the Israeli consulate would be upgraded to an embassy. Prior to that, Selassie was hesitant to associate openly with Israel. One of the main reasons for Ethiopia's reluctance to establish ties with Israel related to the need for Arab votes in the United Nations. As long as the future of Eritrea, the northern province of Ethiopia that sought independence, remained in doubt, Ethiopia could not afford to alienate the Arabs. In addition, Ethiopia hoped to obtain U.N. support for its claim to Italian Somaliland, but that territory became independent Somalia in July 1960.

Ethiopia was also concerned by the threat posed by Nasser, but after his military defeat in 1956, Ethiopia recognized that Israel could help fight communist and Nasserist subversion. Thus, when two Israeli representatives approached Haile Selassie after the Suez War to discuss the possibility of joint political and economic cooperation, the emperor was amenable. Soon after, an Israeli consulate was opened in Addis Ababa and an Ethiopian consul was sent to Jerusalem. By the time the emperor gave Israel *de jure* recognition in 1962, the Israeli secret service, the Mossad, had sent agents to train the Ethiopian police, and economic and cultural relations between the two countries had begun to flourish.[18]

While Nasser vowed to expel Israel from Africa, Israel's presence in Ethiopia grew. In fact, Israel's military mission became second in size only to that of the United States.[19] Israel also ran a variety of foreign assistance programs in education, agriculture, industry, banking, and urban planning. In 1959, for example, an exchange program was established between the Technion in Haifa and the Engineering College in Addis Ababa. One of the most important programs was medicine, with hundreds of Ethiopian nurses going to Israel for training and a number of Israeli doctors moving to Ethiopia. From 1961 to 1964, Israel's Egged company provided the general and technical managers for Ethiopia's bus company and helped reorganize and modernize the transportation system.[20] Nevertheless, the number of Israeli experts in Ethiopia never exceeded one hundred. As for trading benefits, Ethiopia was not a very useful trading partner, since it could not provide for Israel's most pressing needs. Consequently, trade between Israel and Ethiopia never grew beyond small quantities of marginal goods.

Israel's overall influence was much greater than the amount of trade and aid might indicate, however, according to a State Department official who was stationed in Ethiopia from 1969 to 1972. This is how he described the Israeli presence:

> They were all over the place. They were probably more influential than the United States was in Ethiopia during the time I was there. If you really wanted to get to the Ethiopian government, you went through the Israelis, not the Americans. This may be a bit of hyperbole, but the fact is the Israelis were very strategically placed throughout the defense establishment. The Americans were there in greater strength, but, as usual, we were sort of there like the great elephant, but the Israelis were operating like the little gazelle, which is not always the case. They were often very clumsy themselves, but they were very effective in Ethiopia, which I always found one of the real ironies and real frustrations because they were probably in a position to get an awful lot done if they had chosen to use their influence on behalf of the Jews, but it was not a priority of theirs.[21]

CIVIL WAR

The beginning of the decline in Israel's relationship with Ethiopia might be traced to the civil war in Eritrea. Asrate Kassa, appointed as Eritrea's *enderase* (regent) in 1964, advocated close relations with Israel because of his concern about pan-Arabism and the politicization of Islam in the Horn of Africa. Kassa had ten to twelve Israeli advisers on counterinsurgency working closely with him to build and strengthen his police force and commandos. Meanwhile, the Eritrean rebels adopted the familiar revolutionary mantra of the time, vilifying the United States and the "Zionists" for their subjugation. Uthman Salih Sabi, the secretary general of the Eritrean Liberation Front (ELF), for example, insisted that the Eritreans were Arabs and that their struggle against Haile Selassie was part of the war on Zionism. This stand made Sabi and his comrades popular among the Arabs, in particular their revolutionary soul-mates in the Palestine Liberation Organization (PLO). Later, in fact, the Eritrean People's Liberation Front (EPLF) was founded in the PLO's camp in Amman.[22]

The Ethiopian army, according to one Israeli military official, was efficient only in killing innocent civilians and was succeeding only in alienating the Eritrean people. As Kassa's influence waned, he was eclipsed by his rival, Prime Minister Habta-Wald Akilu, who opposed Ethiopia's de facto alliance with Israel and preferred to solve the Eritrean problem by appeasing the Eritreans' Arab allies and by eliminating the rebel organizations through military force. As Akilu's influence grew, Israel's diminished; at the same time, the Arab and Muslim influences in Addis Ababa also increased.[23]

Israel and Ethiopia continued to share common interests, such as sending weapons to the Anya-Aya rebels in the Sudan, but Akilu's pressure on Haile Selassie to sever relations with Israel intensified. In May 1973, Libya used the OAU meeting in Addis Ababa to press Ethiopia to sever its relations with Israel. In the following months, Saudi Arabia also increased the anti-Israel pressure. Similar pressures applied to the rest of black Africa ultimately resulted in all of Israel's friends on the continent severing their ties with the Jewish state. The Arab members of the OAU finally achieved their goal of putting a wedge between Israel and Ethiopia by threatening to move the organization's headquarters from Addis to another capital, such as Cairo. Ethiopia subsequently severed relations with Israel on October 23, 1973, thus breaking the Ethiopian link in Israel's periphery policy. At the same time, the Arabs blockaded the strait of Bab al-Mandeb, thereby obtaining the strategic advantage over Israel that the alliance with Ethiopia had been designed to prevent.[24]

Although the Arabs put great pressure on Ethiopia to sever relations, Chanan Aynor, a former Israeli ambassador to Ethiopia, blames the United States for Haile Selassie's decision and the subsequent rebellion that ended his reign. According to Aynor, the emperor went to the United States in the spring of 1973 to ask President Richard Nixon for urgently needed aid to counter the Somali threat to Ethiopia. Since Nixon was already embroiled in Watergate, the emperor's mission was a failure. Haile Selassie told Aynor that Ethiopia would have to break relations with Israel because it did not have the arms to confront the Muslims. He denied being hostile to Israel but complained that he had no money, and his supply of arms would last only a few days. The emperor's subsequent effort to finance Ethiopia's arms requirements by raising taxes precipitated Ethiopia's social revolution.[25] Breaking relations with Israel hastened Haile Selassie's fall because the withdrawal of his Israeli military advisers disrupted the military. The Israelis served as the only communication link between the lower- and higher-ranking soldiers. Since the top Ethiopian officers were not in the least concerned about the mood of the lower ranks, the departure of the Israelis prevented the top officers from learning of the lower ranks' growing disaffection, which soon expressed itself as a revolution. In addition, when the emperor expelled the Israelis, the Ethiopian people saw this as an indication that the emperor was becoming senile, for they regarded this action as a betrayal of their history and tradition.[26]

When Haile Selassie was deposed in September 1974, a bloody revolution ensued and a Marxist council came to power. Nevertheless, the desire to strengthen the military and counter Arab support for Eritrean separatists led to an improvement in ties with Israel. In fact, in 1975, as civil war erupted, the Dergue apologized to Israel for Selassie's decision to break relations and sought new assistance. Though full diplomatic relations with Israel were not restored, the two nations began to cooperate in economic, military and diplomatic spheres. Thus, for example, trade gradually increased, with Israeli exports to Ethiopia more than doubling from 1975 to 1979; the Ethiopians allowed Israeli missile boats to refuel at their Red Sea islands; and Ethiopia abstained from voting for the Arab-sponsored "Zionism is racism" resolution at the United Nations in 1975. Israel also supplied desperately needed ammunition and spare parts for the Ethiopian army's U.S.-made equipment, helped build new army units, and provided training.[27]

The Arab world continued to support the Eritrean rebels, who were now fighting their fellow Marxists, while Israel backed the central government. Recognizing this, the revolutionary government under Mengistu Haile Mariam secretly invited Israeli military advisers to return to Ethiopia in December 1975. By the middle of 1977, probably no more than twenty-five or thirty Israeli military advisers had been posted to Ethiopia, and they were providing only low-level military training for the Ethiopian troops.[28] They were also carrying out intelligence work for the Mossad, probably with the blessing of the United States whose influence in the country was waning.

Having begun selling the new government small amounts of arms, Israel succeeded in negotiating an exchange of arms for Ethiopian Jews in 1977. That agreement was shattered when Foreign Minister Moshe Dayan revealed the secret Israeli arms pipeline to Ethiopia in a press conference in February 1978. The furious Ethiopians then expelled the Israelis. Within four years, however, the Israelis were back in Ethiopia and were once again selling arms to the Ethiopian government. In the interim, a significant change had taken place in Ethiopia, with the government shifting its loyalty away from the United States and toward the Soviet Union.

AMERICA'S CHANGING FORTUNES

The United States had signed a twenty-five-year military assistance agreement with Ethiopia in 1953 and had established an important listening post at Kagnew station. By 1976, the United States had provided Ethiopia with more than $200 million in military aid, more than half the total U.S. military aid to all African countries during the period. Although the amount of military aid was small, the sum of U.S. economic aid to Ethiopia exceeded the total supplied to other African states.[29] The United States, like Israel, believed the stability of the Horn could be maintained by keeping Ethiopia strong and stable. For that reason, as well as the emperor's own position, the United States opposed Eritrean independence.[30]

Although Ethiopian stability remained important to the United States, the usefulness of the Kagnew base to the United States declined with the increasing availability of satellite intelligence. Gradually, the United States reduced its operations at the base, intending to close it down in 1977. The United States also became increasingly concerned over the behavior of the Ethiopian government, especially in regard to its abuses of human rights. In addition, America's friends in Egypt and Saudi Arabia had begun supporting the Eritreans.

On February 24, 1977, President Jimmy Carter announced that the United States was cutting off all military aid to Ethiopia because of its human rights violations. The unstated reason was the U.S. desire to cooperate with Saudi Arabia to lure Somalia away from the Soviet camp, an effort that was ultimately successful.[31] Ethiopia retaliated by closing the American consulate in Asmara, the Kagnew station, and the U.S. information programs. The following week, the Dergue abrogated the military assistance agreement. The announced reason was: "The American government, which never spoke of the violation of human rights when the Fascist government of Haile Selassie was decimating thousands of the oppressed Ethiopian people, takes every opportunity to create hatred against revolutionary Ethiopia by depicting her as a country where human rights are violated."[32] U.S. officials knew that relations were deteriorating long before the decision to cut off aid. The United States, as always, was suspicious of a Marxist government and those doubts appeared justified when it was learned that Ethiopia had signed a military aid agreement with the Soviet Union. The relationship with the Soviet Union was solidified soon after the break in relations with the United States when Mengistu went to Moscow in May 1977.

While the Israelis foresaw that these actions would give the Soviets their long sought opening, they were still able to retain the favor of the Ethiopians by opposing Arab and Muslim expansionism and the rebellion in Eritrea. When Menachem Begin made his first trip to the United States after being elected prime minister in the summer of 1977, he tried unsuccessfully to persuade President Carter to resume aid to the Ethiopians. The Israelis then blamed the Americans for contributing to the "loss" of Ethiopia to the Soviet camp while the Americans accused the Israelis of naiveté. A State Department official explains:

> The Israelis have always lobbied us on behalf of Ethiopia in general. That, as much or more than anything else, is Ethiopia's side of the equation in dealing with Israel. . . . I think the Ethiopians thought that Israel was their channel into Washington and the Israelis would constantly tell us that we were misreading the situation in Ethiopia, that they really don't want to be driven into the Russian camp, that we should be more understanding, that we should be more forthcoming, blah, blah, blah. Whether they were doing this as their part of some deal, as some quid for some quo the Ethiopians were giving them, I don't think it was quite that neat. The Israelis have always thought that we were too quick to write Ethiopia off. Obviously they have a very profound interest in trying to keep a U.S. presence there. I think that they have been naive about it. I think they have underestimated, perhaps knowingly, the degree of willingness to collaborate with the Soviet Union. I think there is relatively little we could have done. We could have kept more aid going in there and kept a higher level of representation, but I don't think it would have had a significant impact on the Ethiopia-Soviet Union relationship.[33]

Since the Soviet Union was rather slow about moving into Ethiopia, Israel was still able to play a role in Ethiopia, primarily by providing spare parts for American weapons. After the Ethiopian army failed to defeat the Eritrean People's Liberation Front (EPLF) in November 1982, Mengistu invited the Israelis back as technical advisers to his intelligence service.[34] Following the Lebanon war, Israel sold Ethiopia Soviet arms that it had captured from the PLO in Lebanon.[35]

COLD WAR IMPLICATIONS FOR JEWS

The shift in Ethiopian loyalty from West to East had serious implications for the effort to save Ethiopian Jews. For one thing, it eroded all American influence in Ethiopia so the United States could not exert any leverage on the country to force the Ethiopians to allow freer emigration. In fact, the United States' actions were counterproductive and helped stimulate the shift in Ethiopia's loyalty. Moreover, the influence of the Soviet Union within Ethiopia was expected to make the probability of emigration much more remote because of the Russians' policy toward Soviet Jews. For the Ethiopian Jewry activists, it also became clear that denouncing Ethiopia's violations of human rights would have no effect because, unlike the Soviet Union, the leaders of Ethiopia were not believed to be sensitive to public opinion. Although Israel retained some influence in Ethiopia, certainly much more than the United States, little could be done to bargain with the Dergue once the Russians were entrenched and had, in effect, veto power over the Ethiopian government's actions.

CONDITIONS ON THE GROUND CHANGE

In addition to the shift in Ethiopia's loyalty, another important change took place at the end of the 1970s. Many Ethiopians, including Jews, began to migrate to the Sudan to escape the civil war, famine, and persecution in their native country. By crossing the border, many hoped to find not only refuge, but an opportunity to get out of Africa. As the number of Ethiopian Jews in the Sudan grew, the focus shifted from the foreign policy of Israel and the United States toward Ethiopia to their policies toward the Sudan.

Israel's relationship with the Sudan was very different than its relationship with Ethiopia. The two nations shared no historical, religious, political, or cultural experiences. The Sudan is a predominantly Muslim nation, a member of the Arab League, and officially an enemy of Israel. Israelis are not even permitted to travel to the Sudan and so the only Israeli presence in that country is a covert one. Since the Sudan occupies a key geographic location on the Horn and has close relations with other Arab nations, the Mossad maintains important intelligence-gathering operations in the country. This situation created a whole new set of problems for the prospect of rescuing the Ethiopian Jews.

First, no Israelis or Jewish organizations could openly coordinate rescue efforts. Second, the Mossad was in the Sudan for intelligence purposes, not rescue. Third, a large-scale rescue effort threatened the intelligence operations with exposure. On the other hand, since the Sudan was an enemy of Israel, there would be far less hesitation about mounting a secret operation. A similar operation inside friendly Ethiopia would have been, in Professor Haggai Erlich's words, "suicidal and politically stupid."[36] Thus, although the logistics of rescuing people from the Sudan were more formidable, the political obstacles were less inhibiting.

The movement of the Ethiopian Jews to the Sudan also brought the United States back into the picture because it enjoyed very close relations with Sudanese president Gaafar el-Numeiry. The United States provided the Sudan with large amounts of aid, and at the time, the Sudan was in desperate need of that aid because of its economic difficulties and the growing military threat to Numeiry's regime. Thus, unlike Ethiopia, the United States did have leverage over the Sudan, and it ultimately used this leverage to persuade Numeiry to permit the rescue of the Ethiopian Jews from his country.

NOTES

1. Marie Syrkin, *Golda Meir: Israel's Leader* (NY: Putnam, 1969), p. 118.

2. Golda Meir, *My Life* (NY: Dell, 1975), pp. 308–309.

3. Ibid., p. 306.

4. Samuel Decalo, "Israel and Africa: The Politics of Co-operation, A study of Foreign Policy and Technical Assistance" (Ph.D. diss., University of Pennsylvania, 1970), p. 87.

5. Susan Gitelson, "Israel's African Setback in Perspective, " in Michael Curtis and Susan Gitelson, eds., *Israel in the Third World* (NJ: Transaction Books, 1976), pp. 189–190.

6. Gamal Abdel Nasser, *The Philosophy of the Revolution* (NY: Economica Books, 1959), pp. 75–76.

7. Joseph Churba, "U.A.R.-Israel Rivalry over Aid and Trade in Sub-Saharan Africa, 1957–1963" (Ph.D. diss., Columbia University, 1965), p. 252.

8. Decalo, "Israel and Africa," p. 85.

9. Mordechai Kreinin, "Israel and Africa: The Early Years," in Michael Curtis and Susan Gitelson, eds., *Israel in the Third World* (NJ: Transaction Books, 1976), p. 58.

10. Abel Jacob, "Israel's Military Aid to Africa, 1960–1966," *Journal of Modern African Studies* (August 1971): 165–172.

11. Bernard Reich, "Israel's Policy in Africa," *Middle East Journal* (Winter 1964): 25.

12. Mordechai Kreinin, *Israel and Africa* (NY: Praeger, 1964), p. 5.

13. Louis Rapoport, *The Lost Jews* (NY: Stein and Day, 1980), p. 192.

14. Michael A. Ledeen, "The Israeli Connection," in Michael Samuels et al., eds., *The Washington Review* (May 1978).

15. Michael Bar-Zohar, *Ben-Gurion: An Autobiography* (NY: Delacorte Press, 1977), p.263; Dan Kurzman, *Ben-Gurion: Prophet of Fire* (NY: Simon & Schuster, 1983), pp. 405–406.

16. Bar-Zohar, *Ben-Gurion*, pp. 263–264.

17. Rapoport, *The Lost Jews*, p. 192; Haggai Erlich, *The Struggle over Eritrea* (CA: Hoover Institution Press, 1983), p. 57.

18. Walter Eytan, *The First Ten Years* (England: Weidenfeld and Nicolson, 1958), p. 178; Bar-Zohar, *Ben-Gurian*, p. 261; Rapoport, *The Lost Jews*, p. 192; Churba, "U.A.R.-Israel Rivalry," pp. 140–141; Erlich, *Struggle over Eritrea,* p. 57.

19. Jacob, "Israel's Military Aid to Africa," p. 176.

20. Leopold Laufer, *Israel and the Developing Countries* (NY: The Twentieth Century Fund, 1967), pp. 133–135; Ledeen, "The Israeli Connection," p. 7.

21. Confidential interview.

22. Erlich, *The Struggle over Eritrea*, p. 27.

23. Ibid., pp. 58–59.

24. Ibid., p. 59; Raman Bhardwaj, *The Dilemma of the Horn of Africa* (India: Sterling Publishers, 1979), p. 159; Gitelson, "Israel's African Setback," pp. 192–196.

25. Chanan Aynor, interview with author, former Israeli ambassador to Ethiopia, April 1987.

26. Aynor, interview; Professor Haggai Erlich, interview with author, April 1987.

27. Erlich, *The Struggle over Eritrea*, pp. 103–104.

28. Ledeen, "The Israel Connection," p. 7; Jack Anderson, "Israel Aiding Mengistu in Ethiopia," *Washington Post,* January 2, 1985.

29. Peter Schwab, "Israel's Weakened Position on the Horn of Africa," *New Outlook* (April 1978); Joseph Kraft, "Letter from Addis Ababa," *The New Yorker,* July 31, 1978, p. 60; Fred Halliday and Maxine Molyneux, *The Ethiopian Revolution* (England: NLB, 1981), p. 215.

30. Harold Marcuss, *Ethiopia, Great Britain, and the United States, 1941–1974* (CA: University of California Press, 1983), pp. 85–88.

31. Halliday and Molyneux, *The Ethiopian Revolution,* p. 223.

32. Kraft, "Letter from Addis Ababa," p. 60.

33. Confidential interview.

34. *Foreign Report* Economist Newspapers, January 20, 1983.

35. *Africa Confidential,* December 12, 1984; Anderson, *Washington Post;* "Foreign Report" *The Economist,* November 22, 1984.

36. Erlich, interview.

CHAPTER 3

A New Opening
in Ethiopia

I n May 1973, an Ethiopian Jew wrote to the World Jewish Congress pleading for help: "The Christians have started to kill us. They
have told us to move from their lands and some of us left the place. The
Christians say we are sucking their blood. Many of our people were killed a
few weeks ago. Please help us as you do the other Jews. If you will not help
us quickly it is evident for everybody we will not be any more in this world."[1]
The organization that took up the cause of the Beta Israel was David Kessler's
London-based Falasha Welfare Association (FWA). The FWA was established
in 1972 and had grown out of the Standing Conference of Organizations
Interested in the Welfare of the Falashas, which was created to provide aid
in 1961 at the behest of Norman Bentwich by the World Jewish Congress
and American Joint Distribution Committee. Kessler was one of the most
active and vocal supporters of the Ethiopian Jews. While only rare articles
appeared in the press elsewhere, his paper, the *Jewish Chronicle*, consistently
kept the issue in print. In 1973, Kessler visited Ethiopia for the second time
and, after seeing the Ethiopian Jews in some of their remote villages, returned
convinced that "unless help is forthcoming this ancient branch of the Jewish
people will disappear within the foreseeable future."[2]

In 1973, the FWA hired a schoolteacher living in Addis Ababa named Julian
Kay to become its representative in the field. He was in Ethiopia from December 1973 to March 1975 and sent back the following report on April 5, 1974:

While there is no famine in those areas where the majority of the Falashas live the fact that probably over half the provinces in the whole country are suffering to some extent from famine must have some effect on the Government when it comes to discussing (assuming it does) the position of minorities. The evacuation of let's say 20,000 Falashas may mean 20,000 less mouths to feed and therefore is to be welcomed but it must be remembered that as despised as they are the Falashas are known to be hard-working industrous (not the teachers!) and so closely connected by their work in pottery and basket-weaving with the eating habits of the people at large that to let them go would be a highly unpopular move.[3]

The FWA became the conduit for all relief to the Ethiopian Jewish community in the early 1970s. From 1970 to 1974, the Joint Distribution Committee (JDC) provided a trivial amount of aid—relative to the community's need—about $10,000 a year for medical aid. The chairman of the JDC, Ed Ginsberg, reported during the summer of 1974 that "the Falashas are the poorest of the poor. . . . The average yearly income in Ethiopia today is about $50; it is about $30 among the Falashas." Ginsberg said Jewish organizations had long been concerned with the Beta Israel, but "because of the backwardness of the country, political problems, and the general inaccessibility of the communities, assistance has been limited mainly to a modest medical program and educational aid."[4] The JDC then allocated a paltry $25,000 for general assistance.[5]

As with virtually all aspects of the Ethiopian Jewry story, even the FWA's activities became mired in controversy. The Jews did not trust Kay because he allegedly spent too much time with missionaries in Gondar and rarely visited the remote villages. Kay was ineffective and after having aroused the government's suspicion of his activities, he was expelled from the country in April 1975. An Israeli agricultural expert named Rafi Tarfon initially replaced Kay and was given a 1975 budget of $66,000, which was increased to $120,000 the following year. The FWA was subsequently replaced by the JDC and the ORT as the primary organizations providing relief to the Jews in Ethiopia. The World ORT Union began its development program in Ethiopia in 1976 with a $2 million budget raised from the governments of the United States, Canada, Germany, Holland, and Switzerland. Although Rapoport says he was the most effective emissary ever sent to help the Jews, Tarfon was fired by ORT for insubordination. Gershon Levy, who had directed the FWA program, became the head of the ORT project.

THE AAEJ

For decades, interest in the Beta Israel was largely confined to the Europeans. The controversy over whether the Beta Israel were Jews served as an inhibiting force on the willingnes of American Jewish organizations to offer aid. As far back as the 1920s, however, at least one Jewish leader did not view the religious controversy as an obstacle. The president of Hadassah the women's Zionist organization, Henrietta Szold, said in a message on March 18, 1924:

> Among all the fragments, the flotsam and jetsam of Jewish history, none have had a more baffling fate than the Falashas of Abyssinia. Solomon and the Queen of Sheba, their reputed ancestors, shed the glamour of their romance upon them. All we know for certain is that they have been carrying on a historic struggle for the preservation of their Jewish selves for hundreds of years. In the course of the centuries the teachings and principles that make them Jews became more and more attenuated. It takes scholarship to discern that their simple practices express a complete identification with the Jewish people. To the rest of us the supreme vindication of the scholar's view lies in their invincible allegiance to the Jewish heritage—a steadfastness that has been matched only by that of their rescuers.[6]

When Szold learned that Jacques Faitlovitch was seeking money to train Ethiopian Jewish girls in Palestine as teachers, she asked junior units of Hadassah to contribute in an emotional appeal: "Who will reforge the link between this stranded group and the living body of Jewry? Who will enable Palestine to show that it is in truth and spirit the gathering place of the exiles—the centre from which comes forth the law now as it did of yore."[7] Despite such concern, world Jewry contributed only small amounts to Ethiopian Jewish relief prior to ORT's involvement.

American Jewry did not become actively involved until a Jewish social worker named Graenum Berger took up the issue. Berger had never forgotten meeting the Ethiopian Jews in Kfar Batya in 1955. He returned to Ethiopia in 1965 and was shocked by the conditions he found but moved by the commitment of the Beta Israel to their faith. He was sure the American Jewish establishment and Israeli government would help them. "I assumed all I had to do was bring the problems of the Ethiopian Jews to their attention; and with the accustomed response to the Jewish downtrodden they would mount a campaign to save them. I also presumed Israel would rise to the occasion and undertake a resettlement mission. I found myself talking to deaf ears."[8]

In succeeding years, Berger watched the situation in Ethiopia from America with increasing frustration. It was clear to Berger the amount of relief was inadequate; even the $2 million ORT was providing divided among 28,000 Jews was trivial, and that amount had to also be shared with non-Jews. Worse, from Berger's perspective, was the absence of any effort to bring the Ethiopian Jews to Israel. For Berger, the only possible way to prevent the extinction of this remnant of the Jewish people was to bring them to Israel. Berger had enjoyed a distinguished career in Jewish communal service and had begun to raise money for Ethiopian Jews after returning from Ethiopia in 1965.

The money was sent to Aryeh Tartakower in Jerusalem, who headed a committee to assist the Beta Israel. In 1969, Jed Abraham returned to the United States from a Peace Corps assignment in Ethiopia and organized The Friends of the Beta Israel (Falasha) Community in Ethiopia to solicit funds. Berger began to work with this new group. In the meantime, the American pro-Falasha Committee that Faitlovitch had founded in 1922, which had been dormant since the 1950s, was revived by one of the original committee members, A.H. Kavey. Berger decided the activists would be more effective if they combined their efforts. After discussions with the two groups, a new organization emerged in February 1974 known as the American Association for Ethiopian Jews (AAEJ). From that point on, the AAEJ, under Berger's leadership, became the principal American organization advocating on behalf of relief and *aliyah* for the Beta Israel.

A MODERATE BEGINNING

Although Berger came to be regarded as an extremist because of his criticism of what he believed was the Israeli government's lack of action on behalf of the Ethiopian Jews, he did not start out as a militant. In fact, Berger's initial proposal for rescuing the Beta Israel was a modest one. Almost exactly ten years before Operation Moses began, Berger wrote in *Congress Bi-Weekly*:

> If the *aliyah* is to be gradual, it should concentrate on taking the fourteen to seventeen year-olds and placing them in Israeli Youth Aliyah villages, whose record for rescue and adjustment is one of the glories of Israel. Then it would be best to bring the 18 to 30 year-olds, preferably those already married, because they are more likely to achieve quicker assimilation and greater stability. In due course, the Falashas will assist their parents, other kin and friends to migrate and help in their absorption. Most of the Ethiopian Jews could be brought to Israel through this process in the next five years. Since their needs are much more modest, which is in keeping with their gentle demeanor, the costs for effecting such an *aliyah* would be a fraction of what is being spent on other Jewish groups. This investment will reap the fullest rewards, because the Ethiopian Jew will come to Israel to stay—and we would not have to undergo the disappointments of any future *yerida* [emigration from Israel].[9]

When Israel failed to respond to Berger's entreaties, he began to work with a small group of activists to develop a plan to bring young Ethiopian Jews to Israel. The group included Mordecai Paran, head of the Jewish Colonization Association (JCA) of England; Hezi Ovadia; Aryeh Tartakower; and Haim Halachmy, the director of the Hebrew Immigrant Aid Society (HIAS) in Israel. They decided to bring a group of Jews to Israel to study industrial occupations and nursing and to say the Jews would return to Ethiopia after their training. In fact, the group planned to keep the Jews in Israel. At one point seven young Jews were brought to Beersheva for training at a chemical factory. They completed their Jewish studies and Hebrew language instruction, but the local rabbi was withholding their residence cards. Berger mentioned the problem during a meeting with Chief Rabbi Goren, who picked up the phone and called the rabbi. The next day the group received their residence cards and were subsequently permitted to stay.[10]

Although he acquired a reputation as a firebrand, and was later castigated by Israeli officials for being irresponsible and endangering rescue operations by his public bombast, Berger initially heeded Israeli warnings not to make any noise or to demonstrate against the Ethiopian government because such actions might make the situation worse. When he suggested to an Israeli official that the U.S. government could intervene on the behalf of the Jews, he was also discouraged. "What do you want another Jackson-Vanik amendment to kill the project [Falasha immigration]?," General Uzi Narkiss of the Jewish Agency asked him, referring to the congressional amendment that linked U.S. trade with the Soviet Union and the emigration of Soviet Jews, implying the legislation had been responsible for the decline in emigration.[11]

Berger had, in fact, held the same opinion and wrote in 1974 to Howard Lenhoff, a new activist, and future AAEJ president, telling him that the Ethiopian Jews would have to be taken out of Ethiopia quietly without any pressure from any source. "What we don't want to do," Berger wrote, "is get the Arabs to suddenly intervene and force Ethiopia to close its doors to migration. Should that happen, we may then have to undertake a campaign a la Russia, but at the moment we are all convinced at this end that we don't want or need that intervention."[12]

NO REVOLUTION FOR JEWS

In the meantime, the political and economic situation in Ethiopia was rapidly deteriorating. In 1973, it became known that the emperor had suppressed news of the drought that had begun in 1972 and the quarter of a million people who died in the subsequent famine in the northern region of Ethiopia. Chaos soon followed, with a series of protests, strikes, and mutinies in the armed forces that ultimately led to the end of Haile Selassie's reign in September 1974. A military council, the Dergue, took over the government, which ultimately became dominated by Mengistu Haile Mariam.

On December 20, 1974, the new military government declared Ethiopia a socialist state. What followed was a campaign of terror, first perpetrated by feudal landowners who had been stripped of their possessions, and then by the government, which instigated the "Red Terror" to eliminate political opposition. Between 1974 and 1978, U.S. ambassador to the United Nations Jeanne Kirkpatrick said an estimated 30,000 people were summarily executed for political reasons in Ethiopia.[13] The Ethiopian Jews were caught in between the warring factions, with the landowners exacting vengeance against their former serfs, and the government attacking them for suspected disloyalty. At least one massacre was reported in which thirty men, women, and children were killed in the village of Lastah in early 1974 when the Ethiopian Jews there tried to resist Christian landowners who wanted to drive them off their land.[14]

Although the revolution was supposed to provide land to all Ethiopians, including the Beta Israel, and to bring about a new socialist order that would benefit the minorities, Yona Bogale saw no future for the Ethiopian Jews in the country. He told Kay the only hope for the Ethiopian Jews was *aliyah*. "If only 1,500 boys and girls could go to Israel," Bogale said, "this would be enough to ensure the survival of the Falashas."[15] When Louis Rapoport first reported the Lastah massacre in the *Jerusalem Post* in 1974, he agreed with Bogale. "This may be a difficult time to press for Falasha *aliyah*," he wrote, "but it may also be the last chance to save Ethiopia's Jews."[16]

In his final report after being expelled from Ethiopia, Kay said many Ethiopian Jews who had assimilated would return to their faith if they received some encouragement. He also reported that some Beta Israel villages maintained Jewish traditions despite the absence of *kohanim* and synagogues. On the other hand, he was discouraged by the declining number of Ethiopian Jews who attended the annual Siggud celebration in Ambober, a city near the regional capital of Gondar. In theory, Kay wrote, the Ethiopian Jews were supposed to benefit from land reform under the revolutionary government, but they had not, and he could not see them doing so in the future so long as Amharas, who despised them, dominated the peasant committees. "Life in the Ethiopian countryside," Kay added, "is so primitive and savage that so far it has been the absence rather than the presence of the government which has been so inimical to the peace and security of the Falashas."

The greatest threat to the Ethiopian Jews, however, according to Kay, was the missionary activities of the Church Ministry to the Jews. The only counter to the missionaries were the twenty schools supported by the FWA and the Jewish Agency. As an indication of the relative lack of support of Israel for the Ethiopian Jews, Kay's report noted that forty of the forty-six teachers were paid by the FWA with the remainder getting help from the agency. Those schools, although maintained at "a dismal level," educated more than 1,300 students who would otherwise be forced to attend the missionary schools. He concluded that it was essential to send another representative so the Ethiopian Jews would not feel abandoned, but that *aliyah* still was the community's only hope of survival.

Unless there is *aliyah* eventually, there seems little point in teaching a child Hebrew for three or four years. As it is, we have been doing this and leaving them high and dry, miserable in the aspirations we have awakened but which we cannot satisfy. At best, the founding of a school must be regarded as nothing more than a holding operation. Until *aliyah* can be put into effect, or until we can establish a school whose curriculum bears some relevance to the life in the village in which it is situated, it is difficult to reply to the charge of many Falasha elders and *Cohanim* that our schooling does nothing to hinder the ever present threat of assimilation and conversion—on the contrary, it may well prepare the ground for its realization.[17]

What Kay was saying was that nothing had been learned since the 1950s when the Jewish Agency did the same thing by stimulating the Ethiopian Jews' aspirations for *aliyah* and then leaving them, in Kay's words, "high and dry." Moreover, whatever other reasons may be given for why the Ethiopian Jews were not brought to Israel and why world Jewry did not come to their aid, it cannot be said that it was because no one knew what was happening in Ethiopia. Their plight may not have attracted a lot of publicity, but it was reported in the press and was known by the leaders of establishment organizations and the Israeli government.

RELUCTANT ISRAELIS

The attitude of the Israeli government and Jewish aid organizations toward bringing the Ethiopian Jews to Israel remained at best reluctant and, at worst, hostile. For example, Israeli officials dismissed the reports of the Lastah massacre as exaggerations. According to Rapoport, the officials believed that "murder was an everyday occurrence in Ethiopia and that there was no evidence that the Falashas had been singled out for persecution."[18] This argument, that the suffering of Ethiopian Jews was no worse than other Ethiopians, was voiced consistently by both Israeli officials and American Jewish leaders, as if the murders of Ethiopian Jews were justified because other Ethiopians were also being killed. The fact that Ethiopian Jews were suffering, one would have thought, would have been sufficient reason to come to their aid, but apparently many Jewish leaders believed they had to first prove the Ethiopian Jews were being either singled out for persecution or their suffering was in some way greater than that of other Ethiopians. As the *Jewish Post and Opinion* editorialized in 1974, "As to the Joint Distribution Committee and HIAS (Hebrew Immigrant Aid Society) who are entrusted by the Jewish world with aiding Jews to leave the countries where they are in distress and transport them to Israel or to New York or Canada or wherever, they provide double-talk, but lift no finger."[19]

The situation was exacerbated by the Israeli officials most responsible for *aliyah* because they consistently refused to recognize the necessity of bringing the Ethiopian Jews to Israel. An Israeli embassy official in Washington wrote candidly that "Israel is not enthusiastic about the prospect of Falasha immigration."[20] One of the Jewish Agency's top officials, and the man who would later be responsible for the rescue efforts, Yehuda Dominitz, said,

"Take a Falasha out of his village, it's like taking a fish out of water . . . we are told that the *aliyah* potential is tiny—the number that would leave is minute. Most of the ones that come to Israel felt lost and they went home. I'm not in favor of bringing them."[21] Dominitz later claimed he was misquoted. What he meant to say was that he did not believe individual Jews should be taken out of Ethiopia because it would destroy the community.[22] Nevertheless, activists and other critics seized on the Dominitz statement as evidence that Dominitz, and hence the Jewish Agency, were opposed to *aliyah* for Ethiopian Jews. For people such as Graenum Berger, moreover, the "fish out of water" remark was an example of what he believed was the racist attitude of the Israelis toward the Beta Israel. As far as Dominitz's statement that the *aliyah* potential was small, it is unclear where he got that idea since visitors to Ethiopia had suggested that at least 40 percent of the Ethiopian Jews wanted to come to Israel.[23]

Dominitz said the Jewish Agency felt pressure from Tartakower and the committees for Ethiopian Jews, but "as long as there was no proof of inner strife," there was no urgency to rescue the Ethiopian Jews.[24] In 1975, when Dominitz was put in charge of the immigration effort, he said he had changed his mind, but the critics never trusted him. Rapoport, however, believed he did change his attitude and ultimately played a constructive role in the rescue efforts.[25]

A BUREAUCRATIC ROADBLOCK

The one man whose attitude is widely considered to have been the most detrimental to the immigration of the Ethiopian Jews was Yosef Burg, the former Israeli minister of the interior. Burg, the leader of the National Religious Party, once told Rapoport in connection with the Beta Israel that "you might as well write a book about the Martians." Burg was responsible for issuing the necessary documents for Ethiopian Jews to come to Israel.[26]

In 1973, Burg issued edicts to expel four Ethiopian Jews who had reached Israel because he did not believe the Law of Return applied to them. Hezi Ovadia found a hiding place for the four men and then went to Chief Rabbi Ovadia Yosef and obtained the decisive ruling that the Beta Israel were Jews.[27] Prior to Yosef's decision, the rabbis had said the Ethiopians would have to convert before being considered Jews, and Burg insisted they would have to convert before they could immigrate. However, there was no way for them to convert in Ethiopia, and Israel did nothing to facilitate their conversion, so the minister effectively put them in a catch-22 position.[28]

Even after Yosef's ruling, Burg created obstacles to the immigration of the Ethiopian Jews. In November 1973, for example, Chanan Aynor had worked out a plan with Miriam Freund of Hadassah to develop a Youth Aliyah program for the Ethiopian Jews. Youth Aliyah had originally been created in the 1930s to rescue young Jews from Nazi Germany. The Youth Aliyah officials in Israel began discussing how to implement the plan when the Interior Ministry entered the picture and effectively killed the idea. Aynor believed the program would have been very successful, but it was hamstrung by the attitude of Burg and his appointee at the Jewish Agency, Yehuda Dominitz.[29] Burg also delayed implementation of the Chief Rabbi's ruling so that it took another two years before the Ethiopian Jews were recognized as Jews under the Law of Return and eligible for immediate citizenship. Even then, Burg remained obstinate, refusing to issue the Ethiopians identity cards listing them as "Jewish" for nearly two years, despite receiving instructions from the legal advisor to do so in 1975.[30]

Burg, however, denied that he obstructed efforts to help the Ethiopian Jews. In an interview, Burg recounted his childhood interest in "exotic" and "fringe" Jews and said that he had seen two Ethiopian Jews praying in the Orthodox synagogue he attended. In the early 1930s, he said that he met Ethiopian Jews in Leipzig who were studying dentistry. He also was familiar with the rabbinic opinions that said the Ethiopians were Jews, so there was never any doubt in his mind about their Jewishness. The reason he did not favor *aliyah* was initially based on his concern as the minister of social welfare from 1950 to 1974 that the Ethiopian Jews learn Hebrew and a vocation before they came to Israel so that "we won't have a kind of Harlem here." If that were true, however, the Jewish Agency should not have withdrawn its support for the Ethiopian schools it had set up. Burg also denied ordering the expulsion of Ethiopian Jews. He said he might have issued such an order for Ethiopians who said they were Jews but who were, in fact, not. Finally, he did not believe there was any urgency to bring the Ethiopian Jews to Israel because the Ethiopian government was "not a Nazi regime."[31]

ATTITUDES TOWARD BLACK JEWS

Although there are no doubt racists in Israel, like everywhere else, and there were people who opposed bringing the Ethiopian Jews to Israel, most Israelis were far more tolerant. In a poll for the Ministry of Absorption taken two weeks after the Ethiopian Jews were formally recognized under the Law of Return in May 1975, the Institute of Applied Social Research of Hebrew University found that two-thirds of the respondents believed it was worthwhile to make a major effort to bring the Ethiopian Jews to Israel. Fourteen percent did not think it was so worthwhile, and only eight percent were against such an effort. Surprisingly, it was the Orthodox and observant Jews who were most in favor of bringing the Ethiopian Jews to Israel. The problem for the Ethiopian Jews, however, was that the minority view was more representative of the Israelis in key government positions prior to 1977.

The most damaging evidence that the Israeli government did not want to encourage *aliyah* was a secret report written by Yosef Litvek in January 1973 for the Internal Office of Absorption, Planning and Research Branch of the Department of Research of Diaspora Jewry. In that report, Litvek supports the argument that the Ethiopian Jews are "completely foreign to the Jewish people" and that their only awareness of the existence of the Jewish people was brought to them by Jewish researchers and community leaders with national and religious motivations, primarily for humanitarian reasons, due to their depressed living conditions.

The report reiterates the Ethiopian government's position opposing emigration and adds that the failure to respect that position will not only threaten the Jews but also Israeli-Ethiopian relations. "This last point is especially important in view of the growing crisis in the relations between the Africans and Israel, as a result of the efforts of the Arab states with their ample means."[32] Litvek said that *halacha* (Jewish law) does not recognize them as Jews; therefore, they are ineligible to immigrate under the Law of Return. Moreover, encouraging Ethiopian Jews to emigrate anyway would encourage non-Jews to try to enter Israel. Litvek recommended that nothing should be done to increase the identification of the Beta Israel with Israel: "Certainly it is best for the Falashas and for Israel to completely abandon any plans for their emigration to Israel." This did not mean, however, that Israel should be unsympathetic toward those Ethiopian Jews who were already in Israel or who totally linked their fate to the Jewish people and to Israel. He also recommended that consideration be given to family reunification (nucleonic only) for those Jews who had legally entered Israel and had already been absorbed.[33]

The Litvek report was not well known at the time, and it was not publicly disclosed until January 1979, when the Israeli newspaper *Ma'ariv* revealed its existence.[34] The official position of the Jewish Agency, as reported by the American Jewish Committee's Bernard Resnikoff, was that the Agency would assume the responsibility for absorbing any Ethiopian Jews who reached Israel, but they would not encourage *aliyah*. Resnikoff believed the reasons were the uncertainty as to whether the Beta Israel were Jews; the interest in maintaining good relations with Ethiopia; the tremendous strain on resources necessitated by the absorption of other, mostly Russian, immigrants; and the lack of enthusiasm for absorbing "primitive" people. The JDC's position was that there was no justification for a private effort to encourage *aliyah* so long as the Jewish Agency was unwilling to support it.

Prior to 1975, most of the Ethiopian Jews who had reached Israel (the estimates range from 120 to 350) had done so either by jumping ship in Eilat, a Red Sea port city in southern Israel, or by pretending to be Christians. It was ironic that a Christian wishing to make a pilgrimage to Israel had no difficulty acquiring a visa, but an Ethiopian Jew found it almost impossible to get one. Unlike Christians, the Ethiopian Jews were usually required to leave a $600 deposit and purchase a round-trip airline ticket, both prohibitively costly for the poor Beta Israel, so that there would be little likelihood of them trying to stay in Israel. When the Israeli embassy was closed

in 1973 after Ethiopia broke relations, Rapoport said "that solved the minor nuisance of the Falashas for Israel's Labor Party."[35]

A TURNING POINT

The symbolic turning point in Israel's official attitude toward the Beta
Israel came with Chief Rabbi Ovadia Yosef's decision to recognize them as
Jews; however, the political recognition that the Ethiopian Jews were eligible
under the Law of Return did not occur for another two years. The reason
that it occurred even then was a matter of luck according to the people who
believe that Burg would have prevented the recognition. In 1974, Burg went
on a trip abroad, and Shlomo Hillel became the acting minister of the interior for six months. While in office, he discovered a letter from Rabbi Yosef
saying the Ethiopian Jews were Jews and thought that would enable them
to come under the Law of Return. People at the ministry said that it would
be difficult to make any changes, so Hillel summoned the attorney general
to try to find a solution. Before he could, however, Burg returned. Hillel
did not follow up on the matter until 1976 when he again was asked to fill
in as interior minister. At that time, he felt he did not need any advice and
simply made the decision that the Ethiopian Jews were eligible under the
Law of Return.[36] Ironically, it was a secular person who endorsed the rabbinic
decision.

The government's attitude actually began to slowly change even before
Hillel's action. In a meeting at the end of 1974 with Burg's deputy, the director general of the Prime Minister's Office, and his deputy, Tartakower was
told that Ethiopian Jews whose identity was established would be given Israeli
visas without the prior conditions. In addition, the officials expressed the
belief that it would be possible to obtain exit permits from Ethiopia for Jews
who had work contracts from well-known foreign firms.[37] This apparently
was the beginning of a plan to supply Ethiopian Jews with such permits as a
cover for bringing them to Israel.

Gabi Sebag, who worked for Koor, one of Israel's largest companies, initiated efforts to supply Ethiopian Jews with work permits to come to Israel
and work for his company. At the end of December 1974, the first group
arrived. It was originally thought that five hundred Ethiopian Jews could be
brought in this way, but only seven arrived initially. Sebag explained that the
small number was the result of the unavoidable difficulties associated with
starting such a program and the necessity of securing documentation such
as exit visas and health certificates. Ironically, the plan was derailed by the
government's decision to admit the Ethiopian Jews under the Law of Return. An interministerial committee chaired by the minister of justice was
empowered with the responsibility for making the decision about the eligibility of the Ethiopian Jews. When they made their decision, it was supposed
to remain secret because Sebag was in the process of organizing a group of

seventy Ethiopian Jews to enter Israel on work permits for Koor. When the Israeli government and press publicized that seventy Falashas would be flown to Israel "within a week" under the Law of Return, however, the Ethiopian government stopped them from leaving. An Israeli Absorption Ministry official told the *Jerusalem Post* that the announcement was "stupid, wrong, and dangerous to the Falashas during a period of uncertainty in Ethiopia."[38] This was the first of several instances in which publicity harmed the rescue effort. It was not surprising, therefore, that the Israeli government would become sensitive about publicity and that they would become critical of the AAEJ's later efforts in the United States to stimulate press coverage of the Ethiopian Jews' plight. The AAEJ's response would be that their publicity never hurt the rescue effort but it was Israeli publicity, such as in this case, that was responsible for the various suspensions of rescue activity.

No doubt as a response to the Koor fiasco, the government put the subject of Ethiopian Jews under the control of the military censor so that for the next several years Israeli newspapers would be constrained as to what they could publish about the Ethiopian Jews. Once again, this action was seen by critics as an attempt to protect the government from criticism and pressure to help the Ethiopian Jews. The Israeli justification was that censorship was required for the protection of the community and rescue efforts. According to Rapoport, the mention of Diaspora Jews living in countries where the community is endangered, such as Syria, falls under the censorship laws so that the ruling regarding Ethiopian Jews could not be considered unique.[39] The Tartakower group, moreover, endorsed censorship of the issue.[40]

REASSESSMENT

Berger continued to demand greater efforts to bring about *aliyah*. The Koor fiasco, however, led some people to believe that *aliyah* was not practical. This was David Kessler's view. In a reply to an earlier letter from Berger, the British publisher disagreed with the American's view that aid to the Ethiopian Jews undermined the prospects for *aliyah*. Kessler believed the two were complementary and that "every effort should be directed towards raising the morale and standard of living of the community on the spot." He said that he had discussed Berger's suggestion that the JDC assume responsibility for helping the Falashas, but that they had told him it was contrary to their policy and that they preferred to work through the FWA. The FWA's own activities were inadvertently undermined by the Koor plan because their representative, Julian Kay, was expelled afterward.[41] This illustrates that even among the activists there were divergent opinions as to the best strategy to help the Ethiopian Jews.

Despite the setback, the Israelis did not abandon their efforts to find a way to bring the Ethiopian Jews to Israel. Prime Minister Rabin sent emissaries to Ethiopia, but the Ethiopian government remained unwilling to let the Jews leave.[42] Like Dominitz, Burg, and others, General Ephraim Poran (later Prime Minister Begin's military adviser, who was put in charge of the Ethiopian Jewry issue) said there was no sense of urgency so the government did not see an immediate need for large-scale *aliyah*.[43]

In October 1975, meetings were held in Ethiopia between Israeli and Ethiopian officials and the latter expressed an interest in obtaining military aid from Israel.[44] According to a CIA report, Ethiopian leader Mengistu decided that the Israelis could help his army cope with the insurrections in Ethiopia and that this service outweighed any political fallout from Ethiopia's Arab neighbors.[45] That created a slight opening for Israel. According to Shlomo Hillel, when the Ethiopians asked what Israel wanted from Ethiopia to prove its friendship, the Israeli ambassador said, "Send Jews."[46] In that initial October meeting, the Israelis raised the possibility of exchanging arms for the release of Ethiopian Jews, and although no agreement was reached at that time, the foundation was laid for the one that was later consummated.

In the meantime, the Israelis kept channels of communication open and smuggled in small numbers of Ethiopian Jews. An Israeli fishing company in Asmara, for example, took Ethiopian Jews who could reach the port to Israel.[47] Israel also organized a clandestine rescue attempt after an Israeli who had spent time in Ethiopia training the police force suggested that Ethiopian Jews could be taken by bus to Nairobi and then flown directly to Israel. That operation turned out to be a fiasco when twenty-four Ethiopian Jews were arrested and tortured in December 1975 trying to cross the border into Kenya. Eventually, the Jews were allowed to return to their families.[48]

UPHEAVAL IN ETHIOPIA

After the unsuccessful effort in 1975, the Israelis were cautious in their planning for rescues because they did not want to put the lives of either the Ethiopian Jews or their rescuers at risk. It also illustrated how difficult it was to escape from Ethiopia despite the chaos that engulfed the country. In 1974, Julian Kay reported "the country is in such turmoil that . . . even if official sanction for the evacuation of the Falashas was not forthcoming it would be relatively easy to arrange their clandestine departure."[49] In an interview, David Ottaway, the *Washington Post's* correspondent in Ethiopia from 1974 to 1977, agreed that the government had so little control over the country that escape should have been easy.[50] In practice, however, it was much more difficult.

At the end of January 1976, Tartakower informed Berger that an agreement between the Israeli and Ethiopian governments had been reached and speculated that the release of the twenty-four Jews captured in December was the first consequence of that agreement. Tartakower also warned that there should be no publicity about the agreement despite the fact that it was "legal."[51] Two months later, Tartakower told Berger that nearly seventy Ethiopian Jews were prepared for emigration and that if they reached Israel without any problems another group would be selected to be reunited with their families.[52] Problems did arise, however, and Tartakower had to write again in August to say the Ethiopian government remained willing to permit the Ethiopian Jews to leave, but a list had not been submitted because the Jews could not agree among themselves as to who should be included.[53] This was an example of the infighting that often took place among the Ethiopian Jews, which sometimes hindered efforts to help them.

In October, there still had been no immigration. Paran wrote Berger and asked him to encourage his friends to lobby the prime minister and the chairperson of the Jewish Agency because the Agency was not following through on the plan. Paran said that some people were still creating obstacles to immigration, and he hoped that personal rather than public pressure could stimulate the Israelis to act.[54] The following month, Tartakower spoke to Dominitz and was told the Mossad was trying to obtain the consent of the Ethiopians to send a representative of the Aliyah Department to Ethiopia, but the Ethiopian government had a policy of procrastination, and he did not foresee when that consent would be given.[55] This had long been one of Berger's complaints, that is, Israel had not sent a *shaliach*—a person who facilitates immigration—to organize and stimulate *aliyah*. The Ethiopians denied the Israeli request and then the Israelis felt constrained against sending a representative secretly because, Dominitz said, "it would be dirty pool to talk above the table and deal under it." In addition, it was likely that if an unauthorized representative was caught, he would be killed.[56] Dominitz contradicted this version of events in an interview when he said that *shlichim* were sent to Ethiopia, only they were not called by that name. "They went under different covers because they were not allowed to go to Addis as representatives of the Jewish Agency." The AAEJ and several Ethiopian Jews said they never saw any of these messengers, but Dominitz replied, "just because Ethiopian Jews did not see them does not mean that they were not there."[57] This makes little sense, however, because the purpose of the *shaliach* is presumably to encourage Ethiopian Jews to make *aliyah*, so if the Beta Israel did not see them they were not doing their job.

It was true that the Israelis maintained a presence in Ethiopia even after Haile Selassie was overthrown and diplomatic relations were severed. Israel continued to provide counterinsurgency training, spare parts, and light arms to government forces, particularly in Eritrea. No more than twenty-five or thirty Mossad agents were in the country at the time, and there are conflicting reports of their mission. One source, for example, said their work was closely coordinated with U.S. interest in obtaining information after the U.S. embassy staff was cut back.[58] It was reported in the *Los*

Angeles Times, however, that U.S. officials were unhappy about the Israeli arrangement.[59]

ACTIVISTS CHARGE RACISM

As the years passed, and the Ethiopian Jews were not brought to Israel, Berger became increasingly critical and lashed out at Israel's inaction. He had reason to doubt the Israeli commitment to the Ethiopian Jews because officials had consistently expressed views to him indicating their lack of interest. At the end of 1973, for example, General Narkiss of the Jewish Agency told him Israel already had overwhelming problems resulting from the Yom Kippur War and the difficulty of absorbing nearly 70,000 Russian Jews. Berger asked Narkiss if he felt the Jewish Agency could not accept more Ethiopian Jews for practical reasons or if he was personally opposed to their *aliyah*. Narkiss replied that he was opposed to their admission in principle.[60]

The following year, after Ovadia Yossef's decision, the chairperson of the Jewish Agency, Pinchas Sapir, was calling for increased emigration from the Soviet Union, but said the matter of Ethiopian Jewish emigration required further study. When a questioner pointed out that the Ethiopian Jewish population had declined from 100,000 to 25,000, Sapir replied that was all the more reason for additional study. He also intimated that if the Beta Israel were assimilating so easily there was no reason for them to be readily accepted in Israel.[61]

This kind of reasoning infuriated Berger, who was convinced that the Ethiopian Jews were assimilating because they did not have the opportunity to immigrate to Israel and that the Jewish Agency had abandoned them by pulling out its support for their schools. It was impossible for Berger to understand how the nation that had rescued thousands of Jews around the world from oppression could not act on behalf of the Ethiopian Jews. The only explanation he could imagine, and the one he clung to throughout his life, was that Israeli officials did not want to rescue the Beta Israel because they were black. In an interview in 1981, he explained: "I've been working on behalf of the Falashas for 25 years and all along I could never bring myself to think that Israel's reaction was due to racism, but racism is the only reason it could possibly be."[62] He expressed the same sentiments to his friends and fellow activists, telling one, for example, that the Jews would never be saved until the leadership of the American Jewish community and the prime minister of Israel were called "blatant Jewish racists."[63] He also criticized Howard Lenhoff, who succeeded Berger as AAEJ president, for believing the religious issue was holding the government back: "THE ONLY PERVASIVE OBJECTIONS HIDDEN BEHIND A SCORE OF REASONS WERE THAT THE FALASHAS WERE BLACK" (emphasis in original).[64]

Although many of the Ethiopian Jews in Israel also believed the government was racist, most activists on their behalf did not. The more common view was that the problem was the objective realities in Ethiopia, not racism or disinterest on the part of the authorities. Israeli government officials responded to charges they were racist with predictable indignation. They would ask how they could be accused of racism when they had rescued more than 40,000 Yemenite Jews and thousands of Sephardic Jews who had been brought to Israel from North Africa who were not much lighter skinned than the Ethiopians. There is little evidence that Israel was unwilling to rescue the Ethiopian Jews because of the color of the skin. In 1982, Lenhoff wrote an article in *Israel Today* that quoted the passage from Malkah Raymist's 1956 article in *The Jewish Horizon,* which clearly showed that racist attitudes existed but did not prove that was the explanation for Israel's alleged inaction.[65]

It is hard to imagine what Berger and those colleagues who shared his belief hoped to accomplish by branding the Israelis as racist. At best, he apparently hoped to embarrass them into action, which he claimed to have done; however, his main achievement was to alienate Israeli officials. This line of criticism was especially counterproductive because it damaged the AAEJ's credibility with the Israelis and the establishment American Jewish organizations, which saw such attacks as aiding the enemies of Israel who had succeeded in getting the United Nations to equate Zionism with racism in 1975. In addition, the AAEJ was violating one of the precepts of diaspora behavior, namely, to keep all criticism "within the family." It was the AAEJ's insistence on publicizing its condemnation not only in the Jewish press, but the secular press as well that led the establishment to cast aspersions on the AAEJ's motives. This was unfortunate because the AAEJ was the principal organization crusading on behalf of the Beta Israel and Berger and Lenhoff were passionately committed to their welfare.

Even if Israel was not racist, and most of the AAEJ's members did not believe it was, there was still a conviction that the Israelis were not doing all they could to save the Ethiopian Jews. As evidence, they pointed to the 1973 Litvek report, which recommended that nothing be revealed about Ethiopian Jewry and that no action be taken to bring them to Israel. That same year, David Zohar, of the Israeli embassy in Washington, wrote in *Sh'ma* that "Israel is not enthusiastic about the prospects of Falasha immigration."[66]

NOTES

1. Louis Rapoport, "The Falashas: This Year in Jerusalem?" *Women's American ORT Reporter* (May/June 1975): 2; Louis Rapoport, "The Falashas," *Jerusalem Post Magazine* (April 12, 1974).

2. David Kessler, "Falashas Face Extinction," *Jewish Chronicle* (February 23, 1973).

3. Julian Kay, "Report Number 10" (Falasha Welfare Association, April 5, 1974).

4. Ed Ginsburg, "Report to JDC National Council" (Joint Distribution Committee, June–July, 1974).

5. Diane Winston, "The Falashas: History and Analysis of Policy Towards a Beleaguered Community" (NY: National Jewish Resource Center, April 1980), p. 4; Herbert Katzki, letter to Graenum Berger, November 28, 1978; David Kessler, "The Falashas—The Jews of Ethiopia: An Almost Forgotten Community," IJA Research Reports (England: Institute of Jewish Affairs, February 1983), p. 7.

6. Hadassah Newsletter, May 1924.

7. Ibid.

8. Graenum Berger, *Rescue the Ethiopian Jews!* (NY: John Washburn Bleeker Hampton Publishing, 1996), p. ix.

9. Graenum Berger, "The Plight of the Falashas," *Congress Bi-Weekly* (October 25, 1974).

10. Berger, *Rescue*, pp. 45–46, 53.

11. Graenum Berger letter to Howard Lenhoff, January 17, 1976; Graenum Berger, letter to Howard Lenhoff, June 7, 1978; Graenum Berger, letter to Howard Lenhoff, February 15, 1976.

12. Graenum Berger, letter to Howard Lenhoff, October 11, 1974.

13. Thomas Magstadt, "Ethiopia's Great Terror," *Worldview* (April 1982): p. 5.

14. Rapoport, "The Falashas: This Year in Jerusalem?," p. 2; Rapoport, "The Falashas."

15. Kay, "Report Number 10."

16. Rapoport, "The Falashas."

17. Julian Kay, Final Report (Falasha Welfare Association, June 5, 1975).

18. Louis Rapoport, *Redemption Song* (NY: Harcourt Brace Jovanovich, 1986), p. 52.

19. Editorial, *Jewish Post and Opinion*, February 15, 1974.

20. David Zohar, letter to the editor, *Sh'ma*, February 2, 1973, p. 55.

21. Louis Rapoport, *The Lost Jews* (NY: Stein and Day, 1980), p. 53.

22. Yehuda Dominitz, interview with author.

23. For example, Julian Kay, "Report Number 11" (Falasha Welfare Association, April 12, 1974).

24. Dominitz, interview with author.

25. Louis Rapoport, interview with author.

26. Rapoport, *Redemption Song*, p. iv.

27. Moshe Bar-Yehuda, interview with author.

28. Chanan Aynor, interview with author.

29. Ibid.

30. Natalie Berger, interview with author.

31. Yosef Burg, interview with author.

32. At the time of the 1973 war, and the Arab oil embargo, Arab oil-producing nations placed great pressure on African states to break relations with Israel. The black African states did. Israel maintained good relations with several and formal ties began to be restored in the early 1990s as the oil-producers' political power waned.

33. Yosef Litvek, "The Falashim" (Internal Office of Absorption, Planning and Research Branch, Department of Research of Diaspora Jewry), Israel, January 1973.

34. Natalie Berger, interview with author.

35. Rapoport, *The Lost Jews*, p. 53.

36. Shlomo Hillel, interview with author.

37. Mordecai Paran, "Report on Activities in Israel on Behalf of the Falashas" (Jewish Colonization Association in Israel, October 1974).

38. Louis Rapoport and Judy Siegel, "Ethiopian Falashas Recognized as Jews under Law of Return," *Jerusalem Post*, April 15, 1975; Rapoport, *The Lost Jews*, pp. 44–45, 197–198.

39. Rapoport, *The Lost Jews*, pp. 199–200.

40. Chanan Lehmann, interview with author.

41. David Kessler, letter to Graenum Berger, August 6, 1975.

42. Lehmann, interview; Hillel, interview.

43. General Ephraim Poran, interview with author.

44. Memo, regarding meeting between Berger and Israeli officials, October 7, 1975.

45. Jack Anderson, "Israel Aiding Mengistu in Ethiopia," *Washington Post*, January 2, 1985.

46. Hillel, interview.

47. General Ephraim Poran, interview; Aynor, interview.

48. Graenum Berger, letter to Howard Lenhoff, January 16, 1976; Myer Levin, "The Last of the Falashas," *Midstream* (June–July, 1975): 47; Mordecai Paran, Israel Committee for Ethiopian Jews, letter to Graenum Berger, January 26, 1976; Graenum Berger, letter to Bernie and Fran Alpert, June 20, 1977; Dominitz, interview.

49. Kay, "Report Number 11."

50. David Ottaway, interview with author.

51. Aryeh Tartakower, letter to Graenum Berger, January 30, 1976.

52. Graenum Berger, letter to Howard Lenhoff, March 5, 1976.

53. Aryeh Tartakower, letter to Graenum Berger, August, 29, 1976.

54. Mordecai Paran, letter to Graenum Berger, October 10, 1976.

55. Aryeh Tartakower, letter to Graenum Berger, November 29, 1976.

56. Henry Rosenberg, letter to Graenum Berger, approximately December 20, 1976.

57. Dominitz, interview.

58. Michael Ledeen, "The Israeli Connection," in Michael Samuels et al., eds., *The Washington Review* (May 1978).

59. Oswald Johnson, "Israeli Agents Reportedly Training Ethiopian Troops," *Los Angeles Times*, July 23, 1977.

60. Graenum Berger, memo on meeting with General Uzi Narkiss and Isadore Hamlin of Jewish Agency in New York, December 6, 1973, AAEJ.

61. Charles Roth, "Russian, American Jews Yes, Not Falashas: Sapir," *Jewish Post and Opinion*, November 22, 1974.

62. Gary Rosenblatt and Michael Alloy, "Fighting for Falashas," *Baltimore Jewish Times*, February 20, 1981, p. 42.

63. Graenum Berger, letter to Bernie Alpert, August 22, 1977.

64. Graenum Berger, letter to Howard Lenhoff, January 19, 1978.

65. Howard Lenhoff, "Documents Reveal Longstanding Policy Against Falasha Aliyah," *Israel Today*, January 28, 1982.

66. Zohar, letter to editor.

CHAPTER 4

Early Rescue Efforts

B y the beginning of 1977, a new civil war was escalating in Ethiopia as pro- and anti-government forces battled each other. One of the major battlefields was in Gondar province where Ethiopian Jews became trapped between the competing factions. The Ethiopian Jews were pressured to join guerrilla groups seeking to overthrow the government. Many Ethiopian Jews were killed for being "fascists" or "Zionist tools" of the government and others died in the cross fire. The total number of Ethiopian Jewish deaths was at least 300.[1]

When Menachem Begin came to power in Israel in May 1977, he pledged to bring the Ethiopian Jews to Israel, but the American Association for Ethiopian Jews (AAEJ) remained skeptical because of "a small number of bigoted, but powerful people, who threaten to break up his coalition if more than token gestures are made to rescue the Falashas."[2] Their concerns were reinforced when the new government issued guidelines that called for "a constant campaign for the return to Zion of all who yearn for her in the Soviet Union, and for the rescue of the Jewries of Syria and the Arab states," but neglected to mention the Ethiopian Jews.[3] This skepticism was also fed by Israeli actions and statements, one of the most notable being Defense Minister Ezer Weizman's response to a question about the Beta Israel at the annual conference of the North American Jewish Student Network in December 1979, when he said: "Everyone in the Cabinet has their own

problems; you have to bother me with the Falashas too. Falasha, smalasha."[4]
A State Department official commented, "I think he summed up, as only
Ezer can do, the prevailing attitude of most of the people in the government of Israel. Abba Eban put it a bit more elegantly when he said, 'I believe there are larger issues on Israel's political agenda,' or something to that
effect. But that's just an Oxfordian way of saying Falasha smalasha."[5]

It was always difficult for Americans to criticize Israel because of the tradition of keeping dissent within the family, but it was particularly hard for
the AAEJ to argue with Begin since his relationship with the United States
was already tense because of his policies toward the administered territories.
"At the moment," AAEJ president Graenum Berger wrote to Howard
Lenhoff in August 1977, "all of American Jewish leadership is tied up defending Begin against the U.S. . . . So they wouldn't breathe a word of prejudice against him, and we will find ourselves not only ignored but even
repudiated."[6] Simultaneously, it was clear to Berger that Begin was the only
one who had the power to reverse what he believed was the Israeli policy of
neglecting the Ethiopian Jews.

RESCUE PLANS

The Mossad began planning for the evacuation of the Ethiopian Jews
under Prime Minister Yitzhak Rabin, but the operation was implemented by
Menachem Begin. Begin was a man who had long been known for his commitment to saving Jews in distress, so it was no surprise that he was the first
Israeli leader to meet with the Ethiopian Jews in Israel and that one of his
early initiatives as prime minister was to send a message to Ethiopian
strongman Mengistu Haile Mariam asking him to let the Ethiopian Jews immigrate to Israel.

As a result of the earlier failure to rescue Jews through a clandestine operation, Berger became convinced that it was necessary to organize *aliyah*
by some legal means such as that employed with the Soviet Union; that is,
reunification of families. The Israelis shared that belief, and the groundwork
for such an arrangement was laid in discussions regarding the provision of
military aid to Ethiopia. In April 1977, before Begin was elected, the Jewish
Agency sent Haim Halachmy to Ethiopia to arrange for family reunification
on a humanitarian basis. He brought with him the names and addresses of
150 Ethiopian Jews living in Israel and gave it to the Ethiopian minister of
interior. The Ethiopians said they wanted to make a test case of people from
Gondar because it was closer to Addis Ababa. Halachmy was told he had to
provide someone to help the government identify the Jews and check their
names with the list of relatives in Israel. Halachmy brought Gedalia Uria
because he was a teacher who could speak Hebrew. The Ethiopians appointed
Uria to represent the government in Gondar. It took four months for Uria

to identify the relatives of the Ethiopian Jews in Israel and obtain permission for them to leave.[7]

TRADING ARMS FOR JEWS

To some extent, Israel is the victim of its own success; that is, there is a tendency to believe that Israel can do anything it wants; therefore, the AAEJ insisted the reason the Ethiopian Jews were not being brought to Israel was that Israel did not want them. After the revolution in Ethiopia, Israeli officials claimed they could not help the Beta Israel because they no longer had diplomatic relations with the government, but it was later learned that Israel was still providing arms to the Ethiopian government; the AAEJ believed those arms should be traded for Ethiopian Jews.

In a speech at Hebrew University on August 15, 1977, Berger said Israel was sending supplies to Ethiopia, but the planes were coming back empty: "Why couldn't they come back filled with Jews?"[8] Berger had initially hoped to make a speech announcing the triumphant arrival of Ethiopian Jews arriving under the new government, but when it became clear that no Jews were coming, he felt the need to indict the government for inaction. Yehuda Dominitz, General Ephraim Poran, and Aryeh Tartakower all tried to discourage Berger from speaking, but he refused to listen. According to Berger, Poran did succeed in getting the military censors to make sure there was no press coverage of his talk; nevertheless, the *Jerusalem Post*'s Louis Rapoport did attend. When Berger asked Rapoport the following day why no story appeared, the reporter told him that he had been told by two activists that it would lead to the slaughter of the Beta Israel; Rapoport said that "such a slaughter would be on his conscience forever."[9]

On August 25, 1977, ten days after Berger's speech, sixty Ethiopian Jews secretly arrived in Israel on military supply planes in what Israeli officials hoped would be the first of many arms-for-Jews exchanges. Prior to this, critics who were aware of Israel's arms deals with Ethiopia had repeatedly asked why such a deal had not been made and then, after the exchange was arranged, they wanted to know why there were not more planes filled with Ethiopian Jews coming to Israel instead of the supply planes returning empty. According to Rapoport, the problem was Jewish Agency inefficiency; that is, there was a lack of coordination between the Mossad, the Jewish Agency, and the Ethiopian government. Rapoport said an experienced Israeli was available in Ethiopia to coordinate the operation, but the Jewish Agency, "for obscure reasons of its own, vetoed his participation."[10] According to Halachmy and General Poran, however, the reason planes came back empty was that the Ethiopian government only agreed to allow a certain number of Ethiopian Jews to leave and did so reluctantly. Those that did come were allowed to leave; they had not been smuggled.[11] Dominitz said they could have airlifted two hundred from Gondar, "but what," he asked, "would happen to the 28,000 left behind?" Israel feared there would be retribution against the remaining Jews if they airlifted people illegally.[12]

Although the warnings Berger was given were probably to prevent his speech from jeopardizing that operation, the American saw his actions as the catalyst. Berger became more convinced than ever that Israel would act when threatened with publicity despite evidence from two activists working with the AAEJ that showed that long and arduous negotiations were required before the group had been allowed to leave.[13] In fact, the Rabin government had been negotiating with Mengistu for a trade of arms for Jews but had difficulty in securing the Ethiopian leader's approval. Once the first plane arrived, however, the AAEJ was convinced it was a simple trade and there was no reason why all of the Ethiopian Jews should not be able to come out the same way. In fact, Mengistu had only reluctantly allowed the sixty out, but he did agree to at least one more trip and negotiations were continuing. According to Haim Halachmy, the man who represented the Jewish Agency and Hebrew Immigrant Aid Society (HIAS) in the negotiations, the route looked promising and Israel hoped to begin increasingly regular flights.

In September 1977, Begin wrote directly to Mengistu and asked him to permit the Ethiopian Jews to emigrate. The Ethiopian leader responded positively, and Halachmy began to organize another group of Jews, which Tartakower believed would consist of about four hundred people. Actually, Halachmy only planned another group of sixty.[14] Just after Egyptian president Anwar Sadat made his historic journey to Jerusalem in November 1977, and Begin was preparing to meet U.S. president Jimmy Carter in Washington, Mengistu sent his reply, asking Begin for help in securing U.S. aid for Ethiopia's fight against Soviet-supported Somali forces in Ogaden. Mengistu said he needed arms and American spare parts from Israel, but the arrangement had to be kept secret. Begin promised his help in exchange for Mengistu's cooperation on the Ethiopian Jewish issue; however, the agreement fell through when Carter vetoed the idea because of what he felt was Mengistu's poor record on human rights.[15] According to a State Department source, this was the first Israeli contact with the United States on the subject and also illustrated the personal involvement of Begin on this issue, which, according to the source, made a big difference in making the issue a high priority in Israel.[16]

After failing to secure U.S. aid, Mengistu turned to the Soviet Union, which was more than willing to fill the vacuum. Despite Carter's response, Israel's willingness to raise the issue and to provide spare parts on its own—with American permission—created a positive atmosphere that allowed the arms-for-Jews agreement to be finalized. In December, a second group of sixty Ethiopian Jews was permitted to leave.

The AAEJ and other activists were not satisfied by the small numbers, even though there had been practically no one rescued before. "If you told Ethiopian Jewry organizations in Israel or in the United States in April 1977 that 120 Ethiopian Jews would come in," Dominitz said, "they would have been thrilled." Tartakower told the chairperson of the Jewish Agency, Pinchas Sapir, that Israel should bring in 400 or 500 a year. Sapir asked: "What about 100 or 200?" Tartakower replied that Sapir would be a hero. "The 120," Dominitz added, "was a tremendous success. You don't know how difficult it was to get 120."[17] Nevertheless, the Israelis also were not satisfied. When Halachmy said he planned to go to Ethiopia every three or four months and take people out, his superior at HIAS lamented that it would take fifty years to get them all out.[18] At the time, however, it was the best the Israelis could do, and they still hoped the exchanges would become a regular means of immigration.

DAYAN'S DISCLOSURE

The willingness of the Ethiopian government to cooperate came to an end in February 1978 after Israeli foreign minister Moshe Dayan told a press conference in Geneva that Israel was helping arm Ethiopia against its enemies. As a consequence of this statement, the Ethiopian government was put in the awkward position of explaining to its Arab and Communist allies why it was cooperating with Israel, a country with whom it had no diplomatic relations. The government subsequently decided it was prudent to break off arms sales with Israel, though they were later resumed, thereby ending the possibility of exchanges for Jews.

The AAEJ did not know about the Israeli efforts to start a pipeline and considered the Dayan statement as a deliberate act of sabotage and yet another indication of Israel's unwillingness to rescue the Ethiopian Jews—even after 120 were brought to Israel. This view was bolstered by an Israeli diplomat interviewed by *Ha'aretz*, who said the Jews who had been rescued were only meant "to throw sand in the eyes of good American Jews who pressured the government of Israel to act to save the Jews and quiet the conscience in Israel itself." When asked if he believed Dayan intentionally leaked the information about the arms sales, the diplomat replied that "with Moshe Dayan, there were no accidental disclosures. He revealed the matter with intent and forethought and expected that, in their reaction to the disclosure, the Ethiopians would announce the termination of *aliyah*—*aliyah* which in reality didn't exist. Also, in the absence of immigration, it would be possible to accuse the Ethiopians while we would have a clean record."[19] U.S. embassy officials in Tel Aviv believed that Dayan wanted to clarify reports from the United States of Israel's aid to Ethiopia, thinking that the matter was bound to come to light anyway. There was also a second suspected reason but that information was deleted when the cable was declassified.[20]

Other people who knew Moshe Dayan agreed that he would not have made such a gaffe unintentionally; however, none of those interviewed believed that his disclosure had anything to do with the Ethiopian Jews. Shlomo Hillel, for example, said that Dayan was not too good in foreign affairs and attributed the statement to "stupidity." He suspected, however, that Dayan was trying to prove that Israeli-Ethiopian relations were good.[21] This view was buttressed by Aynor who said the day before Dayan's trip, the foreign minister called him. Aynor said he told Dayan the week before that an Ethiopian MIG fighter had intercepted an Israeli transport. Dayan was furious. "At a critical time in Ethiopia's existence, Israel's assistance was critical," Aynor observed, "and Dayan wanted the Ethiopian people to know that they owed Israel."[22] Yet another explanation was provided by Dominitz, who said that Begin told him the Ethiopians were about to sever relations anyway because there was no room for both the Soviet Union and Israel, so he provided them with a pretext.[23] On the other hand, Dayan may have had no particular reason for his actions, as Israeli ambassador Gideon Rafael wrote in describing the former foreign minister:

> It has become an Israeli national pastime, cherished by many and loathed by others, to figure out the true intentions behind the surprise moves of Moshe Dayan. Some appear to be so involved that seasoned Dayanologists believe that he himself is not always clear at the onset of an opaque move of the end he strives for. Rocking the boat is his favorite tactic, not to overturn it, but to sway it sufficiently for the helmsman to lose his grip or for some of its unwanted passengers to fall overboard.[24]

In February 1978, Dayan apparently miscalculated because he tipped the boat over.

PERSECUTION GROWS

The Israelis gradually moved back into Ethiopia, but the immediate impact of the Dayan statement was to cause their expulsion and to put an end to any hope of direct *aliyah* from that country. Despite this political reality, there were still members of the AAEJ who believed it was possible to bring Ethiopian Jews out of Ethiopia and that the Israelis were just making excuses. Lenhoff, for example, again raised the issue of sending a *shaliach* to Ethiopia and was told by Dominitz the same thing the AAEJ had been told earlier; the agency could not send a representative to Ethiopia without that government's consent, something that was not forthcoming.[25]

Meanwhile, the Dergue became more firmly entrenched and began to institute socialist methods of control, such as a national service campaign composed of students selected by the government to help spread literacy and Marxist ideology to the peasantry. Organized efforts were also made to persuade the Ethiopian Jews to give up their traditions. Their practice of *kashrut* (dietary laws) was ridiculed as was their observance of the Sabbath. To undermine their adherence to the laws regarding the Sabbath, the local governor in Gondar made Saturday market day.[26] In addition, in keeping with the Marxist attitude toward religion, the Ministry of Information issued a paper on how to eliminate religion from Ethiopia. Although the paper refers only to churches and mosques, the implications for worshipers in synagogues was clear.

> Today, although the Ethiopian revolution inspires hope, it is (also) evident that places of worship (religious places) have become tools to frustrate the workers' (own) movement. . . . If the revolution is to achieve its ultimate goal, it is of the greatest importance to conduct a campaign against religion and to eliminate once and for all this dangerous anti-revolutionary cancer.[27]

Although the AAEJ publicized that the Ethiopian Jews were being persecuted as Jews, for the most part, whatever discrimination existed in Ethiopia was not sanctioned by the central government. The persecution of the Ethiopian Jews was primarily carried out by their neighbors for historical and cultural reasons rather than political ones. Nevertheless, reports periodically surfaced indicating that Jews imprisoned at various times, usually for trying to escape, were treated worse than other prisoners. As scholar Tudor Parfitt explains, "even sympathizers of the EDU or EPRP were still considered 'good Ethiopians,' whereas the Falashas were viewed as traitors and spies who were trying to reach 'racist' Israel."[28]

ORT IN ETHIOPIA

From 1977 to 1979, the Joint Distrubtion Committee (JDC) provided $150,000 directly to Ethiopia and, in 1980, contributed $456,000 to ORT. The AAEJ's attitude toward the program was typified by Nate Shapiro, who would succeed Lenhoff as president. After a Jewish Federation official told him that ORT was spending the "incredible sum of $400,000" on the Ethiopian Jews, Shapiro thought to himself, "Isn't that wonderful, they're spending $15 or $18 a person on Ethiopian Jews."[29] Though the level of funding was paltry, the impact of ORT's program was exponential. "It was this beginning of Hebrew teaching that reawoke the ancient dream and hope of making *aliyah* to the Land of Zion and Jerusalem," said one Ethiopian Jew who attended an ORT school.[30]

To qualify for grants from governmental sources, ORT had to agree to provide aid on a nonsectarian basis. This provoked criticism from Beta Israel activists in the United States who felt that assistance should only be given to the Ethiopian Jews. Gershon Levy, the director of the program, began to criticize the ORT effort because a non-Jew who was not supportive of the Beta Israel had been appointed to a top position and the extraordinary needs of the Jews were not being met. Levy was later forced to resign because he refused to repudiate his criticisms. The AAEJ, meanwhile, accepted Levy's account and took his reports as an indication of ORT's inability to adequately provide for the Beta Israel.

The reality was that ORT's freedom of action was limited by the restrictions placed on its funding and operation. The Ethiopian government was only willing to allow ORT in the country if it agreed to provide aid to non-Jews as well as the Falashas. This was, as Robin Gilbert had found out in the 1950s, a requirement the emperor had also insisted upon. Despite the restrictions, at least two thousand Jewish families did receive aid from ORT in 1979 in the form of tools, seed, oxen, fertilizer, and agricultural and crafts training. The following year, nine hundred families received aid. In addition, ORT operated twenty-two schools, twenty-five synagogues and two clinics, and was involved in a number of other development projects.[31] The director of ORT's education program said the schools had five thousand students, about 16 percent of whom were non-Jews.[32] One of the other factors the AAEJ did not appreciate, according to one JDC official, was how difficult it was to get anything done in Ethiopia.[33]

Another criticism leveled against ORT and the JDC, mainly by the AAEJ, was that they were not doing anything to promote *aliyah*. The AAEJ did not believe in relief; it demanded that all the Ethiopian Jews be brought to Israel and therefore expected any Jewish organization in Ethiopia to contribute toward that goal. The AAEJ was convinced that neither ORT nor the JDC would do so. Graenum Berger believed ORT officials did play a role in the clandestine operation that brought two groups of Ethiopian Jews to Israel in 1977, but he also thought ORT was unwilling to jeopardize its operations in Ethiopia by promoting *aliyah*. This was a concern for both ORT and the JDC. In fact, Shari Hyman of the JDC admitted her organization always steered clear of *aliyah* because they did not want to risk the programs they had in thirty-three other countries by becoming involved in politics.[34] From Berger's perspective, the organizations were simply more concerned with their bureaucratic interests than saving Jewish lives, so he suggested that the Jewish Agency send a representative to Ethiopia to work on *aliyah* full time.[35]

Unlike nations with whom Israel maintained diplomatic relations, however, Ethiopia would not permit an Israeli representative to promote immigration, especially when the government was adamantly opposed to it. The only way to carry out Berger's recommendation was to do so secretly through ORT and that is exactly what Israel decided to do several months later. In August 1978, Aryeh Tartakower wrote to Lenhoff and informed him that his committee, Haim Halachmy, Yehuda Dominitz and other government officials, had decided to send a special undercover ORT representative to Ethiopia as a medical officer to be in charge of *aliyah* affairs.[36] The AAEJ maintained, however, that no such representative was ever sent and that ORT never did anything to encourage *aliyah*. They were wrong.

AAEJ DIPLOMACY

While the drama was playing out in Ethiopia, the AAEJ set out to educate the American Jewish community, which knew little or nothing about the Ethiopian Jews, and to put pressure on both the establishment organizations and the Israelis to take action to rescue the Ethiopian Jews. The method was to develop a grass-roots constituency that by-passed the establishment organizations that were uninterested in the issue. The AAEJ published a newsletter, sent out speakers, and publicized the plight of the Ethiopian Jews in the press. When Lenhoff became president of the organization in 1978, he focused on publicity and displayed a knack for generating stories in both the secular and Jewish press. He also regularly wrote articles describing the plight of the Ethiopian Jews and criticizing Israel's alleged lack of action. It was almost exclusively through the actions of the AAEJ, and especially Lenhoff, that Americans learned of the existence of the Beta Israel and their predicament.

Members of the AAEJ also had an ongoing dialogue with Israeli officials. Berger and Lenhoff, in particular, regularly wrote to Israel's top officials urging them to act on behalf of the Ethiopian Jews. The tone of this discourse, however, was sometimes disrespectful, souring relations and undermining their message. Though it did not affect their policy, it would only be human nature if the officials were to respond, as many did, with incredulity and a sense of outrage. Here was a group of Americans who wanted to be taken seriously and to have influence with the Israeli government but who seemed to believe that they could do so by insulting the responsible officials.

The Israelis also objected to the Americans' belief that they were entitled to information and explanations from the Israeli government and the Americans' penchant for telling that government what to do. Sometimes the AAEJ went so far as to act as though it was a sovereign government negotiating with Israel. For example, in the summer of 1979 after having met in Begin's office with his advisers, Lenhoff wrote a letter to Prime Minister Begin outlining what he believed Israel and the AAEJ had agreed upon. The AAEJ would hand over to the Jewish Agency the names and locations of all the Ethiopian Jews they located in the Sudan (referred to in the letter as TOC— The Other Country), cease their independent operation in the Sudan, and stop mentioning the Sudan in their publications. In return, the AAEJ expected Israel to "continue and expand its program in TOC with significant numbers arriving in Israel during the immediate forthcoming months by: 1) sending *schlichim* (messengers) to encourage influx into TOC; 2) caring for new people until they are ready to leave for [their] ultimate destination; 3) expediting the process by which the newly found people are checked and approved for transport to Israel; and 4) transport them to Israel expeditiously." The agreement also expressed the expectation that Israel would keep the AAEJ regularly informed of all activities regarding the *aliyah* and absorption of the Beta Israel in Israel.[37] Lenhoff did not like the terms, but felt pressured to accept them.

Though such messages were high-handed, they were not out of character with the behavior of American Jewish organizations, which, on other issues, also believed they should be equal partners with the Israeli government. Still, the Israelis felt they had no obligation to tell the Americans anything. They found their demands arrogant and told them so. At a meeting, for example, in Dominitz's Jerusalem office, General Ephraim Poran told a group of activists: "You all think that you have to know everything in the U.S. You have no right to demand this. Things don't work that way. You will never succeed. We want to hear your ideas. That is all. There are things that are only for the government to know."[38] In an interview, Poran added that things were on a "need-to-know" basis even within the inter-ministry committee he chaired, so it should not have been surprising the Israelis did not think the Americans should be told what was going on.[39]

Barbara Gaffin, an Ethiopian Jewry activist, understood this better than her colleagues at the AAEJ, but she also said it made her job more difficult. "There might have been underground people [working on rescue], but the Israelis are not about to say, 'We have Joe Shmoe the Mossadnik who is getting people out or trying to get people out.' So we kept running into this barrier where the Israelis would maintain there is a secret operation and couldn't tell us it was being done or not being done." Since the AAEJ did not see any Jews arriving in Israel, they interpreted Israel's reluctance to inform them as an indication that the government was not doing anything. Thus, when the Israeli rescue operation was underway, the AAEJ still refused to believe the government was interested in helping the Beta Israel because of their conviction that they had been lied to in the past.

There is a similarity here to the case of Peggy Say, whose brother was held hostage in Lebanon. She went to the White House to complain that the United States was not doing anything to get her brother released. She met with Lieutenant Colonel Oliver North who reassured her by saying, "Peggy, I promise you we are doing everything we can." Like members of the AAEJ, Ms. Say was skeptical, and it was not until later that she learned that North had attempted to sell arms to Iran in exchange for the release of Say's brother and the other hostages in Iran.[40] In the case of the Beta Israel, Israel did trade arms for some Ethiopian Jews and the United States later "traded" foreign aid to the Sudan for President Gaufer Numeiry's cooperation with the airlifts of Ethiopian Jews from the Sudan. Israel also was engaged in other clandestine activities that could not be disclosed to those concerned about the Ethiopian Jews.

Perhaps the biggest mistake the AAEJ made with respect to its credibility was to exaggerate the plight of the Beta Israel. As chapter 10 details, the conditions in Ethiopia were extremely bad in the 1970s, but the tendency to refer to a "holocaust" taking place deflected the debate from the serious-ness of conditions to whether or not a holocaust was indeed taking place. Each time an establishment organization would send a mission to Ethiopia to check the conditions of the Jews, they would come back and say there is no holocaust and the effect was to discredit the AAEJ because it called into question everything they were saying. To its credit, however, the AAEJ was one of the only organizations in the 1970s talking about the issue. There just was no interest on the part of establishment organizations in the Ethio-pian Jews. It was really not until 1980, when the severity of the Beta Israel's plight became accepted and Israel formed an interdepartmental committee to deal with the matter, that mainstream American Jewish groups began to take interest. Even then, it was to be another four years, when the Opera-tion Moses fundraising effort began, before they would become actively involved.

PATIENCE WEARS THIN

Following the Israelis' expulsion from Ethiopia, the AAEJ refused to ac-cept the argument that there was little they could do to help the Ethiopian Jews. Lenhoff wrote, for example, that one thousand Christian Ethiopians came to Israel each year despite the lack of diplomatic relations.[41] An Israeli Sephardic newspaper, *Bamaaracha,* also ridiculed the excuse that diplomatic relations were necessary to save the Ethiopian Jews:

When Mr. Dominitz . . . proclaims that "there is no Israeli diplomatic presence in Ethiopia and it is therefore difficult to work for the *aliyah* of the Falashas, scattered in 490 villages"—then we must say that this is irresponsible drivel. Until 1973 Israel did have a presence in Ethiopia under very good conditions, but the Department of Aliyah and Absorption did nothing for the rescue of the Jews of Ethiopia. Israel then had free access to each of the 490 villages where the scattered Jews of Ethiopia lived, but nothing was done to become involved with them. Whoever was able by his own initiative and effort to make *aliyah* did so. However, Mr. Dominitz' remarks sound like irresponsible drivel not for this reason alone, because everyone knows that Israel has no official repre-sentation in the Soviet Union; yet she turned the world upside down, success-fully, so that Soviet Jews might leave for the Western world. Israel has no rep-resentation in any East European land, except Rumania; yet, remarkably, what exertions Israel is making to save the Jews of Eastern Europe.[42]

It was true that the absence of diplomatic relations did not necessarily rule out all possibility of *aliyah*, but in the case of Ethiopia, it became very unlikely, particularly after the Israelis were expelled and the Soviet Union became that government's primary sponsor. The implications of Soviet in-volvement were twofold: (1) there was only a limited need for Israeli arms and aid and (2) the Soviets' own opposition to Zionism and Jewish immigration was passed to the Ethiopians. Whatever bargaining leverage Israel had before was now gone.

After the publicity of Dayan's statement led to the interruption of the rescue, Israeli officials were particularly sensitive about publicizing the Ethiopian Jewry issue. On June 9, 1979, Prime Minister Begin met with representatives of the Council of Jewish Federations, ORT, HIAS, JDC, and the AAEJ and personally urged them to keep quiet because "any publicity would bring attention to the problem and might jeopardize our efforts."[43] The establishment organizations were willing to heed the prime minister's warning, but the AAEJ was not. Although the AAEJ did believe Begin was sincere in his desire to help the Ethiopian Jews, the leaders were still convinced his subordinates would obstruct his efforts.

Many Israelis and establishment figures resented what they saw as the AAEJ's cavalier attitude toward the Ethiopian Jews and apparent belief that only *they* knew what was best for them. To be fair, it must be said that like any organization, the AAEJ was not a monolith and that while the members were united on the objective, they disagreed about tactics. One example of the extent to which Berger, at least, was willing to go to save the Ethiopian Jews was an advertisement he wanted to place in national newspapers in 1978 that said: "WHY DOESN'T ISRAEL, THE JEWISH AGENCY AND AMERICAN JEWISH LEADERSHIP RESCUE LEGITIMATE BLACK JEWS FROM EXTERMINATION?" Lenhoff and a number of other Jewish leaders who had seen the ad vigorously opposed publication, but Berger was willing to take risks: "As to the effects on the Falashas in Ethiopia by the publication of the ad," he wrote to Lenhoff, "I cannot say or predict. The only thing that the Ethiopian government can do that is worse than what is being done to them now—is exterminate them in one fell swoop. It would be on my conscience for the rest of my days, but it is a chance that has to be taken."[44] Lenhoff and other members of the AAEJ succeeded in persuading Berger that the ad was not in the best interests of the Ethiopian Jews, but Berger was convinced that his threat of publicity once again would stimulate the government to act.

ETHIOPIANS DEMONSTRATE

In Israel, the Ethiopian Jews had also grown impatient with the government and started to discuss the need for a demonstration in the spring of 1978. They continued to wait, however, to see if any action would be taken, but by the end of the year, they became convinced the time to break their silence had come. "The decision was very hard," according to Rachamim Elazar, "but many people, especially teachers, were in prison in Ethiopia and were being tortured and dying. We said we had nothing to lose since people were dying. We didn't believe the government was doing enough because no one came out after the government made promises." Rachamim said the

Ethiopian Jews in Israel were also influenced by the AAEJ and other organizations in the United States and Israel who told them that Israel is a free
country and that they should speak out. Coming from Ethiopia, however,
they did not understand what freedom of speech meant. "We were very
scared," Elazar explained, "we thought that they would put us in jail."[45]

On December 14, a group of the Ethiopian Jews in Israel met in Tel Aviv
and voted to demonstrate on January 7, 1979. The AAEJ encouraged them
and provided money for the demonstration.[46] Chanan Lehman of the Jewish
Colonization Association in Israel (ICA) was sympathetic and told Lenhoff
that people in Israel felt the Ethiopian Jews should be allowed to express
their disappointment "in any way they deem expedient." Lehman also told
Lenhoff, however, that he did not believe that meant his organization agreed
with the AAEJ's criticism of Israeli authorities. "Whereas it is correct to state
that not enough has been done to get the Falasha *aliyah* going, we would
dissociate ourselves from the accusations that the Israeli authorities regard
this subject of low priority, or even worse."[47]

On January 5, 1979, four Ethiopian Jews met with Prime Minister Begin
and several other officials. Begin told them:

> First there is no question about your Jewishness, you are our brothers, our flesh
> and our blood. So the Israeli Government did, is doing and will continue to
> do its best in searching for ways how to bring our brothers here to their home-
> land. We are fully aware of their plight, so we will not let our brothers suffer,
> but the critical problem is lack of direct connections with the Ethiopian leader.
> Even though we work hard to save them.[48]

The prime minister could not give the delegation any commitment but urged
them not to publicize their grievances because it would affect things the
government was trying to do. The Ethiopian Jews, who had been given assurances in the past that proved worthless and were goaded by the AAEJ,
chose to ignore this advice and staged a demonstration so the Israeli government and the world could not ignore their suffering. Two days after the
meeting with the Prime Minister, more than two hundred Ethiopian Jews
demonstrated outside the Knesset and called on the government to take
action to save their families. Absorption Minister David Levy called the protest "unnecessary and irresponsible."[49]

This sort of behavior was unprecedented. In the past, the families of persecuted communities from Syria, Iraq, Iran, and other countries had accepted
the assurances of the Israeli government and trusted officials' judgment when
they said quiet diplomacy would be the most effective method of securing
the freedom of the Jews in these countries.[50] As the Jewish Agency's chairperson, Aryeh Dulzin said, "While the Jews of Iran ask us to keep a low-
key, the Falashas ask us to raise our voice."[51] The Ethiopian Jews in Israel
who had organized the demonstration were also uncomfortable with their
action. "We felt it was almost a crime to demonstrate against the Israeli

government," Ethiopian Jewish activist Zecharias Yona said. "We don't want to hurt Israel, and we understand her delicate position in the world. We preferred to suffer rather than jeopardize Israel." Nevertheless, the decision was made to demonstrate because of the seriousness of the situation. "If our people don't get help," activist Zimna Berhani explained, "they are sentenced to death because they have no hope of aid from Ethiopian authorities or local officials."[52]

Later, Berger received a report that Ethiopia had arrested a number of Jews, executed some of them, and had arrested a group of teachers to eliminate the study of Hebrew. "Latest reports reaching us," the informant wrote, "are that other ORT activities have been seriously hindered, and *this in direct response to your demonstrations which publicized both their plight and their relationship to Israel*" (emphasis in original).[53] This was the type of harmful consequences that Begin warned the AAEJ about, but the group refused to believe that any of their publicity or actions had any negative impact on the Ethiopian Jews.

The Ethiopian Jews did not care about the politics of the situation. All they knew was that their families were sentenced to death and that something had to be done. The AAEJ agreed. Israeli officials also agreed, but they had other things on their mind at that time, notably the peace negotiations with Egypt. While the Ethiopian Jews and their supporters always believed they should be the government's top priority, the reality was that Israel also had other interests that concerned the safety of Jews. Regardless, Shlomo Hillel said the Mossad wanted to do something to help the Ethiopian Jews, but there was not very much they could do to get people into Ethiopia.[54]

STIRRING THE POT

The demonstrations coincided with a worsening of the Jews' plight in Ethiopia. The JDC's Akiva Kohane played down the situation, maintaining that the attitude of the Ethiopian government toward the Beta Israel "had never been better at any time in history." He admitted, however, that thirty-eight Ethiopian Jews had been killed by the government and the anti-government Ethiopian Democratic Union (EDU), though not because they were Falashas, and that eighteen had been sold into slavery. He also reported that 2,500 Ethiopian Jews lost their land.[55]

While the Jewish establishment vigorously denied AAEJ reports of a holocaust in Ethiopia, an Israeli government official confirmed in January 1979 that two thousand Falashas had been killed or wounded by anti-government rebels and that another seven thousand had been evicted from their homes, and many of those had either been sold into slavery or been living as starving refugees. "They are extremely vulnerable since government soldiers are engaged in remote Eritrea and in the Ogaden," a news release stated. "Rebel armies have vowed to wipe them out because they refused to join their insurrection. Even the remnants of Halle Selassie's army have been persecuting them—the craftsmen sold into slavery, the women raped and mutilated and the men castrated."

In addition, the Jews' former landlords, who now were members of the antigovernment EDU, were furious that Israeli arms were being used against them and vented their anger on the Ethiopian Jews, who were accused of being Zionists. "The Falashas," Rapoport said, "have little hope of catching the attention of a world that has long since grown inured to whole peoples being wiped out, let alone a small, isolated tribe."[56] His article, "The Falashas: A Black Holocaust Looms," did not appear in the AAEJ's literature, but in *The New Republic*; hence, the severity of the plight of the Ethiopian Jews was gaining not only greater attention, but also credibility.

This was the type of information the AAEJ was receiving and passing on to congressional representatives who, in turn, asked the State Department to investigate. The State Department issued a report from the embassy in Addis Ababa on the conditions in the Jewish villages in the Gondar region. The report predicted that the condition of the Beta Israel would improve as development aid from ORT arrived and the Ethiopian government's policies of rural land reform and rights for minority groups began to take effect. The visitors "observed no real distinction between the condition of [Amharas and Falashas]; they were both noticeably poor and lacking, except as ORT and the Falasha Welfare Association has provided, water, electricity, education and health services." The report also stated that the authorities had been very cooperative with ORT, including that organization's efforts to improve the spiritual lives of the Ethiopian Jews:

> It is also worth noting that the government openly displayed its tolerance for the religious practices of the Falasha. Since arriving in the Gondar region in 1977, ORT has built 4 new synagogues and has renovated others. Moreover, in eight of ORT's 23 schools, Hebrew is taught, though only offered as an option, precisely for its ecclesiastical value. Both of these activities are reportedly well known to the government officials. Reported also was a secret decision by the Gondar Administration to allow the Gondar city market to open on Sunday so that the Falasha could do their shopping on a day other than Saturday, their Sabbath.[57]

This type of contradictory information was constantly bandied about in the United States, so the issue was often confused; rather than focusing on what could be done to help the Ethiopian Jews, a great deal of time and energy were wasted arguing over whose information was accurate.

CRACKING THE WALL OF SILENCE

The demonstration in Israel succeeded not only in putting the issue higher on the agenda, but also broke through the wall of silence in the Israeli press.

The censorship of the subject was relaxed, and a large number of articles began to appear in newspapers so that for the first time, the Israeli public became informed about the Ethiopian Jews. In addition, Israeli officials encouraged journalists in other countries to write stories about the Ethiopian Jews.[58] Israel also sent a representative to work with the coordinating committee that was set up in New York to bring all of the Jewish organizations interested in the Ethiopian Jews together to work on their behalf.

The January demonstration in Israel also encouraged American activists. The North American Jewish Student Network (the Network), while not a major actor in national politics, did contribute to the process of educating the American Jewish community by bringing Zecharias Yona, Yona Bogale's son, on a two-month speaking tour to the United States. The establishment organizations, meanwhile, continued to resist efforts by the AAEJ, the Network, and others to bring speakers to major conferences of Jewish leaders. When one of these conferences, the General Assembly, was scheduled for December 1979, the AAEJ, the Canadian Association for Ethiopian Jews (CAEJ), the Network, and the Simon Wiesenthal Center requested that a representative of the Ethiopian Jews in Israel or a member of the AAEJ be invited to speak or consulted on the program, but none were until pressure forced the program organizer to invite Yona Bogale. Bogale, who came at AAEJ's expense, told the assembly: "I have come to tell you about how we—the Jews of Ethiopia, the Beta Yisrael—want to rejoin the Jewish people. I want to tell you about how we want to come to Israel to live a Jewish life with other Jews in Israel. Ethiopian Jews want to come home to Jerusalem—to Yerushalayem."[59]

FRUSTRATION GROWS

By the end of 1979, the frustration of the Ethiopian Jews in Israel once again reached the boiling point after the rescue of only 32. At the end of October, they staged another demonstration in front of the Knesset calling for large-scale emigration from Ethiopia. In a statement following the demonstration and meetings with government and Jewish Agency leaders, Avraham Yerday, chairperson of the Association of Ethiopian Jews in Israel, issued a statement in which he said the Ethiopian Jewish community opposed publicly condemning Ethiopia. "Our only reason for having demonstrated twice," he said, "was our conviction that the Jewish Agency, world Jewish leaders and the government of Israel, because they do not want any more Falashas in Israel, have not done enough to rescue our families."[60] The *Jerusalem Post* joined in the protest with an editorial that not only echoed the views of the Ethiopian Jews in Israel, but also the AAEJ:

Israel and the world Jewish community have devoted massive energy and resources on behalf of Soviet Jewry; the government has mounted rescue operations on behalf of the Vietnamese boat people and Cambodian refugees. But the Falashas of Ethiopia, who unlike the Asian refugees are Jews, and unlike the seventy to eighty percent of drop-out Soviet Jews want to come to Israel, have been neglected. And that neglect must be considered mortal, for the Falashas of Ethiopia, who today number only about 20,000 face total physical extinction. The tale of neglect is long. It certainly cannot be placed solely at the hands of Mr. Begin's Government. But it is nevertheless true that this government is continuing this neglect, despite the dangers facing the Falashas. The source of that neglect derives historically from the narrow dogmatism and bigotry expressed on this issue by orthodox functionaries located primarily in the National Religious Party. What is needed is a concerted rescue effort embracing the government and the major world Jewish organizations for history will neither forget nor forgive anything less.[61]

One consequence of the second demonstration by the Ethiopian Jews in Israel was to bring about an admission by the director of World Jewish Affairs in the Foreign Ministry, Shaul Ramati that "the results of our quiet diplomacy did not bear the fruits we had hoped for."[62] This was followed by the first public debate in the Knesset on the issue of Ethiopian Jewry. At the conclusion of the debate, the members voted unanimously to rescue the Ethiopian Jews and bring them all to Israel. The United Jewish Appeal (UJA), which had done nothing to publicize the issue previously, despite claims to the contrary, endorsed this decision and reasserted that the issue had been and would continue to be "a foremost priority" on its organizational agenda.[63]

This time the Israeli government responded to the demonstration by making the issue a top priority. The government officially abandoned its policy of silence, and the Jewish Agency and World Zionist Organization announced, along with the government, an international campaign to publicize the plight of the Ethiopian Jews. Cabinet minister Moshe Nissim told the Knesset: "We shall not rest in our efforts to secure for the Falashas the right to immigrate to Israel. Our Jewish brethren in Ethiopia are suffering from both physical and mental distress. The government is determined to enable them to come to live in Israel." Prime Minister Begin was quoted as saying that he would appeal to the Ethiopian government to let the Ethiopian Jews go.[64]

In November, an interministry committee was established, headed by General Ephraim Poran and composed of representatives of the Mossad, the Jewish Agency, and the Ethiopian Jews. In response to that committee's recommendations, the prime minister sent a message to Sweden's prime minister asking for his help in bringing the Ethiopian Jews to Israel on the basis of family reunification and humanitarian reasons. All of Israel's foreign missions were given background information on the Beta Israel and several were asked to submit official requests for help. A survey was also conducted to determine which countries might have influence with the Ethiopians.[65]

Although the AAEJ repeatedly accused Israel of failing to enlist the help of other governments and insisted it could do the job itself when its real motivation was to scuttle the issue, the Israelis were using all diplomatic channels open to them to seek assistance. In fact, they even tried channels not open to them. In the summer of 1979, for example, the American Jewish Committee asked Senator George McGovern to approach Fidel Castro to see if Cuba would use its influence in Ethiopia to help the Jews.[66] Israel had also asked the AAEJ to approach Cuba, but Nate Shapiro considered the request an attempt by the Israelis to embarrass the organization with the administration.[67] In the end, it did not matter since Castro refused to intervene in Ethiopia's internal affairs.

Another longstanding cause of criticism was also resolved at the end of 1979 when Yona Bogale was brought to Israel. The AAEJ had been claiming that the failure to rescue the aging Beta Israel leader was a prime example of the government's disinterest. In August, the Foreign Ministry secured an exit visa for Bogale through the Mexican ambassador in Israel who was then representing Ethiopia's interests. The Israelis were unsure why the Ethiopian government had agreed to let Bogale go, but they suspected it might have been because the Ethiopian Church in Israel accepted the Israeli requests on Bogale's behalf and recommended that he be given a visa. At the time, the Ethiopians were worried the peace treaty with Egypt might result in the holy places common to the Ethiopian Church and the Egyptian Coptic Church being returned to Egypt's control, so acceding to the request for Bogale, the Israelis speculated, might have been considered an attempt to win Israel's favor. In any event, Bogale arrived in October and became a party to the discussions of the interministry committee.[68]

ORT COMES UNDER FIRE

According to Yehuda Dominitz of the Jewish Agency, ORT's position began to decline in Ethiopia at the beginning of 1979 because of publicity in Israel and abroad. It became impossible for ORT representatives to reach the areas where most of the Ethiopian Jews lived. This, Dominitz complained, meant the Jews were deprived of aid and the Israelis of a means of communication and information.[69] The situation was made worse when Eli Turgeman, the Israeli who had been in charge of ORT's program in Gondar, accused the organization of contributing to the destruction of the Ethiopian Jews. On the basis of Turgeman's accusations, the AAEJ drew up a list of twenty charges and presented them to ORT officials demanding that they be investigated. The allegations included that ORT underestimated the number of refugees in the area under its jurisdiction; that a Christian employee of ORT was responsible for the arrest and execution of an Ethiopian Jewish employee of ORT and the arrest and torture of several Jewish teachers; that

ORT prevented any of its employees from intervening on the imprisoned teachers' behalf and that money had been misappropriated. The AAEJ concluded that ORT should immediately withdraw from Ethiopia.[70]

Although the AAEJ had no way of investigating the charges, they supported the accusations and began a campaign to force ORT out of Ethiopia. One member of the AAEJ board, Edith Everett, was more cautious. She said the AAEJ took issue with ORT's pretension of doing more than they were doing, but she did not agree with all the charges made against the organization. "There are good and forthright people in ORT," she said. "We have to be circumspect in making allegations. There are rules and regulations you have to abide by in foreign countries. It's not fair to say ORT or JDC should do this or that."[71] Nevertheless, that is precisely what AAEJ ultimately did. In typically bombastic fashion, Berger threatened that he would expose ORT's actions publicly if nothing was done. He claimed the Israelis responded by sending Prime Minister Menachem Begin's aide, Yehuda Avner, to Ethiopia. Berger also said that Israel had asked the Ethiopians not to prosecute the teachers for "Zionist activity," but in the meantime, two had died and four others were languishing in prison.[72]

FWA's David Kessler, meanwhile, went to Ethiopia to investigate the AAEJ charges against ORT and reported back that they were all false. Moreover, the Ethiopian Jews were benefitting from the ORT projects. This finding was supported by two representatives of U.S. Agency for International Development (USAID) and a Canadian official who also visited the area. Israel's own investigation into the matter found the charges to be unfounded.[73] The AAEJ denounced all of these reports as lies and efforts to whitewash ORT's guilt. The man who was most closely involved in the situation on the ground, Rachamim Yitzhak, an ORT employee, provided evidence that buttressed some of the allegations but also showed that ORT was not the detrimental organization the AAEJ claimed it to be. One of the difficulties was that the rebels kept them from doing much in outlying areas such as Tigre, so large numbers of Ethiopian Jews could not be helped. Since he taught Hebrew, Yitzhak also found himself under suspicion and constantly followed by representatives of the authorities who wanted him to stop teaching.

The biggest problem, however, was the large number of non-Jewish employees working for ORT. To some extent it could not be helped, Yitzhak explained. He had no choice but to hire non-Jewish teachers because the Jews did not have enough education to teach. What could have been averted was hiring so many non-Jews as administrators. Yitzhak and the head of the agriculture program, David Seyoum, were the only Jews in key positions. Yitzhak tried to tell his superiors that hiring non-Jews was dangerous because of their historical animosity toward the Beta Israel, but they did not listen. Once Christians were employed, he told them, they would know all of ORT's secrets and it would be dangerous to carry on their *aliyah* activities.

A man named Kebede was particularly dangerous because he was a friend of the virulently anti-Falasha provincial governor Melaku Teferra. Kebede reported ORT's activities. Yitzhak, who had replaced Turgeman, agreed with his predecessor's complaints as they related to these non-Jews because he said those employees stole and misallocated resources and accused the Ethiopian Jews of being CIA agents. Of the $2 million ORT budget, only a small percentage actually went to benefit the Ethiopian Jews; most of the money, according to Yitzhak, went to corrupt authorities. Paradoxically, things might have become more dangerous if the non-Jews were fired because the Ethiopian authorities would have been afraid the Jews controlled too much of ORT's activities. Yitzhak took issue, however, with Turgeman's main argument; that is, that ORT was not good for the Ethiopian Jews. He asserted that ORT did make a contribution, although not as great as it could have made. The benefits ORT provided included education, clean water, money for oxen and seed, modern schools and buildings, health centers, and technical education. The fights he had with ORT officials, he said, were over "providing the maximum versus the minimum."

THE END OF ORT'S MISSION

In 1981, when large numbers of Ethiopian Jews were escaping, Yitzhak learned he was to be arrested on suspicion of helping them. At first he did not believe it was true when the non-Jewish director of the school in Ambober told him; but another person gave him the same warning when he went to Gondar, so he found David Seyoum, the head of ORT's agriculture department, and the two of them hired a guide and traveled fourteen days to the Sudan. After spending four months in the Sudan, they were taken to Israel. The situation deteriorated after Yitzhak left. The Ethiopian minister of education prohibited the teaching of Hebrew or religious subjects in the schools. Then, abruptly, at the end of June 1981, the government ordered all of ORT's offices in Gondar closed. Among the reasons given by the Dergue was the suspicion that ORT was serving as an arm of the CIA and "world Zionism."[74]

Yitzhak's successor, Mahariya Roebel, was warned that he would be arrested if he came to the office. He did not even get a chance to collect his property from his office. When two Jewish employees (who are now in Israel) were arrested, Roebel fled to Addis where the ORT headquarters (Gondar was the functional office) was still open. By the end of September, however, the Addis office was also closed. Roebel then found it difficult to get a job because of his connection with ORT. He was arrested in January 1982 for working with a Jewish organization and helping Jews escape and was imprisoned for eight months. When he was released, he still could not get a job because of his recommendation from ORT. He also was prevented from leaving the country, even though his family was allowed to leave. Finally, in 1984, the AAEJ helped him get a scholarship and he was permitted to leave.[75]

Ironically, in 1981, while the AAEJ was complaining that ORT's activities were counterproductive, and that they were not working on *aliyah*, the Ethiopian government decided to expel the organization for involvement in *aliyah* activity. In fact, Rachamim Yitzhak did help stimulate the exodus of Ethiopian Jews to the Sudan that ultimately made their rescue possible. He said that at the end of 1979 he was instructed by Israel to tell people to go to the Sudan and, in 1980, began to organize groups of ten to twenty people to travel with guides via five different routes across the border. He said the head of the ORT program was also aware of his instructions and that the cooperation of the Jews working for ORT made it possible to stimulate *aliyah*.[76] Yitzhak's successor, Roebel, did not receive similar instructions. He maintained it was dangerous going to the Sudan and that he was worried about informers, so he would only help students get papers for scholarships to study abroad whereby they could leave directly from Ethiopia.[77]

The AAEJ was gratified by the Ethiopian government's decision to expel ORT, but the Israelis recognized that this complicated their efforts by eliminating a source of information and a cover for stimulating *aliyah*. This was an example of one of the consistently tragic occurrences during the effort to save the Ethiopian Jews—the tendency for well-meaning individuals to say or do things on behalf of the Beta Israel that turned out to have unexpected consequences that harmed their interests.

By the time ORT was expelled, large numbers of Ethiopian Jews were beginning to move across the border into the Sudan. In response, the regional administrator in Gondar, Major Melaku, began to institute increasingly harsh measures against the Jewish population that remained. These included closing down schools and synagogues, and arresting and torturing people who attempted to escape and were caught. The plight of the Ethiopian Jews was exacerbated by the famine and ongoing civil war. All of these factors combined to make it clear to Israeli officials that the community needed to be rescued, and soon, to prevent its destruction. Any reluctance to bringing the Ethiopian Jews to Israel was, at last, swept away and the beginning of the triumphant redemption of the Beta Israel began.

NOTES

1. Michael Winn, "Falashas: Doomed to Extinction," *National Jewish Monthly*, May 1981, pp. 8–9; General Ephraim Poran, interview with author.

2. AAEJ Information Paper, February 1979.

3. "New Government's Guidelines," *Jerusalem Post*, January 20, 1977.

4. Diane Winston, "The Falashas: History and Analysis of Policy Towards a Beleaguered Community" (NY: National Jewish Resource Center, April, 1980), p. 14.

5. Confidential interview.

6. Graenum Berger, letter to Howard Lenhoff, August 18, 1977.

7. Chaim Halachmy, interview with author.

8. Steven Schloss, "Unsung Heroes of 1986," *The Queens Jewish Week*, January 2, 1986, p. 29.

9. Graenum Berger, letter to Howard Lenhoff and Ted Norman, April 16, 1977.

10. Louis Rapoport, *Redemption Song* (NY: Harcourt Brace Jovanovich, 1986), p. 66.

11. Halachmy, interview; General Ephraim Poran, interview.

12. Yehuda Dominitz, interview with author.

13. Shoshana Ben Dor, letter to Graenum Berger, January 29, 1979.

14. Halachmy, interview; Report to Prime Minister Menachem Begin [undated]; Aryeh Tartakower, letter to Graenum Berger, October 14, 1977.

15. Report Begin; Poran, interview; Tudor Parfitt, *Operation Moses* (England: Weidenfeld and Nicolson, 1985), pp. 37–38.

16. Confidential interview.

17. Dominitz, interview with author.

18. Halachmy, interview with author.

19. Mordechai Artzi'eli, "The Falashas: A Dying Community. The Weakness of Israel," *Ha'aretz*, December 17, 1982.

20. U.S. State Department cable from Tel Aviv to Washington, February 1978.

21. Shlomo Hillel, interview with author.

22. Chanan Aynor, interview with author.

23. Dominitz, interview.

24. Gideon Rafael, *Destination Peace* (NY: Stein and Day, 1981), p. 229.

25. Yehuda Dominitz, letter to Howard Lenhoff, February 8, 1978.

26. Parfitt, *Operation Moses*, pp. 34–35.

27. "How to Eliminate Religion from Ethiopia," vol. 4, 44 Ministry of Information of Ethiopia in Horn of Africa, p. 41.

28. Parfitt, *Operation Moses*, p. 32.

29. Nate Shapiro, interview with author.

30. Quoted in Shmuel Yilmah. *From Falasha to Freedom: An Ethiopian Jew's Journey to Jerusalem* (Gefen Books, 1996), p. 77.

31. Michael Winn, "Falashas: Doomed to Extinction?" *National Jewish Monthly* May 1981, p. 110; "JDC Annual Report," 1980; Louis Rapoport, *The Last Jews: Last of the Ethiopian Falashas* (NY: Stein & Day, 1980), p. 10.

32. Confidential interview.

33. Shari Hyman, interview with author.

34. Ibid.

35. Graenum Berger, letter to Howard Lenhoff, January 26, 1978.

36. Aryeh Tartakower, letter to Howard Lenhoff, August 23, 1978.

37. Howard Lenhoff, letter to Prime Minister Menachem Begin, July 18, 1979.

38. Minutes of meeting held in office of Yehuda Dominitz taken by Frances Alpert, February 23, 1979.

39. Poran, interview.

40. Lee May, "Sister Crusades for Hostage's Freedom," *Los Angeles Times*, April 19, 1987.

41. Howard Lenhoff, "Young Falasha Killed—His Pleas by HIAS and by Israel's Minister of Interior," *Israel Today*, October 25, 1979.

42. *Bamaaracha*, February 1979.

43. Howard Lenhoff, "Jewish Agency Doublecrosses Pro-Falasha Movement," *Israel Today*, November 8, 1979.

44. Graenum Berger, letter to Howard Lenhoff (September, 1, 1978).

45. Rachamim Elazar, interview with author.

46. Shapiro, interview.

47. Chanan Lehman, letter to Howard Lenhoff, December 26, 1976.

48. Zecharias Yona et al., letter to Howard Lenhoff, February 4, 1979.

49. Rapoport, *The Lost Jews*, p. 217.

50. Halachmy, interview.

51. Eli Eyal, background information from World Zionist Organization Department of Information, January 1979.

52. Diane Winston, "The Falashas: History and Analysis of Policy Towards a Beleaguered Community" (NY: National Jewish Resource Center, April 1980), p. 9.

53. Shoshana Ben Dor letter to Graenum Berger, January 29, 1979.

54. Hillel, interview.

55. Aide memo of meeting convened by Ralph Goldman of the JPC, December 12, 1979.

56. Louis Rapoport, "The Falashas: A Black Holocaust Looms?" *New Republic*, February 24, 1979; Rapoport, *The Lost Jews*, pp. 9–10; Parfitt, *Operation Moses*, p. 38.

57. Report by U.S. embassy in Addis Ababa on early July [1979] visit to Falasha settlements in Gondar region.

58. Report to Begin.

59. Howard Lenhoff, "Behind the Scenes at the GA," *The Jewish Post*, December 27, 1979.

60. *Israel Today*, December, 6, 1979.

61. "On Behalf of the Falashas," editorial, *Jerusalem Post*, October 30, 1979.

62. Winston, "The Falashas," p. 13; Simcha Jacobovici, "Ethiopia's Black Jews, A Periled Community," *New York Times*, October 2, 1981.

63. Herschel Blumberg, national chairman of United Jewish Appeal, form letter, May 19, 1980.

64. Rapoport, *The Lost Jews*, p. 232.

65. Report to Begin.

66. Ibid.

67. Shapiro, interview.

68. Report to Begin.

69. Yehuda Dominitz, letter to Raymond Epstein, February 4, 1979.

70. Shapiro, interview; message from Zimna Berhani et al., March 18, 1979; Rapoport, *The Lost Jews*, pp. 10–11.

71. Edith Everett, interview with author.

72. Graenum Berger letter to Rabbi Irving Greenberg, March 7, 1979.

73. Rapoport, *The Lost Jews*, pp. 11–12.

74. Teshome Wagaw, *For Our Soul: Ethiopian Jews in Israel* (MI: Wayne State University Press, 1993), p. 60.

75. Mahariya Roebel, interview with author.

76. Rachamim Yitzhak, interview with author.

77. Roebel, interview.

CHAPTER 5

Escape to the Sudan

T he turning point in the efforts to rescue the Ethiopian Jews
began when they started to escape to the Sudan. The Sudan and
Ethiopia share the longest border in Africa, stretching 1,200 miles
from the Red Sea to Kenya, which makes border control virtually impossible.
Consequently, throughout the 1970s, Ethiopians wishing to escape the civil
war and economic conditions of their country made the arduous journey to
this neighboring country, where most hoped to be taken care of by the international refugee organizations and to eventually reach either the United
States or a European country. Many succeeded, and it was not uncommon
to find Ethiopians in, for example, Washington, D.C.

The first reports that Jews were in the Sudan began to filter out in the
spring of 1978. Eli Turgemann told Graenum Berger and the AAEJ in February that he had informed Haim Halachmy of HIAS that Ethiopian Jews
were in the Sudan, but no one had done anything about it.[1] Nate Shapiro
said Turgemann wrote to Yehuda Dominitz and said that eighteen Ethiopian Jews were in refugee camps in the Sudan and others were walking back
and forth across the border saying, "What's going on? We're here in Sudan,
we want to get out."[2] An Ethiopian Jew also said that he told Halachmy that
there were Jews in the Sudan, that he had received letters from Ethiopia
saying that thirteen Ethiopian Jews were there, but Halachmy did not believe him.[3] A letter from an AAEJ member in Israel to Howard Lenhoff in

May, however, suggested that the Israelis were aware that there were Jews in the Sudan, and they anticipated that the numbers would grow.[4] Nevertheless, the AAEJ flew Turgemann to Chicago to present his version and that, according to Shapiro, "was the signal alerting everyone to the fact that the whole thing was a pack of lies because they had been saying that you can't get across the border, you can't find Ethiopian Jews, nobody's there. Turgemann was saying it's a lie. They can walk across the border. Life is terrible for them there. They want to get to Israel. No one's helping them and Dominitz is covering it up."[5]

In March 1978, before it was widely known that there were Ethiopian Jews in the Sudan, Lenhoff submitted a plan to General Ephraim Poran for rescuing the Beta Israel through the Sudan:

> Through the cooperation of EDU, and with the help of five Falashas, and through bribery, it should be possible to bring thousands of Falashas to the Sudanese border by foot in the matter of one to three days. Once there, and declared political refugees (Christian or Moslem), they can be transferred by truck and/ or rail to Port Sudan where a ship under foreign flag (Greek or Italian) can pick them up and take them to Israel. A ship is better than [a] plane because going to [the] airport is too obvious and housing Falashas arouse suspicion. A ship is less obvious, more people can be saved, and can be used as a hotel.[6]

The letter to Poran implied the plan would be relatively simple to implement. Lenhoff believed that five thousand Ethiopian Jews could be saved in only two months. One of the problems with this outline, however, was that it did not give any consideration to the risks involved nor did it provide answers to such seemingly critical questions as: What if the EDU refuses to cooperate? What if the Jews are caught? What if the Sudan objects?

Nevertheless, the plan was virtually identical to the one actually used, although Israeli officials, including Poran, deny that it was Lenhoff's idea. They claim that Israel had already thought of the idea and find it absurd that only one person could have come up with such a plan. Halachmy told Lenhoff that anyone can have a plan, the problem was to implement it.[7] This may be a response to avoid the embarrassment of admitting that someone else thought of the plan they used or it may be accurate—it is difficult to know for sure.

According to Louis Rapoport of the *Jerusalem Post*, the plan to rescue the Ethiopian Jews via the Sudan was first proposed to Menachim Begin by Baruch Tegegne, an Ethiopian Jew, who had lived for awhile in the Sudan and eventually escaped from there, and other Beta Israel leaders in Israel after they had heard that twelve Ethiopian Jews had gone to the Sudan and managed to get jobs there. General Poran subsequently sent a Mossad agent to investigate and arrange transportation to Israel for the twelve Jews, but the agent was unable to find them until one of the Ethiopian Jews in Khartoum sent a message to the AAEJ who passed it on to the Israelis.[8] Tegegne denied talking to Rapoport and said Halachmy had him meet with two people from the Mossad who brought with them the Sudan plan that Lenhoff had sent. Tegegne told them another Ethiopian Jew named Ferede was in Khartoum and they should contact him. They asked Tegegne what he was doing, and he told them he was going into the army. The meeting ended, but later, before finishing his military service, Tegegne was again called in to meet with the Mossad. The man who eventually became the Mossad's primary agent in the rescue effort, Daniel Longet, told Tegegne that the Mossad wanted him to go to the Sudan.

Tegegne was sent first to Athens where he waited for one month before being recalled to Israel for a more detailed briefing regarding the Sudan. When he met again with the Mossad, however, he was told the operation had been canceled. Tegegne told them that families could be saved and tried to persuade them not to cancel the operation, but the decision was final. He learned later that Longet had already been to the Sudan and contacted Ferede and arranged to work with him.[9]

ISRAEL DEBATES THE AAEJ

By September 1978, the Israelis began to confirm that Jews were in the Sudan. On the fifteenth, Aryeh Tartakower wrote to Lenhoff that fifteen Ethiopian Jews were in the Sudan and that the high commissioner for refugees agreed to have them sent to Israel. He also reported that unofficial negotiations with the Ethiopians were taking place.[10] Tartakower wrote to Lenhoff again in December to tell him there were no more than around twenty Ethiopian Jews in the Sudan, but the number was expected to increase. He said the Israelis were working with the United Nations High Commissioner for Refugees (UNHCR) and to some extent Sudanese officials on the matter. He added that there were no possibilities for legal emigration directly from Ethiopia because the influence of Israel had "disappeared" and that of the Russians had grown.[11]

According to Halachmy, the Jewish Agency did not learn that the Ethiopian Jews were in the Sudan until 1979. When they found out, he said, they asked the UNHCR to look for them, but the relief organization said they could not recognize Jews among the nearly half-million refugees.[12] It was especially hard since the Jews tried to hide and avoid identification as Jews for fear of being persecuted by other refugees. Thus, they did not register with relief authorities as Jews. In 1979, there were continuing reports about the presence of Ethiopian Jews in the Sudan, but the AAEJ was constantly arguing with the Israelis as to how many were there and what was being done and should be done for them. For example, the AAEJ claimed as many as two thousand Ethiopian Jews were in the Sudan in January while the Foreign Ministry's Alon Liel said Israel did not have proof yet there were any Jews in the refugee camps.[13]

The AAEJ decided to send its own people to the Sudan to investigate and that led them to the conclusion that the Israelis were lying to them. The establishment Jews, however, were willing to believe the Israelis. Shapiro found their naiveté incredible:

> Dominitz would write them a letter or someone would speak to them, but the information that always got back was that the borders were closed; there weren't any Ethiopian Jews in Sudan; if they are there, you can't find them; if you can find them, you can't get them out. None of it made sense. You just had to read the press or go to Washington D.C. or New York and there were Ethiopians all over, all coming out of Sudan. Europe was loaded with them. So I was very disturbed that these people, as intelligent business people, were willing to accept what I view as absolute nonsense. If Sudan had a [half] million refugees as was reported, how did they get there if the borders were closed? They didn't climb over a 75-foot wall with barbed wire. They walked across. The border had to be open. It was silly. If thousands of Ethiopian Christians were coming into Sudan, as they were, as refugees, it seemed absurd that a country that did all that Israel had done in all the wars didn't know how to get Jews out.[14]

According to Shlomo Hillel, "The Mossad did as much as possible to shake the kibitzers" and get the government to act. He also suggested the Israelis might have known more than they were revealing to the Americans. "They may not have admitted they knew about the Ethiopian Jews in Sudan, I wouldn't".[15] The AAEJ thought it was being deceived. Shapiro, for example, said he tried to get an appointment with Dominitz to discuss the matter, but he could not get one. Instead, Dominitz called him and spoke in a whisper as if what he was saying was secret. Shapiro said he just wanted to know what was going on, and Dominitz whispered that he could not tell him. "It was such a fake act from my perspective to whisper into the phone. That left a sting in my memory," said Shapiro. "It was like the guy was acting it out to make me believe that it was cloak and dagger stuff."[16] Rather than considering that such deception might be necessary, the AAEJ took it as an indication that Israel was trying to cover up the fact that there were Jews in the Sudan and thereby avoid rescuing them. Israel did inform the AAEJ in February that it brought one Jew to Israel from Ethiopia and received exit permits for two more through diplomatic channels. This demonstrated that the government's efforts were continuing even though success was limited.[17] In April, Begin raised the issue with President Jimmy Carter and asked other people in Washington for help. In the meantime, nine Ethiopian Jews were located in the Sudan and Israel arranged to rescue them.[18]

MAN UNDERCOVER

The groundwork for the Israeli operation in the Sudan was laid primarily by one man, Ferede, who helped build up a network of people that arranged for internal travel permits from the Interior Ministry and police and documents from the Red Cross and Sudanese refugee officials. Ferede would take these documents and alter the photographs so that whole families could be added. In many cases, the "families" were just a group of Ethiopian Jews whom Ferede made into a family for the purpose of getting them out.

The story of how Ferede became involved began in 1978 when he escaped from Gondar to the Sudan. He made it to Khartoum and contacted the ORT office in Geneva asking for help in getting out of the Sudan. He sent a second telex on December 2, 1978, to Graenum Berger whose address he had obtained in Ethiopia. Ferede received a letter from Geneva telling him to meet two U.N. workers in Khartoum. He met them and they helped him to get a visa to Greece. Ferede had not received a reply from Berger who, it turned out, had passed on the information to Dominitz. Berger was upset that the Jewish Agency did not seem to want to rescue Ferede, but Dominitz could not tell him they had other plans in mind for him.[19] Dominitz apparently passed on the information about Ferede to the Mossad, who sent Daniel Longet to meet Ferede in Khartoum while he was waiting for his flight to Athens.

Longet wanted to know if Ferede knew other Ethiopian Jews in the Sudan, and Ferede told him that he did not. Longet told him that he had come to the Sudan to help the Ethiopian Jews, and Ferede agreed to help him. They spent the next two weeks checking refugee camps for Ethiopian Jews and found none. Thus, the Israelis were not lying to the Americans when they said they looked and could not find anyone. Longet left the Sudan but gave Ferede money to continue looking. At the beginning of February 1979, Ferede found an Ethiopian Jew he knew in Gedaref. In the next few days, he found a total of four and sent a telex to the address that Longet had given him and asked for help to transfer the people. Longet returned to the Sudan and helped Ferede get the four to Khartoum. Longet left again and told Ferede to begin processing documents and to look for more Ethiopian Jews. Longet returned a third time and gave Ferede enough money for twenty-one days and to pay for eight people. Later, Ferede received about $20,000 in Sudanese pounds every two weeks to distribute to refugees in the camps.

One of the most difficult parts of the operation for Ferede was to secure a safehouse in Khartoum where groups of Ethiopian Jewish refugees could stay and not attract attention. As an added complication, the rental housing market in Khartoum was very limited. Ferede finally got help from an Eritrean woman who ran a call-girl operation and was able to rent a house next door to a brothel. As many as fifty or sixty Ethiopian Jews sometimes stayed in the safehouse, which attracted the attention of neighbors who sometimes complained, but Ferede always succeeded in avoiding trouble. Eventually, he found a more private safehouse.

The refugees were usually taken by Landrover from Gedaref on a five-hour trip to Khartoum. The drivers were paid for each person they successfully delivered to Khartoum. They always traveled at night so that when they returned early in the morning no one would see the refugees being unloaded and transferred to the safehouse. The refugees were then taken in groups of fifteen or thirty, never more than sixty, to the Khartoum airport where they were flown to Athens on Olympic Airways and then to Israel by Olympic or El Al.[20]

THE AAEJ'S EMISSARY

The AAEJ sent Bill Halpern to the Sudan in April 1979 to see if he could have more success finding Jews than the Israelis were reporting. While he was waiting for Longet to return the third time, Ferede had received a telegram from Halpern saying that he was coming to the Sudan. Ferede had met Halpern in Ethiopia but still was suspicious of him when he said that he had come to rescue Ethiopian Jews. Ferede did not understand why Americans were there, since Longet had not said anything about other people coming to help with the rescue. Nevertheless, Ferede agreed to help Halpern because he was afraid and confused.

Halpern told Berger that Jews were not only in refugee camps, but scattered in villages from Port Sudan to the southernmost border with Ethiopia. He suspected there were hundreds, but had only identified eight. Halpern's effectiveness was limited because the Jews were suspicious of being approached by "a stranger, by a white man and by an American." Berger told Halpern that if the Hebrew Immigrant Aid Society (HIAS) was able to get out the Jews they knew about, then the AAEJ would have to rethink its involvement in rescue activities, since it was their responsibility in the first place. If neither HIAS nor Halpern could get them out by the middle of June, then Berger said he might have to agree with the Jewish Agency and HIAS that it was impossible to get them out of the Sudan. To prove otherwise, he told Halpern, it was imperative that he show results quickly.[21]

The eight Ethiopian Jews that Berger referred to in that conversation were rescued by Longet, who told the Jews "not to have anything to do with Halpern or else they would not be helped."[22] The Israelis did not like the idea the Americans were also looking for people in the Sudan. The Jewish Agency told them it was dangerous for both to be there, but, Halachmy said, "the AAEJ was interested in public relations" and continued their efforts despite the warnings.[23]

When Ferede brought eleven Ethiopian Jews to Khartoum, he decided not to tell Halpern about them. Instead, he cabled Longet and planned to give the Jews to Halpern only if the Israeli did not show up. Longet did come, however, and helped Ferede arrange for two Jews to go to Israel via Athens in April. Then he sent one more person; then six more. An Ethiopian Jew described the final stage of preparation:

It took Ferede a week of working in secret to fix us a travel permit from Gedariff to Khartoum . . . nothing could stop us worrying that the scores of police carrying out checks at the stops on the way would seize us in their grip. . . . We all changed clothes and shoes so as not to stand out at the airport as village people. For two weeks Ferede prepared and trained us in all the things that had to be correct for the flight. . . . He gave everybody new names and made the ones without family into members of one of the group's extended families. He drilled us in our new names and gave minute instructions in how to get through all the airport procedures. . . . We carried out all our instructions, passed safely through one stage after another, until at last we were sitting in a Dutch KLM plane bound for Athens. Until the moment the plane lifted into the air, there was not one of us who believed that we would get out of Sudan in the wished-for direction.[24]

Longet encouraged Halpern to leave, but he would not listen to reason or accept a bribe. He only wanted to see Ethiopian Jews. Halpern and Tegegne then went to Gedaref and brought twenty-eight people back to Khartoum. Ferede went to the place where they were staying and found that many of them were Christians. He told the four Ethiopian Jews he found that he would send them to Israel and took them to the safehouse where his people were staying.

PUTTING ISRAEL TO THE TEST

In May, an agreement was reached between the AAEJ, HIAS, and the International Red Cross (IRC) to rescue those Ethiopian Jews who were in the Sudan. The Jewish Agency agreed to accept all the Ethiopian Jews processed by the IRC and the AAEJ in Khartoum. The names were to first be submitted to HIAS, which would clear them with the Ethiopian Jews in Israel and, within three days, all those who were approved were to be picked up by HIAS's agent in Khartoum for flights to Athens and then Tel Aviv. Although the AAEJ would later claim there was a quota, Gaynor Jacobson of HIAS assured Berger that the Jewish Agency set no limit on the number of Ethiopian Jews they were willing to accept. After the meeting, Berger noted that it was essential the AAEJ avoid any separate rescue operations from Khartoum to any transit point, including Kenya, until July 1 to see what the Israelis would do.[25] On one hand, Berger demonstrated the willingness of the AAEJ to let the Israelis carry out the rescue, but, on the other, he displayed the same arrogance that the organization had become noted for by setting a deadline for Israel to act.

Berger said the AAEJ discovered there were eighteen Ethiopian Jews in the Sudan and that his group sent people to rescue them. When the organization's team arrived in the Sudan, they found thirty-two Ethiopian Jews. Israel agreed to rescue them. When those thirty-two arrived in Israel, the AAEJ team said ninety more were waiting in refugee camps. "I told them [the Israelis] I'd give them 30 days," Berger said. "Either they rescued the ninety Jews or I would go to the *New York Times* with the story." As a result of his threat, Berger believed, the ninety were soon rescued.[26] Regardless of whether Berger was correct, the AAEJ had proven it could find Jews and facilitate their immigration to Israel.

Shapiro believed the Israelis, including Yehuda Dominitz, Aryeh Dulzin and David Kimche, had agreed that if the AAEJ could find any Ethiopian Jews in the Sudan, they were welcome to go and rescue them, so the AAEJ sent Halpern to the Sudan. "Everybody used to say to go to Sudan. Once you took them up on it things were different," Shapiro explained. "They thought everyone was afraid. Only they would risk their lives. Once people saw that we put our asses on the line, everything changed."[27]

Not everyone in the AAEJ was so confident that their organization should be involved. Edith Everett, for example, said that she agonized over the decision of whether the AAEJ should rescue people. "What if they get killed?" she asked herself. "I was at a public phone in a cold sweat," she recalled, "wondering if I have the right to do this." In hindsight, she believes, the AAEJ made the right decision.[28]

In June 1979, Halpern sent the AAEJ a progress report on his rescue efforts. He said five hundred to one thousand Ethiopian Jews were in the Sudan, distributed from the north (Port Sudan) to central (Sennar) Sudan with the majority concentrated near Gedaref. All of the Jews were persecuted if the other Ethiopians discovered they were Jews. Halpern and Tegegne went to the refugee camps in Gedaref and picked out Ethiopian Jews to bring them to Khartoum. They made lists of the Jews and sent them on to the Jewish Agency and the AAEJ. They also enlisted the help of a Christian who had connections with the EDU (the Ethiopian antigovernment party) and was willing to help people cross the border. Daniel Longet, whom Halpern believed was from HIAS (or at least that was what he wrote), assumed responsibility for most of the refugees once he was confident they were Jews. Halpern said that "excessive noise" caused by the other group, presumably the Israelis, was creating confusion and that the Sudanese employees of UNHCR had reported the HIAS and Israeli activities to Sudanese security. Tegegne said Ferede was known to Sudanese security as an Israeli agent.[29]

The problem was that the private AAEJ rescue operation was competing with the Israeli operation and the Israelis were not too happy about it. Shlomo Hillel said that out of his five years of experience working undercover saving Jews in Egypt, Lebanon, Syria, and Iraq, there were always dogooders getting in the way. He said he did not know of any specific instances where that happened in the Sudan, "but I swear in any court that at times you cross paths and endanger each other. There could be no question that it was not responsible. When I heard of their activities, I believed there could be nothing more dangerous." Because of his background in clandestine rescues, Hillel thought he was a credible source and that the Americans should believe him when he said that things were being done and that they should stay out of the way, but they would not listen.[30] Halachmy told Lenhoff that rescue is like a band. Each person plays a different instrument, but there can only be one conductor, which in this case was the prime minister of Israel. The problem, he said, was that the AAEJ also wanted to be the conductor.[31] In response to Lenhoff's suggestion that Israel coordinate activities with the AAEJ—another effort to help "conduct the band"—Dominitz replied, "We see no need or possibility to integrate operational activity in the field. Such activity can and must be done only by a body of full authority and competence."[32]

The AAEJ had never wanted to become involved in rescue activities. The group believed that rescue was the responsibility of the Israelis who had the experience and expertise to carry out the operation. The only reason they sent people to the Sudan, Shapiro said, was because the Israelis did not and told them they could try to rescue the Jews themselves if they wanted to. The AAEJ then hoped that by sending a team to the Sudan they could prove, first, that there were indeed Ethiopian Jews in the refugee camps awaiting rescue and, second, that rescue was possible via that route.[33]

The AAEJ believed they had accomplished this when, in June 1979, Dominitz told Lenhoff the AAEJ should stop its rescue efforts and Israel would begin to rescue sixty to one hundred Jews from the Sudan each month if they did. Dominitz, Halachmy, and General Poran all vigorously denied that any such deals were ever made. "I could never have made any agreement with the AAEJ," Dominitz said, "because we were doing all we could. I could not morally commit myself to 300, 700. . . . I could only agree to do my best."[34] General Poran added that the only thing he was willing to do was speak to the Americans. "Sometimes they brought ideas we'd been working on for a year. There were no agreements," he insisted.[35]

In July 1979, a Christian who was taking money from Ferede, and was supposed to be distributing the funds to the Ethiopian Jews in Gedaref, blew the whistle on the operation. Ferede decided it was no longer safe in the Sudan, so he left with sixteen other Ethiopian Jews. He also thought, incorrectly, that no more Jews were in the Sudan.

A month later, Dominitz told Lenhoff that only ten of twenty-seven names that Israel had received from the AAEJ were actually Jews. Only three of those, he complained, had been turned over to Israel for handling, and one of them was not Jewish. Lenhoff had sent a list of another seventeen names in July, and Dominitz said that eight of those were not Jews and the other nine could not be confirmed because of a lack of details. Halachmy was responsible for verifying identification and he did so by referring to the 1976 census of Ethiopian Jews for the name of the person's father. If the name was not on the list, he would ask Yona Bogale for verification.

At about the same time that Dominitz was trying to get the AAEJ to stop its activities, Halpern was in Geneva meeting with Nissim Gaon, a Sudanese-born Jewish millionaire. Gaon agreed to give Halpern an advance of 6,000 Sudanese pounds per month (approximately $10,000), which he expected to be reimbursed for by either the Jewish Agency or the AAEJ. Gaon told Halpern that he had access to five hundred Ethiopian passports that could be used to transport Jews out of the Sudan. He also said he would look into the possibility of chartering a plane to fly them out.

Halpern also had learned in August that thirty-five of the sixty Falashas under his care had been arrested because of charges made against them by "friends of Ferede." They were later released and were waiting in Khartoum, but Halpern said the arrests jeopardized the security of the Ethiopian Jews in the Sudan. Nevertheless, he told Berger that a steady flow of refugees was coming from Ethiopia now that it had become fairly well known that the Sudan was the point of departure for Israel. Berger told Halpern to try to use the Gaon's Ethiopian passports to get ten Falashas to Rome, where he hoped the Jewish Agency would take responsibility for bringing them to Israel. "I still believe this is Israel's and the Jewish Agency's responsibility and not ours to keep doing forever," he added.[36]

Ferede returned to the Sudan in October because he knew that more Ethiopian Jews would begin to cross the border. At one point he sent a phony list of twelve Ethiopian Jews to Geneva to convince Israeli officials he should remain in the Sudan. Then, by chance, in December, Ferede's mother and sister reached the Sudan and found a way to contact him. Ferede met them in Gedaref and took them to Khartoum before cabling Geneva again. Longet then came with money but without documents. A month later, Ferede obtained the necessary documents and, in February 1980, sent his family to Israel. More of his relatives began to leave Ethiopia and he arranged for them all to go to Israel.

THE FRANKFURT OPERATION

Tegegne and Halpern managed to bring a group of Jews to Frankfurt, Germany using false Ethiopian passports. Ferede learned that twenty-two people went to Germany, but he was not sure if they were Jews and asked Longet to check them out. This escape route was cut off shortly thereafter when Germany stopped accepting the passports because too many people tried to use them. The Israelis blamed the AAEJ for ruining this route by using false passports and upsetting the Germans.

A letter to Halpern dated November 2, 1979, from an American lawyer working with refugees in the Sudan, meanwhile, noted that there was growing opposition to the rescue operation in the Sudan. He wrote that this was caused by rumors spread by Ferede and his group, who were apparently saying such things as Halpern's team was selling the Jews to Israel to do their fighting for them. They also gave the Sudanese authorities the name of one of Halpern's most active workers, who was subsequently arrested and beaten for his alleged part in the action against the interests of the Sudanese people. After a great deal of effort to persuade the authorities that the charges were false, the man was released.[37]

The AAEJ continued its operation as well as its efforts to enlist the co-operation of the Israelis. According to Aryeh Dulzin, the Israelis had approached Halpern on a number of occasions and asked him to supply them with names of people they could help rescue, but that he had not provided any names.[38] A short time later, however, Halpern submitted a report to the AAEJ in which he claimed to have transmitted a number of names to HIAS, but said that he had not heard of any being approved since June.[39]

Meanwhile, a number of representatives of the Ethiopian Jews in Israel wrote to U.S. Senator Rudy Boschwitz in December urging him to stop all support for Halpern's activities because he was endangering the rescue project. According to the Israeli Association of Ethiopian Jews, Halpern refused to cooperate with their organization and exposed himself by telling people that he was looking for Ethiopian Jews and mobilizing huge sums of money. [40] The senator received another contradictory letter a few days later from Yehuda Dominitz indicating that there were not hundreds of Ethiopian Jews in "countries close to Ethiopia—contrary to information you may have received from other sources."[41] Generally, though, legislators were being kept informed by the AAEJ and tended to be unresponsive to the Israeli complaints. As Representative Stephen Solarz's aide, Dawn Calabia, explained:

> Obviously no government wants private operations except someone like Ross Perot, when you can't do it any other way. They prefer to control those operations that are taking place and I think the Israelis realized that and their operations increased because they criticized private operations and the difficulties they were causing professional operations. They had to increase their professional operations. When they would call up to criticize that so and so was doing this or so and so was doing that; so and so was running around this country; this busload got stopped here; there was a roadblock there. We'd say fine, you do it. You do it much better. But do it.[42]

There were at least a couple of reasons why there was so little agreement about what was really happening in Ethiopia or the Sudan. First, the AAEJ received most of its information from Ethiopian Jews. The versions supplied by these Jews frequently conflicted with those of the Israelis, but the AAEJ always believed the former. Second, the Jewish establishment had few if any independent sources of information and relied entirely on the Israelis, dismissing the AAEJ as gadflies. "It was ridiculous," Edith Everett explained. At NJCRAC meetings, the establishment figures would say to her "show me a list" of Ethiopian Jews in the Sudan. She would say, "Why should I, Edith Everett, businesswoman and housewife tell you? Why can't the Mossad or Israel get names? They didn't see the nonsense in us bringing Israel names."

Despite the arguments and the operational difficulties, a total of thirty-seven Ethiopian Jews were rescued in 1979 from the Sudan. Berger claimed that the AAEJ was responsible for finding them all, but Zecharias Yona said the Israelis were looking for them at least three months before anyone from the AAEJ was in the Sudan and that half of the thirty-two said they were originally found by the Israelis.[43] The AAEJ certainly played a role, but the Israelis were also involved in the Sudan and accepted all those Jews who were identified and could, therefore, justifiably claim to have rescued them all.

THE ERITREAN CONNECTION

Baruch Tegegne came to the United States and told AAEJ's Nate Shapiro that he had made an agreement with some Eritreans prior to leaving the Sudan to pay them $200 for every Ethiopian Jew they found. The Eritreans found out that Tegegne was at Shapiro's house in Chicago and would call him in the middle of the night asking what he was doing. "You asked us to find Jews," they would tell him, "we've got all these Jews here and we're feeding them and where are you?" Shapiro could not believe the Eritreans suddenly found two or three hundred people just because they were offered $200 a person so he picked up the phone one day and heard someone telling Tegegne: "What kind of people are you? You ask us to find these people and now they are all starving to death and it's costing us a lot of money."[44]

Since the AAEJ had agreed in May not to go back to the Sudan, they set up a meeting between the Christian Eritrean that Tegegne had made the deal with, Haile Temeskin, and the Israelis. After they met in Europe, Temeskin called Shapiro and told him that Israel was not going to do anything. Then the vice consul of the Israeli consulate in New York, Benjamin Abileah, wrote to the AAEJ in January 1980, indicating that meeting with Temeskin had been a waste of time and effort. Tegegne convinced Shapiro, however, that Temeskin could get people out of the Sudan because he had been the one to get him out. So Shapiro decided that they had to prove that Temeskin could get people out.[45] In mid-January 1980, Berger was informed by Temeskin that he had twenty Ethiopian Jews under his care and wanted to fly them to Frankfurt where the AAEJ decided to have Tegegne and Zecharias Yona meet them to certify that they were Jews. According to Berger, the Israelis would not deal with Temeskin, and HIAS would not intervene before clearing the names. Temeskin was not willing to wait.[46]

Meanwhile, Lenhoff apparently forwarded the names to Benjamin Abileah at the consulate in New York and was told that Israel had seen the same names the previous July and found that they were not Jews. Abileah said someone met with the AAEJ's man in Europe and was given twenty-five names, seventeen of which were already known by the Israelis. The other eight could not be verified because the AAEJ representative knew only their names, but nothing else about them. "Surely, if one can honestly claim that he knows a certain person to be a Jew he can be expected to have enough access to that person to obtain this data," Abileah wrote skeptically.[47] Strangely, a few days earlier Dominitz had complained to the editors of the Jewish Student Press Service that Berger and his colleagues had not supplied Israel with any information about names and locations of refugees.[48]

The AAEJ flew six people into Frankfurt, but the Israelis refused to give them visas. Shapiro said the Israelis kept them in the airport three days while they tried to determine if they were Jews. Israeli activist Rachamim Elazar went to Halachmy to vouch for their identities, but Halachmy said he could not find out so quickly, so Elazar went to the Jewish Agency and got approval for them. Rachamim then went back to Halachmy who immediately called the Israeli ambassador in Germany and arranged for visas. Shapiro said Lenhoff threatened to go to the newspapers and that all of the organizations that had ignored the issue suddenly got upset because they thought Israel would get bad press and fundraising would be affected. Halachmy countered that it just took time to verify that the people were Jews. Not all of them turned out to be Jews, so some were denied visas.[49]

Later, two more people were flown to Frankfurt and Israel only accepted one; the other was a Christian who returned to the Sudan and hung himself. This created some anxiety among the fourteen Ethiopian Jews waiting in a safe house in Khartoum, so the AAEJ decided they had to be evacuated quickly. Finally, Shaul Ramati, director of World Jewish Affairs in the Israeli Foreign Ministry, and Chaim Aynor agreed those fourteen could be flown to Germany and Israel would take them to Israel. Then, they told Shapiro, the AAEJ would have to disband their activities and allow the Israelis to take over.

The AAEJ stopped its rescue operation again after Dominitz insisted, but the Ethiopian Christian who had been arranging escapes for the AAEJ continued to pass names of Ethiopian Jews he found to the AAEJ, which, in turn, forwarded them to the Jewish Agency. The agency, however, ordered them to stop collecting names, which the AAEJ took as yet another example of the Israelis' disinterest in acting. The Israelis simply did not think AAEJ's list gathering was necessary, since they had their own sources of information and claimed to already have the same names. Meanwhile, the Israelis were telling people in America that there were no more Jews in the Sudan. Shapiro would go to meetings in New York and argue with Abileah:

I'd say they are there and he would say that they are not there. And all the Jewish organizations would get up and say that we are lying, that they are not there. At the end of the meeting, I gave them a list of two and said to check them out. Three or four days later, there would be a meeting of the same people, Israel's defenders, HIAS and ORT and JDC. Everyone was there defending the Jewish Agency. Abileah would say, "yes, I checked, they're there, but there are no more." I'd say there are hundreds, thousands, but they didn't want to admit they were there. I'd get another list and show it to them. By this time they

began taking people out because it was a terrible embarrassment. I said there
were hundreds more and Abileah began to shout: "there are no more, there
are no more." I said there are hundreds, and he said you won't give me one
more name, and I took out a list of 60.[50]

Shapiro said Abileah complained that the AAEJ was hiding people from
them. Shapiro admitted the Eritreans were hiding them because they wanted
to collect their $200 per person. He said the Israelis would look for the
Ethiopian Jews and then try to steal them away from the Eritreans. Then
they would come to the meetings in the United States and try to prove that
the AAEJ was conning the Jewish organizations. Finally, Shapiro said, they
made a deal and Israel agreed to take 290 people for which the AAEJ had
names and bring them to Israel. They found the Eritreans and took the
Ethiopian Jews away from them "because they wouldn't give anyone the
pleasure or the satisfaction of saying we were helping the people and the
AAEJ had to turn the names over to the Israelis to help Israel. They stole
the people," Shapiro said laughing, "but we didn't care. We were delighted.
From our perspective that was great. They had them and that was their responsibility."[51]

DOUBLE-CROSS?

The AAEJ was not satisfied, however, and continued to monitor the number of Ethiopian Jews arriving in Israel. They considered the failure to bring
in the number that they claimed was promised to be a "double-cross." In
July, Lenhoff issued one of the AAEJ's typical veiled threats in a letter to
Abileah: "I want to reemphasize our desire for discretion, but the activities
must continue at 400 per month and there must be some pipeline of information so that I can quiet many of our restless membership."[52] Once again,
the AAEJ was making demands on the Israeli government and assuming that
it was possible to regularly bring in large numbers of Jews and that failure
to do so was "proof" that Israel did not want the Ethiopians or was not
making enough of an effort to save them.

The AAEJ was also upset because they did not believe the Israelis were
doing anything to encourage the Ethiopian Jews to go to the Sudan after
the escape route had proved workable. Based on his experience in illegal
immigration, Shlomo Hillel said that such emissaries were not necessary.
"When you show that you can rescue people from the other side of the border, I knew people would move across the border themselves."[53] Hillel acknowledged that some Ethiopian Jews might be stuck in refugee camps for
months or even years, but he believed that was better for them than staying
in Ethiopia because, once they reached the Sudan, Israel had a chance to
rescue them. Nevertheless, when large numbers of Ethiopian Jews did begin to cross the border in 1981, Rachamim Elazar went to Halachmy and

asked him to send someone to Ethiopia to stimulate movement. At first Halachmy told him it was a bad time, but three months later a teacher was sent.[54] In addition, the education director for ORT had been instructed by Israel to encourage people to cross the border and had done so until he had been forced to flee the country himself.[55] Parfitt wrote that a handful of Israeli Beta Israel were recruited by the Mossad and sent back to villages in Ethiopia to tell the people that their moment of redemption was at hand and that they could reach Israel from the Sudan.[56] According to General Poran, tourists were also used to send messages to the Jews still in Ethiopia.[57]

NO EASY WAY OUT

While it was more tenable to rescue the Beta Israel via the Sudan than directly from Ethiopia, risks were still involved. Although the Mossad was originally created to help rescue Jews from Europe during World War II, its priorities had long since shifted to intelligence gathering, and those operatives who were in the Sudan were hesitant to jeopardize their missions. The Sudan is an Arab country that was officially at war with Israel; therefore, the Israelis could not work openly in that country to rescue the Ethiopian Jews, and any such efforts would threaten the exposure of their intelligence network, which was needed to keep tabs on developments not only in the Sudan, but throughout the Horn of Africa. Those involved in the rescue efforts were also in danger, since anyone caught could be accused of espionage. According to Chanan Aynor, the job probably could have been done better by another type of organization. The problem, he said, was bureaucratic; that is, "the Mossad is very powerful and did not want any competition," and that definitely included the AAEJ.[58] It also took a long time to develop the networks needed to obtain documents, transportation, and the other prerequisites for moving the refugees from place to place and ultimately transporting them to Israel. The AAEJ was impatient and believed Israel could carry out a large-scale rescue quickly despite the fact that it took their own people months to arrange the rescue of handfuls of Ethiopian Jews. "You can afford to be patient," Shapiro said, "if people are living and are able to stay alive while you are planning something." You cannot be patient, however, "when you know that while they are taking their time people are dying."[59]

The Israeli position was that they were not "taking their time," but that it did require preparation to arrange rescues. "Up until Operation Moses," Aynor said, "refugees got permits, but that couldn't be organized in large numbers and could not be directed easily. It required a lot of effort for small numbers."[60] Hillel also reflected on his experience and said the younger generation felt they had to prove they could do a better job of rescuing people than his generation did, but "you had to start with a small stream like when I tried to get people out of Iraq through Iran. At first I got 10, then 12, etc. You couldn't just push a button for Operation Moses, it took a lot of preparation. It's a building process," Hillel explained. "It's not like the military when all the elements are in your hand and, for example, you say we'll take Suez in two days. If it was that easy, we'd just do it." It was also impossible for Israel to have anticipated the number of Jewish refugees that would come to the Sudan when the flow across the border started. "No one knew how many would come or where they would go. We didn't have a plan in the drawer to bring them out. We had to make plans as the situation developed," said Hillel.[61]

The AAEJ also was unaware of the fact that Israel was planning larger operations. They did not know, for example, that the Mossad was working with Sudanese security officials to build an airstrip in the desert near the refugee camps so the Ethiopian Jews could be flown directly to Israel. That airstrip took two years to complete. "I couldn't tell them [the AAEJ] we were building this," General Poran said. "These people were not connected with any way of control."[62] Prior to building the airstrip, it was almost impossible to take large numbers of Ethiopian Jews out of the Sudan at any one time. One reason for this was that the Sudanese police (or civilians who would report it) would have a much easier time spotting large numbers of refugees moving from place to place. A second problem was finding and maintaining safe houses without arousing suspicions. It was also more difficult to feed and transport a large group of Jews. All of these problems increased the risk of exposing the entire operation.

The AAEJ believed that if their "amateurs" could make small rescues then Israel's professionals ought to have no trouble with large ones. The Israelis found this reasoning faulty. What the activists did not understand, General Poran argued, was that trying to do too much too quickly could endanger the entire operation. "It is not a big deal to smuggle a few people. Anyone can do it. We needed to bring a stream and we were afraid that stream would be fouled up by their efforts."[63] The AAEJ maintained that they were using different routes and that none of their operations interfered with the Mossad. "First of all," Shapiro responded, "when we brought out five they were bringing out nobody. So it wasn't five against 1,000. They were bringing out nobody. We were careful when we chose our spots. During 1980–81, when they were taking some people we didn't go back in. Once they were taking 5, 6, 7, 800, it wasn't necessary. Once they stop, then the demonstration has value."[64]

The problem was that when people did not come out of the Sudan, the AAEJ attributed it to a lack of effort while, in many cases, it was simply a matter of planning for the future or the need to lay low after a close call. The Israelis insisted, moreover, that their operations [were] undermined in some instances and that there was always the threat that the AAEJ's team might be arrested or get into some difficulty that would alert the Sudanese authorities as to what was taking place and perhaps embarrass them or in some way create a situation in which the rescue effort could not continue. What the Israelis failed to admit was that they were having plenty of trouble with their own people.

NUMEIRY'S BALANCING ACT

Another prohibiting factor that the AAEJ did not seem to take into account was the political situation in the Sudan. The president of the Sudan, Gaafar el-Numeiry, was a close ally of Egypt's president Anwar Sadat and had endorsed his peace efforts, so it was not surprising that Begin was reported to have asked Sadat to intervene with Numeiry regarding the Beta Israel. Sadat, however, refused.[65] While Numeiry's willingness to support the Israeli-Egyptian peace treaty attracted support from the United States, it also resulted in pressure from the Arab world, which saw his action as traitorous. Sudanese opposition figures also opposed the treaty and the net result was that Numeiry's position was undermined both within the Arab world and his own country. One indication of the unrest in the Sudan was a trial in May 1979 of a group accused of attempting a coup. In February 1980, six thousand demonstrators marched on the Egyptian and American embassies in Khartoum to protest the exchange of Egyptian and Israeli ambassadors. Numeiry had already withdrawn his ambassador from Cairo and expressed "deep grief" at the ambassador exchange. In an effort to head off the unrest inside the Sudan, Numeiry tried to reconcile with some of his opponents and to improve relations with his neighbors. He also offered to mediate in the war between the Ethiopian government and the Eritrean rebels.[66]

Throughout the period of the rescue operations in the Sudan, this political unrest was a factor that hindered the Israelis; nevertheless, when both Begin and U.S. diplomats asked Numeiry to allow the Ethiopian Jews to leave the Sudan, he agreed to turn a blind eye to discreet and small-scale operations to rescue the Ethiopian Jews. Many Sudanese officials were willing to cooperate with the rescue on humanitarian grounds and in keeping with Islamic notions of justice; others could be bribed. The agreement was not widely known, however, so the Israeli operation was constantly threatened by exposure from Sudanese security officials who were not privy to the agreement. Numeiry was particularly wary after his friend Sadat was assassinated in October 1981, at least in part, because of his "collaboration with the Zionist enemy."[67] This was another reason the Israelis were so sensitive about publicity and reacted so angrily to the AAEJ's activities.

In addition to the perils faced by the rescuers in the Sudan, the Ethiopian Jews faced great danger in trying to reach the Sudan. The journey was long and arduous, and travelers had to be on guard against bandits. Many Jews, especially the very young and elderly, did not survive the trip. Moreover, attempting to leave Ethiopia illegally was considered a crime of betraying the revolution and was punishable by lengthy imprisonment or, under "grave circumstances," death. In July 1980, for example, ninety-six Ethiopian Jews were arrested trying to cross the border, and after five months, eighty-eight were released unharmed, but eight others, suspected as ringleaders, were still in jail nearly a year later.[68] Many of those who were caught at other times were tortured, and some were crippled by being beaten on the soles of their feet. Those Jews who tried to escape sometimes made things worse for those they left behind because the remaining members of the family would then be punished.

THE END OF FEREDE'S MISSION

Throughout 1980, Ferede forged exit and tourist visas as well as passports and eventually learned how to send Ethiopian Jews to Greece without transit visas. In April, however, Ferede was arrested with 600 names and 249 forms and pictures for documents. So, despite what Israel and its defenders claimed, it was not only the AAEJ who had people arrested in the Sudan with compromising documents. Ferede got word to Daniel Longet not to get too close so that he would not be implicated, but the Israelis ignored the advice and went to ask the Sudanese why Ferede had been arrested. Longet told the police that he worked for the United Nations and that Ferede worked for him as a driver (Ferede did not have a license). The police would not let Ferede go, but told him that they would if he gave them money. Ferede gave his guards money, and then they charged him with bribery. Longet tried sending a U.N. official to get Ferede out as a refugee but failed. The police tried to get Ferede to admit what he was doing, but he refused. They released him for a short time before arresting him again in May. He bribed his way out that time and went back to work.

Most of the rescue operation was carried out by Ferede himself. Besides bringing money, the Mossad agents were primarily supervisors who came to the rescue in emergencies, such as the time when some of the Jews were accidentally placed on a Saudi Arabian plane and had to be discreetly removed. According to Louis Rapoport, the Sudanese had no idea as to the extent of the Mossad operation, although they knew something was going on.[69] Although the AAEJ criticized the numbers of people being rescued, it was Ferede and not the Israelis who was making the decisions. Israel would ask for ten and he would send one hundred. One day, for example, Longet came and Ferede said he only had eleven passports, but he showed the Israeli a room full of people. Longet said that they could not all go, but Ferede sent them anyway.

In June, Ferede went to Gedaref and brought thirty-nine people back with him to Khartoum. There was already a group in Khartoum, but Ferede decided it would be safer to put the second group in a different place. He then flew to Port Sudan and rented a small boat. He photographed the area and looked for safe houses. That evening, he flew back to Khartoum and went to see the first group of Ethiopian Jews and found the police were inside. It turned out that an Ethiopian Jew who had been arrested earlier and tortured had told the police where the safehouse was. The person took the police to the house and then they waited for Ferede to return. Ferede knocked on the door of the house and when he saw the police he ran. He was captured and denied being an Ethiopian Jew or knowing anything about the house. He said that he had gone to the wrong house and was released.

Ferede then met up with Longet and went to the second safehouse. Longet gave him money and arranged to meet Ferede later. When Ferede got inside the house, he found that a child had died. He told the father that it would have to be buried in the house because the operation had been exposed. Ferede then went outside and slept in a tree "tortured with fear." At 5 A.M., he went to a prearranged spot to meet with Longet. He told the Israeli that he could not stay in the Sudan any longer because he would be arrested and sent back to Ethiopia and then killed. Longet wanted him to stay another two weeks, but Ferede said that he could not, so the Israeli got him a plane ticket, and Ferede left the Sudan for the last time on June 29, 1980. When Ferede reached Tel Aviv he was debriefed and asked if Longet was in danger. Ferede said that no one knew him so he was safe.

While he was in the Sudan, Ferede felt some competition from the AAEJ's team, but contrary to Israeli contentions, they had not interfered with his work. On the other hand, the AAEJ's accusations that the Israelis had pulled Ferede out of the Sudan because they lost interest in rescuing Ethiopian Jews and only wanted to compete with the American effort were also spurious. Ferede left because the operation was compromised and his life was in danger. Moreover, after Ferede returned from the Sudan, the Israelis asked him for all his contacts and told him to tell another Ethiopian Jew, who was subsequently sent to the Sudan, to continue the operation.

NOTES

1. Graenum Berger, letter to Howard Lenhoff, June 21, 1979.
2. Nate Shapiro, interview with author.
3. Rachamim Elazar, interview with author.
4. Bayla, letter to Howard Lenhoff regarding Aryeh Tartakower's meeting with Menachim Begin's staff, May 12, 1978.
5. Shapiro, interview.
6. Howard Lenhoff, letter to General Ephraim Poran, "Outline of Plan for Illegal Immigration of Falashas," March 7, 1978.
7. General Ephraim Poran, interview with author; Chaim Halachmy, interview with author.
8. Louis Rapoport, *Redemption Song: The Story of Operation Moses* (San Diego: Harcourt Brace Jovanovich, 1986), p. 67.
9. Baruch Tegegne, interview with author.
10. Aryeh Tartakower, letter to Howard Lenhoff, September 17, 1978.

11. Aryeh Tartakower, letter to Howard Lenhoff, December 3, 1978.

12. Halachmy, interview.

13. Alan Liel, Israeli Ministry of Foreign Affairs, letter to Howard Lenhoff, February 8, 1979.

14. Shapiro, interview.

15. Shlomo Hillel, interview with author.

16. Shapiro, interview.

17. Liel, letter to Howard Lenhoff.

18. Charlotte Jacobson, chairman World Zionist Organization, letter to Miriam Rosenthal, April 24, 1979.

19. Yehuda Dominitz, interview with author.

20. Rapoport, *Redemption Song*, pp. 74–83.

21. Graenum Berger, memo regarding call from Bill Halpern to Berger, April 26, 1979.

22. Report of call from Bill Halpern to Graenum Berger, May 18, 1979.

23. Halachmy, interview.

24. Shmuel Yilmah, *From Falasha to Freedom: An Ethiopian Jew's Journey to Jerusalem* (Jerusalem: Gefen Books, 1996), pp. 56–57

25. Graenum Berger, notes on conference call with Carel Sternberg (IRC), Gaynor Jacobson and Leonard Seiderman (HIAS), and Ted Norman (AAEJ), May 29, 1979.

26. Steven Schloss, "Unsung Heroes of 1986," *The Queens Jewish Week*, January 2, 1987, p. 29.

27. Shapiro, interview; Nate Shapiro, "Setting the Record Straight," *Sentinel* (December 26, 1985), p. 13.

28. Edith Everett, interview with author.

29. Bill Halpern, "International Rescue Committee: Preliminary Report," AAEJ June 30, 1979; Baruch Tegegne, letter to Howard Lenhoff, undated, probably 1979; Baruch Tegegne, interview with author.

30. Hillel, interview.

31. Halachmy, interview.

32. Yehuda Dominitz, letter to Howard Lenhoff, August 6, 1979 (reply to July 18 letter from Lenhoff); Halachmy, interview.

33. Shapiro, interview.

34. Dominitz, interview; Halachmy, interview.

35. Poran, interview.

36. Graenum Berger, memo of phone call from Bill Halpern, August 14, 1979.

37. Memo to Bill Halpern from unidentified U.S. lawyer working with refugees in Sudan, November 2, 1979.

38. Aryeh Dulzin, letter to Nate Shapiro, November 2, 1979.

39. Bill Halpern, "Confidential Report to AAEJ," AAEJ, December 1979.

40. Avraham Yerday et al. of Association of Ethiopian Jews, letter to Senator Rudy Boschwitz, December 4, 1979.

41. Yehuda Dominitz, letter to Senator Rudy Boschwitz, December 16, 1979.

42. Dawn Calabia, interview with author.

43. Richard Giesberg, letter to Peter Jackson, n.d.

44. Shapiro, interview.

45. Ibid.

46. Graenum Berger, memo regarding the Frankfurt operation, January 17, 1980.

47. Benjamin Abileah, letter to Howard Lenhoff, February 21, 1980.

48. Yehuda Dominitz, letter to the editorial board of the Jewish Press Service, February 11, 1980.

49. Shapiro, interview; Halachmy, interview; Elazar, interview.

50. Shapiro, interview.

51. Ibid.

52. Howard Lenhoff, letter to Benjamin Abileah, July 15, 1980.

53. Hillel, interview.

54. Elazar, interview.

55. Confidential interview.

56. Tudor Parfitt, *Operation Moses: The Untold Story of the Secret Exodus of the Falasha Jews from Ethiopia* (NY: Stein & Day, 1986), pp. 66–67.

57. Poran, interview.

58. Aynor, interview.

59. Shapiro, interview.

60. Aynor, interview.

61. Hillel, interview.

62. Poran, interview.

63. Ibid.

64. Shapiro, interview.

65. Rapoport, *Redemption Song*, p. 68.

66. *Africa News*, Numeiry's Subtle Diplomatic Game," March 3, 1980, pp. 8–9.

67. Parfitt, *Operation Moses*, pp. 43–53.

68. Michael Winn, "Falashas: Doomed to Extinction?" *National Jewish Monthly*, May 1981, p. 42.

69. Rapoport, *Redemption Song*, pp. 77–84.

CHAPTER 6

American Pressure

Throughout this period, the American Association for Ethiopian Jews (AAEJ) maintained the position that Israel was not committed to helping the Ethiopian Jews because they could see no results. The truth, they said, was that no one was coming to Israel. Actually, no one was rescued in 1978, but 37 were rescued in 1979, 679 in 1980, and 598 in 1981. It was about this time that the AAEJ reached a major turning point in both the tone of its rhetoric and its actions. The shift coincided with the change in leadership from Howard Lenhoff to Nate Shapiro, a businessman from Highland Park, Illinois, who became president in 1982, and adopted a less combative tone, more effectively lobbied American officials, on the Ethiopian Jews' behalf, and initiated a private rescue campaign.

Shapiro got involved in the Ethiopian issue in 1978 after reading a newspaper article that said Israel was not allowing black Jews from Ethiopia into Israel. He cut the article out and took it to his rabbi and asked him for an explanation because he was sure that it was incorrect. The rabbi told Shapiro that he did not know the truth and suggested that Shapiro talk to a person named Bernie Alpert who had been in Ethiopia and had taken two Ethiopian Jewish children out with him. Shapiro spoke to Alpert, who explained to him that Israel was not going to take black Jews to Israel and that he felt they had to place a full-page ad in the *New York Times* proclaiming it. Alpert believed the religious people did not want the Ethiopian Jews in Israel and that if he could physically take two children out of Ethiopia then Israel could do it. Alpert gave Shapiro some material to read and, several months later, Shapiro decided he wanted to help. "I thought it was very simple," Shapiro said in an interview. "We would just buy a boat, take the boat to Ethiopia, and take the people. I was willing to help buy a boat."[1]

Shapiro wanted to talk to Graenum Berger, but the veteran activist did not want to meet him. Shapiro later learned that Berger felt it was a waste of time; anyone associated with the "establishment," such as Shapiro, would be dissuaded from believing his version of Israel's attitude toward the Ethiopian Jews. Berger believed that Shapiro would talk to people at the Jewish Federation, a local Jewish agency that supports the United States, and be persuaded that he was misinformed and to drop the issue, so Berger did not want to waste his time. Shapiro finally succeeded in speaking to Berger at length and subsequently invited him to Chicago to meet two very prominent Jews because "I felt that if indeed this was as much of an injustice as it appeared to be, once exposed or raised by important people, something would give." Shapiro introduced Berger to A. N. Pritzker and another man of prominence in the Israeli bond drive and in the United Jewish Appeal (UJA). Both promised to help. The person deeply involved with the federation was quickly dissuaded in precisely the way that Berger had said he would be. "He came back and told me," Shapiro said, "that secret things were happening and the rest of the garbage." A. N. Pritzker, on the other hand, played a constructive role. Shapiro credits him with quietly pressuring the Israelis. "Whatever he was asked to do, he did. He was a wonderful friend to the Ethiopian Jews. He quietly went about it and made more noise by calling the Israeli consul general than anyone could imagine, plus he leant his name to the cause for years. He was remarkably helpful here in Chicago, certainly concerning fundraising and dealing with the consulate."[2]

A key point in Shapiro's involvement occurred when he went to Israel and met Haim Halachmy, who spent a couple of hours explaining to Shapiro why everything he had been told was incorrect and reassuring him that Israel was doing secret things. Shapiro found the whole meeting odd: "I had a couple of thoughts. One was why in heaven's name would someone involved in rescue come from Tel Aviv to explain to someone who was meaningless that he's doing something. It made no sense to me." Later, Shapiro understood:

> They were trying to kill it. Here I was with the ear of Pritzker who was one of the richest and most powerful Jews in America and they didn't know whether it would matter to him if he found out they were lying. They certainly didn't care about me. I was like any other worker at the Federation. I contributed, but they could live without me. But Pritzker had significance to them and everyone knew we were very good friends and that bothered them. They didn't like that. It makes sense in that respect, but only in that respect.[3]

Shapiro returned home and told Alpert and Berger that they had to give Israel more time, that they were doing secret things and that Halachmy was going to go back to Ethiopia and that something positive would take place. Alpert and Berger were very disappointed in Shapiro because they believed he had sold out. Soon after, Alpert was told by Halachmy that everything had been called off in Ethiopia, nobody could go back there, and Israel would not be able to do anything for at least six months. That convinced Shapiro that he had been lied to and prompted him to become more actively involved with the AAEJ.

CHANGING AAEJ'S TONE

Many of the people involved in the Ethiopian issue in the United States praise Shapiro for giving the AAEJ credibility by reducing the level of criticism of Israel and focusing instead on nonconfrontational methods of pressuring Israel to rescue Ethiopian Jews. Doug Cahn, a legislative assistant to Representative Barney Frank, for example, credits Shapiro with approaching Congress with greater sophistication "instead of damning the world through the press or their direct mail appeals."

> Nate was a different kind of guy. He was low-key, but forceful and he could talk to members of Congress whereas others could not. He knew how to be helpful to members of Congress politically and was a very quick study on how to lobby and that meant all sorts of things. It meant that he was willing to come here in person and talk to members. He was willing to funnel a contribution here and there, to a member of Congress who was in trouble, for someone who had been very helpful on the issues. I would have to credit Nate with giving the organization credibility to talk about the issue with Congress. He used political connections the way they are supposed to be used in Washington and he is quite good at it. I think that Nate was someone that members of Congress respected and continued to respect. They don't always agree with him, but you don't have to. Nate was someone that members could talk to, he built relationships and that was very important.[4]

Shapiro consciously tried to redirect the AAEJ's activities as well as its rhetoric. This is how he explained his approach:

> The one thing that is clear is that this is a wonderful cause, everyone is for it. If you make it confrontational and controversial, you begin to argue over the facts as you present them rather than the cause. On top of that, the shriller the argument becomes, the more personalized the issue becomes. So that one thing you could see developing was character assassination by everybody. You slandered Berger, Lenhoff, or somebody else. So my idea was to depersonalize it and turn it into a cause. If you depersonalized it and just talked about the Ethiopian Jews' rights, without attacking anybody, then you couldn't be attacked.

If I go in and attack someone, then I'll be attacked and then the focus is me and not the issue. So that's why I decided it was just the wrong approach. And, of course, in Washington, D.C., that makes more sense; no one's interested in controversy. Controversy is unproductive and polarizes people. What is politics? It's the art of compromise. You're in the political arena so if you go at an issue without compromise, you're going to polarize the issue and that's a big mistake. Senators don't want that. They want to help you, but they don't want to get involved in a fight. The same thing for congressmen. That was the most deliberate thing of all. Depersonalize the issue and make it a cause.[5]

To accomplish his objective, Shapiro had to solidify his power within the AAEJ; otherwise, he would have been unable to control the more militant members of the organization, notably his two predecessors, Berger and Lenhoff. Like any good administrator interested in creating an organization that will support his views, Shapiro brought in people who agreed with his strategy and whose votes ensured that his positions would be adopted.

Shapiro's approach reduced some of the hostility that was felt toward the AAEJ, at least in the United States. He took three other concrete steps that made the organization more effective. First, he involved some of the American Jewish community's wealthiest and most respected citizens in the issue, people such as Pritzker. This was necessary to show both the Israelis and American officials that influential people were concerned with the issue. These individuals also provided the much needed financial support to maintain the organization.

Second, the organization needed to be more politically savvy. Although Shapiro had not been actively involved in politics, he quickly realized American officials could be induced to pressure Israel. Shapiro gives credit to Berger and other AAEJ members for getting congressional representatives involved, but he was the person who made lobbying a priority. The style he favored, as already suggested, was considerably milder than that used by the organization in other contexts. Shapiro explained:

We never accused Israel of not doing. We said they couldn't do it. It was different. If we had been faced with a situation that they can but they won't, which is what it was, it would have been one thing. We didn't say that, certainly not to most congressmen and senators. To someone very close we might say that they're not doing their best, but we were never going to walk in and tell a senator who loved Israel that Israel was terrible. First of all, I would not want to do it personally. I want to help Israel not hurt it. I wasn't in Washington to make an impact against Israel. We'd go to Washington and say the Israelis have no relationship with Sudan, the U.S. has a great relationship. They can't get them out. That's exactly what the Israelis were saying, so it fit, it was beautiful.[6]

Despite the fact that U.S.-Ethiopia ties had been severed after the Russians moved into Ethiopia, the United States still retained some measure of influence that could be tapped. A State Department official told Louis Rapoport about the AAEJ's approach:

> They went after young congressmen and government aides like Tom Lantos, Steve Solarz, and Ted Weiss and soon developed a cadre of people on Capitol Hill who were interested. . . . The mobilizing of U.S. officials is what started the ball rolling. The American congressmen put the pressure on the State Department, and this in turn is what put pressure on the Israelis to meet the challenge. There was no high-level approach by Israel to the State Department until August 1984. That was months after people around here had been energized.[7]

The Israelis were not very happy about the AAEJ's agitation on Capitol Hill. According to Barbara Gaffin, the establishment was saying, "'Don't involve Congress, it's too dangerous. You shouldn't be going outside of the Jewish community. Plus, the U.S. has no influence with Ethiopia, so don't waste your time.' My feeling," she explained, "was that we may not have influence today, but we might have influence tomorrow. I want to be sure that the members of Congress know about the issue so that when we need to call on them, we don't need to start from scratch and come in one day and say, 'do you know what a Falasha is?'"[8] This lobbying effort later paid dividends in obtaining congressional support for Operations Moses and Sheba. That success was only possible, however, after a prolonged period of lobbying.

The third component in Shapiro's plan to make the AAEJ more effective was to become directly involved in rescue activity. The AAEJ subsequently began to rescue people from the Sudan and argued that if their "amateurs" could do it, the Israeli government should be able to do even more.

GOING TO THE HILL

The grassroots efforts of the AAEJ and its Capitol Hill lobbyists helped to put the issue of Ethiopian Jewry on the agenda in Washington. In fact, the issue became a matter of sufficient interest that a congressional caucus for Ethiopian Jews was formed. The caucus, like those on other issues, met occasionally and ultimately had more than fifty members. Its existence symbolized congressional concern. The Israelis were not too happy about the caucus because they saw it as implied criticism of their government's policy.

Since Washington did not have relations with Ethiopia, legislation was not likely to help the Ethiopian Jews. "There were limits to what we could do," Cahn explained. "We could not mandate that Ethiopian Jews shall go to Israel."[9] Despite these limits, Dawn Calabia, an aide to Representative Stephen Solarz, said, the United States did have commercial relations with Ethiopia and other contacts. Many of the Ethiopians in government had been trained in the United States and came to visit frequently, so American officials did have opportunities to express their concerns. In addition, the United

States tried to get the message across to other countries in the region, such as the Sudan, Kenya, and Somalia, "that if Ethiopian Jews showed up in those countries they were not to be mistreated or pushed back into Ethiopia, that they should be granted temporary asylum, that they understood that the United States considered it a kindly gesture and an important one to facilitate those people being able to go to Israel."[10]

One small contribution made by Congress was the decision to amend the bill that provided Israel with money to help resettle refugees from the Soviet Union and Communist countries in Israel. Although it was probably unnecessary from a legal standpoint, Charles Percy, the senator representing the AAEJ's base in Chicago, was the author of an amendment to the bill that said refugee aid was for not only Soviet Jews but also refugees from other countries. Later, the language was made explicit to include Ethiopian Jews. The effect of the legislative amendments was primarily symbolic in order to show that Ethiopian Jewish refugees were considered no less important than those from other nations. Skeptics among the AAEJ would later charge that the reason the Israelis brought more Ethiopian Jews to Israel was that they needed to justify the need for this resettlement aid at a time when the flow of Jews emigrating from the Soviet Union had all but stopped, but the truth was the Israelis were not particularly concerned about the resettlement funds.[11] In fact, later, after Operation Moses, when some congressional representatives were trying to restore resettlement funding that had been cut, the Israelis, according to one aide, "couldn't manage to find somebody at the embassy to take enough interest to say, 'We could really use this money, maybe you guys could help us out.'"[12] This disinterest might be contrasted with the Israeli concern with Soviet Jews. The Israelis had someone at the embassy who was always available to provide information regarding Soviet Jewry, but there was never a similar person responsible for Ethiopian Jewry. Congressional aides said they could usually obtain more reliable information from the AAEJ than from the Israelis.

The second major AAEJ lobbying success on Capitol Hill was that the Ethiopian issue became part of House hearings on religious persecution as a violation of human rights in August 1982. The hearings were useful, according to Cahn, because, for the first time, they provided a record of concern on the matter. Moreover, the hearings "helped to educate members of Congress that there was a problem and gave those who had heard about the problem from their constituents an opportunity to say, 'I'm aware of the problem and I'm doing what I can.'"[13] The Israelis, on the other hand, were anxious about the hearings, fearing that they would make "too much noise" and endanger their rescue operations.[14] A few months earlier, a Jewish Agency official noted the growing campaign in America for the Beta Israel and "wryly wondered aloud if they were planning to invade Ethiopia."[15] Rachamim Yitzhak, an Ethiopian Jew from Israel, came to testify at the hear-

ings along with Henry Rosenberg and Graenum Berger of the AAEJ. Yitzhak
told the committee:

> The royal families and the landlords who lost their land and privileges ran away
> to the western parts of the country to an area where the majority of the Falashas
> were located. There they established what they call an anti-revolutionary party.
> Their first target was the Falashas. First they came to the Falasha villages and
> confiscated their meager possessions. Then they threw them out of their houses
> and the little land they had. This action uprooted the Falashas from their land
> before the land reform proclamation was implemented. As a result, several thou-
> sand Falashas became refugees, youngsters were kidnaped to serve in the army
> of the anti-revolutionary parties. The central government could not defend the
> Falashas because of the war with the Somalia and the Eritrea.
>
> Now, politically, the Falashas are accused by both the central government and
> the anti-government parties of not being loyal. The central government blames
> the Falashas as if they were collaborating with the anti-government parties,
> because of their location. Likewise, the anti-government accuses them as if they
> were collaborating with the central government. The two provinces of Gondar
> and Tigre rebelled against the central government and the Falashas were caught
> in between two cross-fires. Due to this, hundreds of Falashas were killed or taken
> to prison.[16]

Yitzhak explained that the central government did not issue an order to
persecute the Ethiopian Jews, but because of the weakness of the central government, certain provincial governors had acquired dictatorial powers. The
governor of Gondar, Major Teferra Melaku, was the primary offender.
According to Yitzhak he had decided to halt education and religious practices of the Ethiopian Jews as well as illegal immigration.

> He closed down 22 elementary schools and the only high school. In addition,
> four vocational schools were shut tight. Some 78 Falasha teachers were dis-
> missed and forbidden to work, and a selected group of teachers were sent to
> jail and tortured. Every Falasha had to carry a special identification card or pa-
> per which also restricted his travel. The Falasha, being mostly farmers, had to
> sell their products in the market. Market day was changed to Saturday, and as
> they were Sabbath observers, they could not and would not go to the market
> to sell their wares on the holy day of the week.[17]

When asked to compare pre- and post-revolutionary Ethiopia, Yitzhak said
that during Haile Selassie's reign the Falashas were at least free to practice
their Judaism, but now, especially in Gondar, they were prohibited from
doing so. Although theoretically they should be better off because of land
reform, he said, "we did not see it in practice."[18]

Since no one from any of the other American Jewish organizations appeared to testify, Henry Rosenberg was asked why the American Jewish com-

munity had been silent on the issue. Rosenberg replied, "It is just too remote for them. . . . The main thing is, though, let the Israelis do it. They
are there. They can do it. The Israelis did Entebbe. They can do anything,
you see? So we do not want to do it. I mean, we are not equipped, let's stay
out of this, be quiet, do not say anything. If you say anything, it is going to
endanger them."[19] Berger told the committee that about two hundred Ethiopian Jews had completed the equivalent of high school and would be eligible for studying abroad, but they needed, as Rosenberg pointed out, a
scholarship to an American university, a guarantor and an entry visa to the
United States. Rosenberg said the American consular official in Addis Ababa
had never issued a visa. The subcommittee chairperson, Don Bonker, said
that he would speak to the State Department and request that they be more
cooperative about the issuance of visas. The visa problem was explained by
Calabia:

> We have a visa law that can be very difficult and if you want to be very strict in
> your interpretation you can make it very difficult, especially in a place like Ethio-
> pia, and especially for an oppressed minority who shows up at the embassy
> having gotten an exit visa, having gotten a passport, having gotten a police clear-
> ance by answering questions about their ability to benefit from an education
> in the United States after completing the equivalent of the 10th grade in an
> Ethiopian school. You start asking about whether they really intend to return
> to Ethiopia, which is one of the criteria for getting a nonimmigrant visa, or a
> visa to come to the United States for medical treatment. . . . We were just in-
> censed when we found out about the problems the consulate was causing for
> the Ethiopian Jews. . . . They did come around. . . . People in Washington can
> make inquiries about certain treatment of certain kinds of cases of certain kinds
> of minority groups and indicate that it's in the best interest of U.S. foreign
> policy if certain people are aided and facilitated. That doesn't require the visa
> officer to do any of those things, because he or she is the sole judge, but you
> certainly sensitize people to the fact that somebody's watching you in Wash-
> ington and that there are individuals, congressmen and senators and organiza-
> tions that are going to raise cases of people who were denied. This is not go-
> ing to go unnoticed. This is not one of the great unwashed that will sink back
> into the cracks. The situation finally changed when they changed the person
> in charge and new instructions were issued.[20]

Although none of the other Jewish organizations sent anyone to testify
at the congressional hearings, the National Jewish Community Relations
Advisory Council (NJCRAC) did submit a statement that minimized the
threat faced by the Ethiopian Jews: "Although Ethiopian Jews live in a primitive area of Africa, in a country where poverty, disease, and famine are ram-
pant, they are not faced with the danger of physical annihilation. Their plight
is most serious, but descriptions of the situation of Beta Yisrael in terms of
Holocaust and genocide are inaccurate."[21] Once again, the discussion was
diverted from the issue to the accuracy of the terminology used to describe

the plight of the Ethiopian Jews. More important, other parts of the NJCRAC statement were contradictory. The statement said, for example, that hundreds of Ethiopian Jews live in "chronically desperate conditions marked by hunger and disease." The statement also noted that the pace of assimilation had accelerated and that the Organization for Rehabilitation and Training (ORT) schools and others in Gondar had been closed; nevertheless, NJCRAC had no policy recommendations to offer.

For the next two years, several congressional representatives voiced their support for the Ethiopian Jews in the *Congressional Record* and members such as Tom Lantos, Stephen Solarz, Barney Frank, Tom Wolpe, Gary Ackerman, and Mickey LeLand took a particular interest in the issue. On the Senate side, Rudy Boschwitz was involved early, although he was rumored to have been under pressure to drop the issue and, at one time, did try to get other politicians to take the lead. Alan Cranston was another senator who would later play the key role—along with Alfonse D'Amato—in obtaining the signatures of all the senators on a letter to the president urging him to do what he could to resume the rescue after Operation Moses was halted. All of these men, and several other representatives, wrote to Israeli officials and met with Israeli embassy staff and made it clear they were concerned about the issue of Ethiopian Jewry.

CONFLICTING STORIES

The Israelis, in most cases reluctantly, provided the congressional representatives and their staffs with information. In one meeting, for example, Representative Frank was told that the problems were "logistical" and that Israel was involved in a quiet campaign for fear that the unusual arrangements used to rescue the Beta Israel might be jeopardized. At the time of the meeting, April 1981, the embassy official said that one planeload of Ethiopian Jews was coming from the Sudan each month. The official remarked that they were having problems determining whether everyone who claimed to be a Jew was in fact a Jew. This was an issue that caused some dissension between the AAEJ and the Israelis, but Frank told the official that "it would be wiser to err on the side of allowing more to enter Israel than were deserving than to risk denying entry to those who had a legitimate right."[22]

The Israeli response evolved over time, according to one congressional aide.

"At first they didn't want to talk to us. They didn't want to admit that there was a significant problem or, I suppose, they were concerned that to talk about it would jeopardize what they might or might not be doing at the time. It was hard for us to know exactly what they knew and what they didn't know. We knew they didn't want to talk about it. The reason we knew that is whenever

we asked to be briefed on whatever the latest was, there always was a predomi-
nance of interest in the secrecy issue. They couldn't spend enough time telling
us how sensitive the issue was and how we ought not be discussing it in this
way because of the sensitivity of the issue and that lives were at stake. In general, members of Congress who listened to that understood quite well that this
was a serious issue that required some sensitivity. . . . What we got from the
Israelis was confirmation of information which we had received from others."

Other aides also said the Israelis, and sometimes the Jewish establishment
organizations, would come to them and say Israel was doing all they could
and the issue was sensitive and should not be publicized. Members of Congress understood and did not issue any newsletters, called no press conferences, and made no statements. "Having worked up here for a long time,"
Calabia said, "that's not too common." On the other hand, she said that
when Represenative Solarz received complaints about publicity and the actions of the AAEJ, his position, which echoed that of the AAEJ, was, "Tell
me how it hurts. I'll be happy to stop, but prove to me how it hurts. Prove
to me that we do not have the right as Jews to speak out about an oppressed
minority."

When the AAEJ sent rescue teams to the Sudan and the Israelis complained
that Solarz's office was aiding and abetting their efforts, Calabia told them
that the United States is a free country and that as American citizens those
activists have every right to speak out about the Ethiopian Jews. She conceded that some of the activists may be hotheads, and they may make rash
statements from time to time, but she said, "tell me a Jewish organization
that doesn't have that. Tell me any kind of organization where those kinds
of passions don't get raised."[23]

In November 1983, thirty-two members of Congress sent Israeli Ambassador Meir Rosenne a letter commending Israel for its efforts and reiterat-
ing their desire to help Israel with its rescue endeavors. Israel's friends in
Congress repeatedly offered to help, but the Israelis consistently refused their
assistance. Some members acted on their own and introduced legislation anyway. In addition, several congressional representatives went to Ethiopia on
fact-finding tours and raised, or tried to raise, the Jewish issue with Ethiopian leader Mengistu Haile Mariam. In 1981, for example, Representative
Mickey Leland planned a trip to Ethiopia, but canceled it when Mengistu
said he would not talk to him about the Ethiopian Jews. Two years later, in
the summer of 1983, Leland was part of a delegation that visited Ethiopia
and succeeded in meeting with Mengistu. The Ethiopian leader gave the
group the traditional line that Ethiopia was composed of many different
groups of people and that he could not give the Ethiopian Jews preferential
treatment. If the Jews were taught Hebrew, he said, the Muslims would demand to be taught Arabic. The Ethiopian leader told his guests the revolution was meant to eliminate such demands.[24] According to the AAEJ's

Washington representative, Lisa Freund, when congressional members would ask the Ethiopians to allow a family reunification program to be set up so Ethiopian Jews could be reunited with their relatives in Israel, they would say they had no objection to such a program, but there would be no structure set up to implement the idea. "The congressmen would leave and, in writing, try to follow up," Freund said, "but then the Ethiopians were no longer interested in pursuing it. There wasn't anybody staying behind to set up this program."[25]

PRESSURING THE BUREAUCRACY

The U.S. Congress played a particularly important role in stimulating the State Department to become better informed about the plight of the Ethiopian Jews and to be more involved in trying to rescue them. For many years, the department was reluctant to intervene, as evident from this letter to Senator John Tunney in response to a letter Lenhoff had written to the senator in 1974:

> We do not believe, however, that it would be either appropriate or useful for the United States Government to become involved in this matter with the Ethiopian or Israeli Governments. The new government of Ethiopia is fully preoccupied with questions of internal administration and foreign relations at this time, and it is unlikely that it would react favorably to an approach by a foreign government on behalf of one small group, particularly since there is no indication that the Falashas have been objects of any organized persecution. Moreover, they regard such an approach as intervention in their internal affairs, something about which all governments—and new governments in particular—are very sensitive.[26]

Ironically, this was written at about the same time the secretary of state was negotiating with the Soviet Union regarding the immigration of Soviet Jews, a matter the Russians also considered an internal affair.

A former Ethiopian desk officer at the State Department in the mid-1970s said that he never saw a single piece of correspondence on the subject of the Beta Israel during the year he held the position. "It simply was not an issue for the United States government at that point," he explained.[27] When Henry Rosenberg and Rachamim Yitzhak approached one of that official's successors at the Ethiopian desk, they were told the official would not become involved because "it's not a holocaust yet."[28] Calabia had a similar experience in 1979 when she went to talk to the desk officer and explain that the plight of the Ethiopian Jews should be a concern of the United States. She said the man was quite knowledgeable, but at the end of their forty-five minute conversation the official said, "Well, I still don't understand why you care about these people."[29]

THE STATE DEPARTMENT GETS ON BOARD

When the United States cut off aid to Ethiopia and the Soviets moved in to fill the vacuum, the State Department was not only less anxious, but also less able to become involved in the issue. In 1982, for example, when Congress held hearings on the plight of the Ethiopian Jews, department officials were forced to admit that their reports were not based on eyewitness accounts because they were unable to visit Gondar. Representative Steve Solarz found such excuses unacceptable. In a letter to Chester Crocker, the assistant secretary of state for Africa, Solarz wrote: "It seems to me that if tourists are able to enter the area, that we should be able to get permission for a State Department officer to also travel in Gondar."[30] This kind of pressure led the department to include the condition of the Ethiopian Jews in its annual human rights report and, each year, Shapiro said, the report came closer to what the AAEJ was saying about their plight.[31]

Although the State Department became increasingly interested in the Ethiopian Jews, problems occasionally arose. For example, when the AAEJ was running its rescue operation in the Sudan, Henry Rosenberg was arrested while carrying letters of introduction from Representatives Solarz and Wolpe to the American embassy. The letters said the congressmen wanted Rosenberg to report back to the subcommittee on Africa about the conditions in the Sudan and what he thought the United States could do to assist the country in terms of humanitarian aid. Calabia said she received a call from someone in the American embassy who was hysterical because Rosenberg was arrested. The official told her it was irresponsible and outrageous for an American citizen to be running around in a foreign country waving letters from congressmen claiming he had the protection of the Congress to help people. Calabia told the embassy caller that Rosenberg was an American and had the right to free speech. "I'm not going to tell him he can't travel and you have no right to tell him he can't travel," Calabia said. "If he's broken the laws of the Sudan, then he's going to have to accept those responsibilities, but you had better protect him and see that he has an attorney and you also better know that there will be several inquiries if the embassy fails to assist him in protecting his rights as an American." State Department officials were angry because they had been put in such an embarrassing position, and they told Calabia not to let Rosenberg go back to the Sudan. She told the embassy staff they would see him again. "If not him, someone else. This is an issue that is not going to go away, because people care passionately about this issue. They are American citizens and they have every right, in fact, they have an obligation as Jews, as humane people, to do something about this constituency."[32]

The AAEJ's Washington representatives, first Marilyn Diamond, then David Feltman, and later Lisa Freund, kept pressure on Congress which, in turn, pressured the State Department and was instrumental in prodding that bureaucracy to act on behalf of the Jews. In November 1983, for example, ninety-five members of the House wrote to Secretary of State George Shultz expressing their concern about the Ethiopian Jews and urging the administration to reply promptly to requests for aid to drought-stricken Ethiopia. That same month, the Senate moved to support Ethiopian Jews by adopting a resolution that expressed the will of Congress that the president should: "(1) express to relevant foreign governments the United States' concern for the welfare of the Ethiopian Jews, in particular, their right to emigrate; (2) seek ways to assist Ethiopian Jews through every available means so that they may be able to emigrate freely."[33] The measure was unanimously passed by the House. The Israelis were nervous about the actions of Congress and feared they would generate publicity that could jeopardize their operations. They were particularly worried about the tendency that the members of Congress displayed for criticizing the Ethiopian government. Knesset member Mordechai Ben-Porat, for example, told Dawn Calabia that Israel did not mind if the resolution was given a hearing, but he hoped the people testifying would be nice to the Ethiopian government.[34]

THE JEWISH ESTABLISHMENT

On most issues of concern to the American Jewish community, the major Jewish organizations act independently, but, when it came to Ethiopian Jews, the matter was thrown into the lap of an umbrella organization known as the National Jewish Community Relations Advisory Council (NJCRAC) (now the Jewish Council for Public Affairs [JCPA]). The issue was first included in the council's 1975 Joint Program Plan, which devoted two paragraphs to the Ethiopian Jews and recommended that Jewish community relations agencies provide information about the Beta Israel and mobilize public opinion in favor of *aliyah* and assistance to Jews in Ethiopia.[35] Little was done to implement this recommendation, however, and the issue was not made a high priority until 1979 when a standing committee was created to plan programs for the education and guidance of the Jewish community. This committee was established at the same time the interdepartmental committee in Israel was formed and was meant to coordinate activities in the United States.

Soon after the committee was created, the executive vice-chairman of NJCRAC, Albert Chernin, admitted that the American Jewish community was guilty of inaction:

> While there are some who point a finger at Israel in terms of this situation, we also have to point a finger at ourselves. There are very few leaders either among the lay leadership of the Jewish community who are unaware of the situation of the Falasha. Perhaps our reluctance to act on this issue grows out of our doubts about their Jewishness—doubts that we don't entertain in regard to

white Jews who are identified as Jews, even though in the Soviet Union, for example, there's been a severe problem of intermarriage. Others say it grows out of our deference to Israel including our concern about the potential of the Falashas for successful integration into Israeli society or our concern about the security of the State of Israel in and around the Horn of Africa. Others question whether we can have any kind of effect on Ethiopian policy because of the negligible influence that the United States has on that government.

Such considerations have not paralyzed us in regard to the plight of Jews elsewhere such as the Soviet Jews or Syrian Jews. When we launched our campaign in 1963, we had no illusions as to the formidable character of the challenge we were agreeing to undertake. We recognized that the influence of the United States was negligible; that Israel's relationship to the Soviet Union was delicate and that we possibly might do harm to Soviet Jews themselves by such a campaign. Nevertheless, we chose to move forward on this campaign, and we have seen the results of doing so.[36]

Despite this expression of concern, activists complained that NJCRAC did little or nothing to help and also actively obstructed their efforts on behalf of the Ethiopian Jews. The activists believed NJCRAC was taking orders from Israel to be quiet and to try to silence the AAEJ and others. Establishment leaders had to obey Israel to keep their jobs. According to the AAEJ's Eli Rockowitz, for example, Abe Bayer of NJCRAC told him that he agreed with the AAEJ, but could not say so or he would lose his job.[37]

The AAEJ was initially included in the committee; however, the leadership of the AAEJ decided to withdraw because of NJCRAC's: "(a) inability to take any decisive action, (b) sole reliance on Israeli government apologists for its information, (c) reluctance to seek out information from the Ethiopian Jews, (d) failure to organize a fact seeking mission to Ethiopia and surrounding countries, (e) publication in (May 1981) of an inaccurate cover-up for the Jewish Agency on the state of current *aliyah* and *klitah* [absorption] of the Ethiopian Jews, (f) reluctance to pressure for the RISHUT [authority] as requested by the Falasha leadership, and (g) failure to keep American Jews informed about the changing situations of the Ethiopian Jews."[38]

The bottom line was that the NJCRAC committee accepted Israel's claims to be doing all that it could and was more willing to take marching orders from the Israelis responsible for the rescue than from the AAEJ. Even when NJCRAC responded to Howard Lenhoff's complaint about the failure to send a fact-finding mission to Ethiopia by doing just that several months later, the AAEJ remained dissatisfied because the delegation came back and presented a report that did not fit with the AAEJ's view of the situation. The AAEJ subsequently charged NJCRAC with a cover-up. The AAEJ was right about the Israelis giving instructions to the Americans. The Israelis did their best to discourage the AAEJ from taking actions that the officials thought were detrimental to the rescue effort, but they had no success in persuading members who were convinced the Israelis were liars. Even when Israel sent unofficial representatives such as Hirsh Goodman, then a highly respected military correspondent for the *Jerusalem Post*, to persuade the AAEJ that their actions were endangering Israeli operations, they were ignored.[39]

NJCRAC repeated the Israeli line that everything possible was being done to rescue the Ethiopian Jews and that the activists were threatening the Israeli operations. In an address on January 11, 1982, Bennett Yanowitz, the chairman of NJCRAC, acknowledged that the Ethiopian Jews did indeed face "hardships and deprivations" because they were Jews, but explained why it was necessary not to publicize the issue:

> The rescue effort is being conducted by a special unit that has a magnificent tradition of insuring the security of the people of Israel and the emigration of Jews from troubled lands. The effort of this unit dates back to the days of *Bricha* when Holocaust survivors were snatched from Hitler's clutches and the closing doors of Stalin's East Europe in the late 40s. This is the same unit that magnificently saved whole Jewish populations in North Africa almost intact from within hostile Moslem countries. Their tradition is to do their work without attention and exposure, which they shun as being detrimental to the achievement of their task. Security to insure the success of the rescue operation is their primary consideration. Their record of achievement inspires our trust. Their long experience has demonstrated that such secrecy has increased the possibilities of success. It is Israel that has the highest competency and resources for achieving undertakings, such as the physical rescue of Jews from oppressed countries not the inexperienced. Therefore, we believe that this rescue can be best carried out by Israel.[40]

At about the same time, the national chairman of the United Jewish Appeal, Herschel Blumberg, issued a confidential memorandum in which he spelled out the "establishment" position and took issue with critics, using the same argument about Israel's history of rescuing endangered Jews. Blumberg also challenged one of the basic tenets of the AAEJ's campaign:

> It is not true that any action on behalf of the Falashas—no matter how precipitate or reckless—is justified because "there is nothing to lose." There is, in fact, in the deepest Jewish sense, everything to lose . . . there are many precious Jewish lives—both rescuers and those who must be rescued—squarely on the line. For, just as it is eternally true that if we save a single life, it is as if we have saved the entire world—it is equally and immediately true that if through indiscretion, we lose a single life, it is as if we lost the entire world.[41]

"It really came down to a matter of faith, whether you believed the government or not," the Anti-Defamation League's (ADL) Roberta Fahn said. The ADL and other establishment organizations had faith in Israel. "The Israelis also were more believable," Fahn added, "because of the lack of credibility of the AAEJ, which was considered irresponsible."[42]

THE NUMBERS GAME

The AAEJ did not have the same faith in the Israeli government. The group acknowledged that Israel had indeed done great things in the past for persecuted communities, but remained convinced that Israel was not doing all it could for the Ethiopian Jews. The AAEJ's position was that people were not well enough informed to realize that nothing was being done. They would point to the numbers of Ethiopian Jews who arrived in Israel as evidence. The fact that the number had jumped from zero in 1978 to 598 in 1981, the year preceding Yanowitz's speech, was of no consequence to them because they believed that Israel could bring all of the Ethiopian Jews to Israel, just as they had rescued those communities referred to by Yanowitz—if they wanted to.

In a letter to Rabbi Irving Greenberg, Yehuda Dominitz of the Jewish Agency devoted seven pages to explaining Israel's actions. He objected to the AAEJ's use of the number of Ethiopian Jews brought to Israel as evidence of Israeli inaction:

> Why is it necessary to measure the dimension of efforts to rescue the Falashas, using the number of *Olim* [immigrants] as a yardstick? If 10 were to arrive in January, 80 in February, and none in March, would this be an accurate reflection of the efforts made in those months? What is true of months is also true of years. If the past months have brought with them some notable success, is this the true criteria for our present efforts or those of the past years? Even though our success in past years was minimal, despite occasional breakthroughs, does this prove that our concern was likewise? Would we be less "racist" if, instead of 700 *Olim* in 1980, 800 had arrived? 1,000? Would we be judged more "racist" had the number been 500? 300? 100? How does one quantify racism?[43]

Even the State Department official with connections to the AAEJ acknowledged that the critics of Israeli policy, including himself, were unfair. "I am not recanting the view that they were not doing enough," he said, "but I think they were doing more than their American critics have been willing to give them credit for simply on the basis of the results. Something *was* happening."[44]

The AAEJ agreed that it was Israel's responsibility and that "amateurs"—a clear reference to the AAEJ's efforts—should not be involved in rescue. The AAEJ believed, however, that unless they showed that rescue was possible, even by amateurs, Israel could claim that it could not be done. Moreover, it remained AAEJ's contention that Israel would only act after their organization brought people out. While establishment figures like Yanowitz claimed that the high profile of organizations such as the AAEJ endangered the rescue effort and only relatively small numbers of Ethiopian Jews could be brought out without jeopardizing the entire project, the AAEJ insisted that none of their actions could be shown to have had any detrimental effects nor would they accept that larger numbers could not be rescued. In fact, the AAEJ was convinced at that time that Israel had a quota of how many Ethiopian Jews they would bring in each year.[45]

OTHER ACTIVISTS

In addition to the AAEJ, other people were not completely convinced that Israel was doing as much as it could for the Ethiopian Jews. One such person was Barbara Ribacove. Ribacove went on the same trip to Ethiopia in 1981 with Barbara Gaffin and returned to the United States with a similar desire to become involved. She said the Israelis told the group to be quiet after the trip, but the Ethiopian Jews in Israel told them to go public. She did not believe massive publicity would be helpful, but the American Jewish community needed information, and she wanted to arouse interest and compassion without making too much noise. The problem was that Ribacove could not relate to what was perceived as the AAEJ's anti-Israel campaign. "Many people wanted to work for Ethiopian Jewry, but not in a position against Israel," Ribacove said. "Whatever the failures of the past, we felt that Prime Minister Begin was committed to the existence of *aliyah* of Ethiopian Jews. We just did not feel it was appropriate to criticize Israel when they were doing something."[46] As a result, Ribacove founded the North American Conference on Ethiopian Jewry (NACOEJ).

Despite NACOEJ's moderate tone and objectives, the organization still had a difficult time gaining credibility. "Everyone was patient and sweet," Ribacove said, "and gave us nothing to do." When she met with establishment people, they would give her a lecture on the AAEJ, and she would try to tell them that NACOEJ did not want to make trouble. "As time went on," Ribacove adds, "we became more acceptable, but some people still don't like us because we are not under their control." NACOEJ provided an outlet for people uncomfortable with the AAEJ, played an important role in distributing information on the plight of the Ethiopian Jews, and sponsored missions to Ethiopia that ensured that a regular stream of visitors would remind the Ethiopian Jews that they had not been abandoned. NACOEJ had only a minor role in the lobbying effort in Washington and was less active and visible in its rescue activities than the AAEJ; nevertheless, the organization did make a significant contribution to the cause by building its own grassroots constituency.

When Gaffin returned from the trip to Ethiopia, she used her skills as a professional in the Community Relations Council (CRC) in Boston to publicize the issue. She went on speaking tours, appeared on television and radio, and maintained a very high profile. The CRC belonged to NJCRAC, which tried to discourage her from publicizing the issue. According to Gaffin, all of the big Jewish decision-making bodies said the same thing: "It was a recording. They're doing all they can. Anything you do will hurt the efforts. You should not be publicizing. You should not be speaking. My feeling was, even if they were doing all that they can, times change, situations are fluid. Why don't we help them or have conditions ready for when times do change."[47]

The Union of American Hebrew Congregations (UAHC)—the institutional arm of Reform Judaism—also was involved, albeit on a more limited scale. According to Glenn Stein, the organization passed its first resolution on Ethiopian Jews in 1967 or 1968 and consistently encouraged the governments of Israel and the United States to do what they could. When legislation was before Congress, the UAHC mobilized around it and helped create the support necessary to get it passed. The UAHC also was directly involved in relief activities in Africa. When news of the famine broke, the UAHC worked with Israeli philanthropist Abie Nathan to build three model tent cities that came with a field kitchen and hospital and could accommodate ten to twenty thousand people. The tents all had red Stars of David on them that said, "From Jerusalem With Love." The UAHC also sent volunteer doctors to Gondar to provide medical care to Ethiopians, including Jews, in the region.[48]

The primary organization responsible for lobbying the U.S. government on behalf of Israel is the American Israel Public Affairs Committee (AIPAC). They were uninvolved in the issue but were not heavily criticized because they did not cause problems for the AAEJ on Capitol Hill—and they could have. "I respect AIPAC tremendously because they didn't get involved in the issue," said Nate Shapiro. "They didn't like what we were doing, but they never said a word against us. They stayed out of it completely. AIPAC could have killed us if they wanted to."[49]

No one disputes that the AAEJ was the most active and vocal spokesman for the Ethiopian Jews in America. The issue was always whether their tactics were appropriate. When Israel's rescue efforts accelerated, and they were being urged to be quiet, for example, the AAEJ continued to agitate and lobby members of Congress to put additional pressure on the Israelis. One of the main reasons for the AAEJ's activism was that they were being told to pressure Israel by Ethiopian Jews in Israel.

ETHIOPIANS OFFER ENCOURAGEMENT

Throughout the AAEJ's campaign, they were guided by the Ethiopian Jews themselves who they believed were more credible than the government. The relationship was reciprocal because the AAEJ would often give the Ethiopian Jews instruction regarding whom to pressure and what to say. The Ethiopian Jews in Israel who were interviewed for this book were unanimous in their praise for the organization and its efforts. Part of this has to do with their genuine gratitude for the role the AAEJ played in their rescue, but their attitude may also be related to the fact that the AAEJ provided funds to meet various needs and they recognized there was nothing to be gained from criticizing the one organization that actively worked on their behalf.

NOTES

1. Nate Shapiro, interview with author.
2. Ibid.
3. Ibid.
4. Doug Cahn, interview with author.
5. Shapiro, interview.
6. Ibid.
7. Louis Rapoport, *Redemption Song: The Story of Operation Moses* (CA: Harcourt Brace Jovanovich, 1986), p. 92.
8. Barbara Gaffin, interview with author.
9. Cahn, interview.
10. Dawn Calabia, interview with author.
11. Marilyn Diamond and Lisa Freund, memo to AAEJ Executive Board, March 6, 1984.
12. Confidential interview.
13. Cahn, interview.
14. David Matnai, congressional aide, interview with author.
15. U.S. State Department cable from Tel Aviv, April 1982.
16. U.S. Congress. House. "Religious Persecution as a Violation of Human Rights—Coptic Christians in Egypt and Falasha Jews in Ethiopia," U.S. House of Representatives Hearings and Markup, August, 5, 1982, pp. 580–581.
17. Ibid., p. 581.
18. Ibid., p. 584.
19. Ibid., p. 587.
20. Calabia, interview.
21. Hearings, p. 911.
22. Rep. Barney Frank, letter to Judy Wolf, April 1, 1981.
23. Calabia, interview.
24. Bert Silver, notes on meeting with staff of U.S. House Africa subcommittee.
25. Lisa Freund, interview with author.
26. Linwood Holton, assistant secretary of state for congressional relations, letter to Senator John Tunney, December 19, 1974.
27. Confidential interview.
28. Shapiro, interview.
29. Calabia, interview.
30. Rep. Stephen Solarz, letter to Chester Crocker, January 29, 1982.
31. Shapiro, interview.
32. Calabia, interview.
33. U.S. Congress. Senate. Concurrent Resolution 55, Capitol Hill Update, AAEJ, December 5, 1983.
34. Marilyn Diamond and Lisa Freund, memo to AAEJ Executive Board, March 6, 1984.

35. "Joint Program Plan of NJCRAC, 1975–76 and 1976–77," p. 15.

36. Albert Chernin, "A Survey of World Jewry and the Role and Responsibility of the American Jewish Community."

37. Eli Rockowitz, interview with author.

38. Howard Lenhoff, letter to Daniel Shapiro, August 10, 1981.

39. Parfitt, *Operation Moses*, p. 46.

40. Bennett Yanowitz, address to NJCRAC Plenary Session, Houston, Texas, January 11, 1982.

41. Herschel Blumberg, "UJA and the Falashas of Ethiopia," January 5, 1982.

42. Roberta Fahn, interview with author.

43. Yehuda Dominitz, letter to Rabbi Irving Greenberg, May 10, 1981.

44. Confidential interview.

45. Shapiro, interview; Simcha Jacobovici, *Falasha: Exile of the Black Jews*, from transcript, Matara Film Production, 1983.

46. Barbara Ribacove, interview with author.

47. Gaffin, interview.

48. Glenn Stein, interview with author.

49. Shapiro, interview.

CHAPTER 7

A Trickle of Jews

The Ethiopian Jews in Israel remained dissatisfied with the pace of the rescue operations and staged another protest march in December 1981. They also presented a petition with thirty-eight thousand signatures to Prime Minister Menachem Begin's adviser, Yehuda Avner, who offered the familiar refrain that the government was doing everything it could to help the Ethiopian Jews and that anyone who said otherwise was slandering the people and government of Israel.[1] The American Association for Ethiopian Jews (AAEJ) echoed the Ethiopians' concern. Despite the fact that nearly 1,300 Jews had been rescued in 1980–1981—after only thirty-seven were rescued in 1979—the AAEJ continued to complain the numbers were too small, that Israel had a quota, and that officials were dragging their feet. According to AAEJ's Nate Shapiro, Chanan Aynor met him in Chicago and told him that Israel would take 1,000 people per year for seven years and "we're not going to do one bit more."[2]

NEW ESCAPE ROUTES

By the end of 1981, the AAEJ had returned to threatening the Israelis. At the General Assembly meeting in St. Louis in November, Graenum Berger said that if Israel did not bring in at least three hundred Ethiopian Jews per month, the AAEJ would have no choice but to set up its own rescue team, go to the American Jewish community for money, and advertise the reasons for their actions in full page ads in major newspapers.[3] The AAEJ, of course, already had a rescue team and had been soliciting money for years. As was the case with all the AAEJ's threats, they caused great consternation within the American Jewish community and in Israel.

The Israelis, on the other hand, did not need the Americans to tell them that they were not rescuing enough people. They were also frustrated because they realized it would take too long to rescue the Ethiopian Jews by the original Khartoum route at a rate that could never exceed sixty per week without risking the exposure of the entire operation, so they began to look for alternative routes. The problem was that development of these options took time. Since the AAEJ was not informed of the Israeli plans, the Americans kept up their criticism. "We were always looking for new ways to take large numbers of people," said General Ephraim Poran. Beginning in 1982, for example, Ethiopian Jews were taken by truck or bus to a relatively secluded part of Port Sudan, a town called Suakin, four hundred miles from the refugee camps, and loaded, as many as 350 at a time, on boats. Instead of illustrating Israel's commitment to rescue, the operation only reinforced the AAEJ's conviction that Israel could rescue large numbers of Jews at one time if they wanted to. Once again, Israel's success helped create unreal expectations.

The truth was that it took months to prepare the sea route, with Mossad agents and Israeli frogmen charting the entire harbor area so there would be no accidents along the dangerous reefs. A total of nineteen ships, including Dabur missile boats, beach-landing craft, and a special American-built speedboat that could carry up to forty passengers were used to evacuate hundreds of Ethiopian Jews. Some Jews were even brought out by submarine. Use of this route came to an end in early March 1982, when eleven Dabur boats waited offshore to pick up more than two hundred Jews. Two Mossad agents and an Israeli Ethiopian Jew were helping the refugees out of the trucks when a group of Sudanese soldiers appeared. The Jews were frightened and began to flee; several were captured. One Jew was wounded when the Sudanese opened fire, but the soldiers were driven off when the Israelis returned their fire. There were several casualties, including the sea route itself.[4]

Even before the sea passage was closed, however, the Mossad had begun work on another route in cooperation with Sudanese security officials. It took about two years, but the cooperative effort resulted in the construction of a 1,000-meter airfield in the desert, exactly halfway between the two refugee camps Tuwawa and Umm Rekuba, where most of the Ethiopian Jews were living. On March 16, 1982, the first unmarked Israeli C-130 Hercules transport touched down on the strip to pick up one hundred Ethiopian Jews. However, one thousand Jews had shown up because the list makers had let the information about the flight out too early, and it had become common knowledge in the camps. No one wanted to be left behind. After seeing the refugees rush onto the plane in a panic, the pilot succeeded in lifting off, though with only half the plane full, leaving hundreds of frustrated Ethiopian Jews behind, some of whom were injured when an overcrowded truck returning a group to the camps overturned. Although the selection process later became more organized, the Israelis still believed it was too risky to use the desert landing strip too often for fear that it would be discovered by Sudanese army officers unaware of the deal made between the Mossad and the Sudanese security service. Over the next twenty-five months, six operations took place involving a total of nine planes. A medical team was on each plane and a unit of commandos who would cover the operation.[5]

The AAEJ was not informed of this operation, so they remained unconvinced that the Israelis were doing everything possible to carry out the rescue and could not understand that the number of refugees that were being taken out was as large as officials thought was safe without putting the operation at risk. Also unknown to the AAEJ was that the Sudanese had agreed to the plan on condition that it was kept discrete, which meant that large numbers could not be rescued. "Good people from the United States complained," General Poran remarked, "but we can't tell them secret information." This was something the AAEJ had difficulty accepting. Poran was even less inclined to inform them given his opinion that "they didn't do anything but damage. Some were crooks and took lists of people Israel brought and said that they did it." General Poran said that he trusted the public committee headed by Shlomo Hillel because of his past involvement in illegal rescue. He hoped that Hillel would tell the Americans that he checked out their complaints and found that Israel was doing a lot.[6] Hillel said he did just that, but the Americans refused to believe him.[7]

The AAEJ believed that it had received promises from the Israeli government that it was obligated to keep. Thus, for example, when Israel rescued more than 500 Ethiopian Jews in the first part of 1982, Berger was unsatisfied because he believed Israel still "owed" the AAEJ another 237.[8] The Israelis denied making any such deals. Moreover, they resented the Americans' attitude and feared that telling the AAEJ about what they were doing in the Sudan would risk a leak. Since the AAEJ had already demonstrated what the Israelis considered gross irresponsibility in their actions and willingness to disclose information to the press, they had every reason to fear that an indiscreet member of the organization might give away the operation and endanger their operatives. As it was, the AAEJ was publicizing their own rescue efforts in what Israelis considered an irresponsible fashion that threatened the Mossad's efforts.

The AAEJ's leaders, the Israelis believed, were only interested in self-aggrandizement and raising money to keep the organization going. The organization's leaders, they conceded, were well intentioned but essentially egomaniacs who wanted to claim they had saved the Ethiopian Jews. It was particularly galling to Israelis who were working quietly to save large numbers of Ethiopian Jews to see the AAEJ trumpet their success in saving handfuls. To the credit of the AAEJ, much of the Israeli criticism was unfair. The AAEJ was composed primarily of selfless individuals who dedicated their time and money to the cause of rescue. While the organization did not operate like a secret intelligence service, it is an exaggeration to suggest the AAEJ was disclosing secrets that jeopardized Israeli operations. Since Israel did not tell the AAEJ about most of its activities, there was nothing to disclose even if they had wanted to. As far as seeking to perpetuate the organization, the AAEJ was no more guilty than any other advocacy group of trying to raise the funds needed to accomplish its mission. As we shall see, unlike virtually every other advocacy group, once the AAEJ's goals were achieved, it disbanded rather than invent a reason for its continued existence.

COMPLICATIONS

According to Nate Shapiro, the Israelis rescued four or five hundred people in 1982, but then the Lebanon war started and they saved only a small fraction of that number from May until December 1982.[9] The AAEJ did not acknowledge that the war might be a higher priority at that time; rather, they decided to send in another rescue team of their own that summer.

Contrary to AAEJ claims that they never interfered with Israel's operations, their representative, Haile Temeskin, discovered when he visited the refugee camps in September that the Beta Israel elders were reluctant to help him because Israel already had started a program in the same place. Nevertheless, he went ahead and tested out a route to Kenya by sending five non-Jews to Nairobi by air via Khartoum and another five to Kenya by land via Uganda. He said the Ugandan route was the safest because there were already 120,000 Ugandan refugees who complicated security measures. The air route was very difficult because a group of 140 Jews had been arrested on the way from Gedaref to Khartoum, and two of the organizers had told everything they knew to security officials. Temeskin said this compromised operations and made the Jews inside and outside the Sudan hesitant to go anywhere. Shortly thereafter he suspended his operation.[10]

Shapiro called Ferede, who had previously been involved in rescuing Ethiopian Jews, and told him to go to Nairobi to meet Henry Rosenberg, a Manhattan attorney, who offered to help rescue Ethiopian Jews from the Sudan. The Mossad sent people to Nairobi to tell Ferede to go back to Israel and to stay out of the Sudan. Ferede told them that he was not in the Sudan. His old Mossad contact, Daniel Longet, was then sent to Nairobi to inform Ferede that a big operation was being planned and that relations with the Sudan were good. When Ferede continued to balk, the Israelis agreed to let Ferede work in the south of the Sudan while they worked in the north.

The AAEJ team now decided to try driving Ethiopian Jews from the Sudan to Kenya. Another member of the team, Sandy Leeder, was sent to Khartoum. Ferede sent a Christian to Gedaref to get Ferede's two brothers and then Leeder drove them to the Kenyan border where Ferede met them and drove them to Nairobi. In Nairobi, Ferede gave a list of eighteen Ethiopian Jews to an Israeli who arranged everything. In fact, despite all of the complaints from Israel about the AAEJ activities, the Israeli embassy staff in Nairobi was extremely cooperative with the AAEJ's efforts. A total of eighty-three people ultimately reached Israel via this route.[11]

According to Ferede, the Israelis grew more nervous about his activities as preparations for their own big operation—what would be known as Operation Moses—neared completion. He believed they arranged for Kenyan security guards to look for him at Henry Rosenberg's house in Nairobi. The guards searched the house and confiscated all his documents but did not arrest him. Instead, they took him to a hotel where he managed to call the Israeli embassy and Rosenberg. Three days later, he was told he would have to leave the country. At first they were going to put him on an El Al flight, but Ferede was afraid the Israelis would arrest him. He managed to convince the Kenyans to return his passport and allow him to fly to Rome. In September 1983, he returned to Israel.[12] The AAEJ apparently was undeterred by the fact that the Mossad had been upset by their activities and saw to it that Ferede was expelled. The AAEJ sent in another team after he left that proved to be the most controversial and, according to some sources, the most irresponsible of all the AAEJ's actions.

A DANGEROUS BUSINESS

Ferede was replaced by an Israeli, Gabe Galambos, and an American, Thomas O'Rourke, who were sent to Khartoum and told to stay out of the Israelis' way. Their plan was to take the Ethiopian Jews from the refugee camps to Israel via a circuitous route whereby they would first go to Khartoum and then be flown to the Sudanese city of Juba where they would be picked up by trucks that would take them across the border to Kenya and ultimately to Nairobi where they would be flown to a European city and then change planes for the final trip to Israel. According to Shapiro, the AAEJ made a deal with the Mossad:

> We wanted to take people out of Sudan in the summer months and the Mossad didn't want us going through Khartoum or the Red Sea. So our deal was that we wouldn't do anything unless we told them up front, which we did. They didn't care if we went through Kenya. So we had to go down through Juba and then into Kenya. It's a very long trip. But the purpose wasn't to prove that it was the best route, it was to prove that if we could do it, they could do much more. But they would never have considered taking refugees from Gedaref

through Juba into Kenya. It's insane. All they had to do was land the C-130s in the desert and take them out.[13]

The Sudanese did not care either, according to Shapiro. "Would you care if it was 129 degrees and somebody wanted to move some dirty old people," he asked. "They had nothing to do and some white guys are moving a bunch of black people up the highway. He has no guns, he has no radios. What do they care? As long as you never have a gun or a radio," he explained, "you weren't a security threat. Here's a bunch of black people moving out of the refugee camp. From their standpoint, they wished they would all leave."[14]

The first week in the Sudan, O'Rourke and Galambos rented a car and drove to Gedaref with an Ethiopian Jew, Robell Adane, who was being used to identify the Jews in the camps. Robell had originally worked for the Mossad, but they had enough people working for them so he went to work for the AAEJ. After a five-hour drive to Gedaref, the Ethiopian Jew was let out of the car, and the two other men pulled the car off the road and parked behind a boulder outside Gedaref and slept until midnight. An alarm clock then woke them and they went back to Gedaref and picked up Adane who had three kids and three adults with him. The number of people he brought with him was determined by the size of the car the American had obtained.[15] On the return trip, they passed two checkpoints without incident and arrived safely in Khartoum where they checked the six Ethiopian Jews into a hotel. The next day Adane took them to a safehouse near the airport.

Two days later, Galambos and Adane returned to Gedaref where Adane found five teenagers—three men and two women. Galambos described what the drive back to Khartoum was like:

> There was a tremendous feeling of excitement in the car not only because the people were scared and anxious to be off, but because they were on their way to freedom. These were real people, Jews, I was helping, who soon would be in Israel. In that moment I felt more pride and gratification than I had the whole time I served in the Israeli army. These were lives I would always be able to point to and know I helped save.[16]

It was this feeling that motivated all of the volunteers who risked their lives in the AAEJ's operations as well as those who contributed indirectly to the rescues.

When they arrived back in Khartoum, the Ethiopian Jews were dropped off at the safehouse with the others who were brought earlier. That same night, Henry Rosenberg came to Khartoum and brought money to cover the operation's expenses. The next day, Rosenberg and O'Rourke went to Gedaref, but since they were unable to find Adane before they left, their trip was unsuccessful as they could not find any Ethiopian Jews. This was an indication that finding the Ethiopian Jews in the camps was not as easy as the

Americans believed and also highlighted the importance of having an Ethiopian Jew in charge of finding people. In fact, though the Mossad has been given most of the credit for the rescue efforts, it was the Ethiopian Jews themselves who did most of the work and took the greatest risks to save their people.

The AAEJ had a contact who was a travel agent who could have gotten them tickets for the Ethiopian Jews under assumed names on Sudan Air, but there was an Islamic holiday (Ramadan) that caused all of the Sudan Air flights to be chartered to Mecca. As a result, Rosenberg paid for a private charter with a small outfit called Niles Safari. The charter company was run by an Englishman named Jack Cadcaddy. Rosenberg did not want to use the company because it was expensive to charter planes, and he considered Cadcaddy and his pilots "dangerous characters," but he had no choice.

The following day, Rosenberg saw the eleven Ethiopian Jews who had been in the safehouse off on a Niles Safari plane. Rosenberg believed it was possible to move twelve to twenty people every week this way and devised a schedule to that effect. In the meantime, Galambos and O'Rourke went with the eleven Ethiopian Jews to Juba and were met there by a Niles truck that took them to their rendezvous in front of a leather shop where a Land Rover was to pick up the eleven and take them to Nairobi. An hour later, the car arrived with an African driver named Chemuka who picked up the Ethiopians while Galambos and O'Rourke flew back to Khartoum.

A few days later, O'Rourke and Adane went back to Gedaref to pick up another group of Ethiopian Jews. On the way back, however, they were stopped by the police, and the Ethiopian Jews with them were arrested for moving without the necessary documents. O'Rourke went to another police station to get release papers and then returned to where they had been arrested. Apparently they were unguarded because O'Rourke simply walked in and took them out. The security had been tightened at the various checkpoints and the group debated whether they should try to maintain the schedule they had established. They decided to stick to the plan and Galambos and Adane made another trip to Gedaref. This time Adane hoped to find someone to take his place so that he could leave with the next group for Israel. When they got to Gedaref, however, Adane was unable to find the person he had in mind and returned with an old man and woman, their five year-old grandson, and two teenage girls.

The next day, Galambos and O'Rourke flew to Juba again with Niles Safari. This time Adane came along. Once again a Niles truck picked them up at the airport in Juba and this time drove them to the Malakia Market cab stand. Chemuku was supposed to meet them at the airport but did not show up. Galambos and O'Rourke decided to take the Ethiopian Jews to the house of a non-Jewish Ethiopian named Heile who they had approached on the previous trip and arranged to use his home as a safehouse. When they arrived at Heile's house, he was not there, but some men who claimed to be his friends were. An hour later, security and soldiers arrived and took them to the police station. On the way, Galambos and O'Rourke devised a cover story, in which they claimed to be representatives of a Christian Bible group sent to aid refugees. When they got to the station, they were interrogated by three people, none of whom spoke English well. When they were searched, the police discovered that they were carrying copies of telexes, names, and codes. It was this kind of carelessness that the Israelis would later be furious about and lead them to justifiably accuse the AAEJ of irresponsible and amateurish behavior. In the meantime, Galambos and O'Rourke's passports and papers were confiscated, and they were placed under house arrest. Every day, the Sudanese officials promised Galambos and O'Rourke they would give them an answer "tomorrow" regarding their fate so they did not see any reason to approach the United States AID or the UNHCR offices in Juba. In addition, they did not want those organizations to know what they were doing.

The Sudanese then arrested Chemuka along with three of the Ethiopian Jews, including Adane, and imprisoned them. After that, O'Rourke and Galambos went to the AID office and explained their predicament, but not the whole story of why they were in Juba. An AID official informed the U.S. embassy in Khartoum of their whereabouts but did little else. They also spoke to the head of UNHCR in Juba, but he did nothing to help them. A couple of days later, the two men were told they would be sent to prison. When they arrived at the prison, they found that the only people incarcerated were those waiting to be tried, lunatics, and political prisoners. After three days in prison, they were taken to the office of the security officials where they spent two nights. "By this point," Galambos said, "we were really concerned that if we were sent to Khartoum, as some of the African security people were saying might happen, they would possibly find out in some way that I was not only Jewish, but Israeli. For the first time in my life, I felt an absolute gut-wrenching, sickening fear of being Jewish." In addition to the immediate danger, he felt a sense of déjà vu: "My parents had been in concentration camps, we were refugees when we escaped from Hungary in 1956. I had always heard stories about how the Americans did nothing to help European Jews as U.S. AID didn't seem to care about us, and of how some Jews betrayed others, as one of those security Ethiopians was doing to us if he really was from the 'tribe' [as he said that he was]."

Galambos and O'Rourke were finally released, but they decided it would be prudent to flee to Zaire. On October 10, 1983, a contact picked them up and took them to the border where they were met by a local to guide them on foot to Zaire through the bush. They reached a border town but were arrested by immigration officials and detained for five days. They tried to explain that they were backpackers who had lost their passports in the

Sudan and had decided to go to Kinshasa for new ones. On the fourth day, they were told they would be released the next day, but that fifth day, a Sudanese security official showed up and said that their passports had been found. The Zaireans took all their money and then extradited them. Once they were back in Juba, they learned that the Sudanese had notified all the neighboring border towns that two men had escaped from their custody.

A week after they had been put back in Juba's prison, an AID official came to check on them and ask if they wanted to inform their families, the press, and Congress about their arrest. Needless to say, they told him they did. Three days later they were taken to the airport and flown back to Khartoum where they were met by security officials who took them for the first of several visits to the intelligence compound. A little more than two weeks later they were deported. They learned later that Chemuku had escaped to Kenya. Adane and the other two Ethiopian Jews in prison in Juba along with those who had stayed in Heile's hut the entire time were released after three months and, with the help of the UNHCR, sent back to Gedaref where they were later taken to Israel by the Mossad.

REPERCUSSIONS

Although everything turned out all right, the Israelis considered the entire episode a disaster. In his book *Operation Moses*, scholar Parfitt claimed the Mossad had to get the AAEJ's men out of jail and the Kenya route through which he says more than six hundred Jews had been rescued, had to be closed down after the *Nairobi Standard* reported the incident.[17] One of the Ethiopian Jews in Israel disputed the claim that the AAEJ had caused the abandonment of the Kenya route. He said he thought the Israelis had pulled out seven months earlier because of a disagreement with the Kenyans.[18] In addition, the Mossad had nothing to do with the release of Galambos and O'Rourke. Shapiro contacted Illinois senator Charles Percy who put pressure on the State Department. Within two weeks, the U.S. ambassador personally intervened and got them out of jail.[19]

Louis Rapoport of the *Jerusalem Post* quoted a State Department official as saying the Juba incident threatened the entire rescue effort and a Mossad agent who warned the AAEJ that the route was too dangerous, but the AAEJ "knew better."[20] Shapiro conceded that the Israelis did not want them involved and the Mossad hated making deals with them, but, he said, "to the complete credit of the State of Israel, they were unwilling to hurt anybody. They wished that we would stop, but they would not ever do anything to jeopardize us physically." He also made it clear that the Mossad warnings had little effect. "They tried to persuade Rosenberg in New York that this was a terrible thing and not to do it, that there would be severe repercussions. But Henry is extremely courageous. He thought about it long and hard and then went ahead and did it anyway."[21]

The AAEJ continued to insist, moreover, that no Mossad operations were harmed by their activities and simply dismissed Israeli contentions that their operations were threatened as an effort to discredit them. The Juba affair was not a "screw-up," according to Shapiro. "The Mossad had people arrested all the time. They must have had twenty or thirty people in jail in the Sudan during the period. We had two. There were no screw-ups." Shapiro argued that their actions actually stimulated the Israelis to act. After the Juba incident, he said, the Mossad took more Jews out of the Sudan than ever. "It really got in their way," he added sarcastically, "because the movement out of Sudan accelerated. We never got in anyone's way."[22]

One Israeli official, Mordechai Ben Porat, complained that the AAEJ promised several times to stop their operations but, from time to time, sent Ethiopian Jews into the Sudan. He said the AAEJ's operatives were caught with valuable papers, which was true, but he also repeated the erroneous claim that Israel had rescued them. Ben Porat said Israel was afraid the arrested men would give information to the police so they had to give up two unspecified routes. He claimed that he also personally witnessed phone conversations from AAEJ members in the United States to Israel and Kenya during which numbers of people and migration were discussed. He warned them not to do this because of enemies listening off Israel's coast.[23] General Poran provided a specific example regarding the AAEJ's use of the route through Frankfurt. He said that when the police caught one of their group it spoiled Israel's relations with the Germans and ruined arrangements they had been using. "We lost that channel," he said.[24]

In fairness, it must also be stated that the AAEJ's people were not the only ones who committed blunders and were arrested. As Shapiro noted, a number of the Mossad's people were arrested or had to flee before being apprehended, including their first operative, Ferede. According to one of the Ethiopian Jews who had worked in the Sudan, "several times Israel's groups were caught and tortured on the way to Khartoum. We bought them out several times."[25] The ability of the AAEJ to carry out the rescue was not the only issue. There was also the more philosophical question of who is responsible for Jews. "I believe that since 1948, as a Jewish State, Israel claims responsibility for the Jewish people," Yehuda Dominitz asserted. "The AAEJ are good people, but dangerous and irresponsible. You can't operate in an enemy country or even a friendly one with different arms. It's nonsense to believe that a private organization could have the means to rescue Jews," he added. "The leading role must be for Israel."[26]

Rapoport does give Henry Rosenberg credit for abandoning his operation after he realized he might be endangering the Mossad effort. After the Juba fiasco, in late 1983, Shapiro said the AAEJ agreed to pull out of the Sudan and the Mossad promised to clean out the refugee camps.[27] Shapiro thinks the Israelis just saw things had gotten out of hand and that as long as there were refugees in the camps there were crazy people who would try to rescue them. Then Israel started to take people out of the Sudan "like only the State of Israel can do it. It was perfection. Sensational."[28]

THE VOLUME RISES

The other source of mutual recriminations involved the publicity surrounding the Ethiopian Jewry issue. The AAEJ's efforts intensified in 1983 when they began to receive reports that thousands of Ethiopian Jews were dying of disease and starvation in the refugee camps in the Sudan. Once again, disputes arose over the figures that the AAEJ was using—they said their numbers came from the Ethiopian Jews—and this diverted people from the real issue, which was not *exactly* how many were dying, but the fact that hundreds and perhaps thousands *were* dying.

From Israel's perspective, there was nothing wrong with publicizing the plight of the Ethiopian Jews at this point. What the Israelis strongly objected to, however, was what they considered the AAEJ's indiscretions in mentioning the Sudan and exposing the rescue efforts. Since Israel was technically in a state of war with the Sudan and that country had to maintain the appearance of hostility for the benefit of its relations with other Arab countries, the Sudan was generally referred to in written correspondence as "the other country," "TOC," or "a neighboring country." Prime Minister Begin was furious, for example, when he agreed to a meeting with AAEJ's Howard Lenhoff and then found Lenhoff had already prepared an agenda that included mention of the Sudan. Although Lenhoff did not see any risk in using the name of the Sudan in a meeting in the prime minister's office, the Israelis saw this as another example of the AAEJ's irresponsibility. In addition, according to a participant in the meeting, Begin told Lenhoff no one should make agendas for *his* meeting.[29] It was this type of behavior the Israelis found arrogant.

The most serious breach of security cited by both Rapoport and Parfitt as examples of the AAEJ's destructive actions were articles that appeared in newspapers revealing rescue efforts.[30] In 1981, an article appeared in the *Miami Herald* that the two authors say revealed "sensitive information." In that article, a board member of the AAEJ, Henry Parnes, was quoted as saying that a national drive to raise $10 million for the rescue of three thousand Ethiopian Jews in the Sudan was set to begin. He also said the AAEJ had received commitments from several European countries to grant temporary entry visas for Ethiopian Jews. Parnes charged the Jewish Agency with dragging its feet and "willfully preventing the *aliyah* of significant numbers of Falashas."[31]

In a letter to Lenhoff, Dominitz complained about the *Herald* article and said it jeopardized the availability of escape routes.[32] By this, apparently, he meant the article's reference that Switzerland, France, West Germany, the United States, and other unnamed countries would provide visas. In a reply to Dominitz, Parnes explained that he was an Israeli and that he spoke out because of the Jewish Agency's inaction. He also admitted the article was "fraught with errors" such as his claim that the AAEJ arranged for visas when it was in fact the Israelis who had done so.[33]

An even greater flap erupted in 1983 when the *Nairobi Standard* published a story about the capture of two members of the AAEJ who were caught in Juba, Sudan, trying to rescue Ethiopian Jews. The story revealed details of the "underground railroad" taking Ethiopian Jews out of the Sudan through Kenya. Rapoport and Parfitt claim that a third article, which appeared in the July 1983 *London Observer*, nearly put an end to the entire rescue operation. That article revealed that

> An underground network is channeling the Falashas . . . out of their homeland to become settlers in Israel. The network is largely financed by Jewish pressure groups in the United States and Canada. The operation is being conducted in the greatest secrecy because the Falashas' only "escape route" is through the Sudan, an Islamic country. Some of the emigrants are taken out by air from Khartoum; others are thought to have left by boat from the small Sudanese port of Suakin, sailing up the Red Sea to Eilat. . . . A key role in this campaign has been played by the American Association for Ethiopian Jews, founded by Graenum Berger.[34]

These leaks reinforced the Israeli view that the AAEJ could not be trusted. The AAEJ maintained that they did keep silent and did not reveal details; moreover, they argued that the rescue was not stopped. Since the rescue continued, they concluded, the revelations were not harmful.

One Ethiopian Jew now in Israel said the Ethiopians did watch the demonstrations in Israel and reports in the United States. "It made them angry and also made them think," he said. "Sometimes it helped, sometimes it didn't. The publicity forced the government to think before acting."[35] Nevertheless, the Israelis did overreact to stories such as the one that appeared in the *Miami Herald*, since it was unlikely that these reports would either filter back to Ethiopia and the Sudan or be of any interest. Had the stories appeared in the *New York Times* or *Washington Post*, however, it would have been difficult for those countries to miss or ignore (although chapter 8 will show that the disclosure of Operation Moses in the *New York Times* did not cause that rescue to be halted).

Some Ethiopian Jews also became increasingly critical of the AAEJ's actions. One group issued a statement saying the "involvement of non-professional, voluntary Diaspora groups and individuals in rescue efforts will not help, but to the contrary, can only hurt those Ethiopian Jews in refugee camps and will endanger and cause interruption of the overall rescue." The statement, which was distributed at the National Jewish Community Relations Advisory Council (NJCRAC) meeting in February 1983, said Israel should be solely responsible for rescuing the Beta Israel and that publicity "can only be harmful to them personally and to their future rescue."[36] The circumstances surrounding the statement and the credibility of some of the signers became a matter of controversy, but the point was that the AAEJ did not have the unanimous support of the Ethiopian Jewish community in Israel, although they argued that the overwhelming majority backed their positions.

While the AAEJ received all of the blame for unwanted publicity and indiscretion, the fact was that others made similar mistakes. The notorious *Miami Herald* article, for example, also contained a quote from Hertzel Fishman, a member of the Jewish Agency's board of governors, who told the reporter that the agency was involved in "'secret, delicate' negotiations to get the Falashas out of both Sudan and Ethiopia."[37] The Israelis were understandably concerned that their operations would be jeopardized by publicity, especially of details of the escape routes provided by loose-lipped Americans. For its part, the AAEJ denied responsibility for the leaks, except the *Miami Herald* story, which it blamed on an overzealous member.

AAEJ officials also maintained that when they were informed that Israel was about to launch a major operation, what turned out to be Operation Moses, and were told to keep quiet by a State Department official whom they trusted, they stopped all their publicity. Even then, however, there were members, notably Berger, who refused to believe that Israel was really going to act. Consequently, according to Rapoport, Berger continued to write newspaper articles discussing the Ethiopian Jews in the refugee camps and specifically mentioning the Sudan.[38] The AAEJ also, despite its claims of maintaining silence, continued to run advertisements soliciting funds for rescue during the operation. The AAEJ was also accused of giving out misleading information. For example, Rapoport quotes an American Jewish leader as criticizing Lenhoff for writing that Israel had hardly rescued anyone until the AAEJ "showed the way" by rescuing 120 people in May 1983 when, Israel rescued 2,000 Ethiopian Jews during the six months from November 1982 until May 1983 (the AAEJ's own figures show that more than 300 were rescued from January to May).[39] Haim Halachmy also criticized the AAEJ for what he said was their tendency to say things that were not 100 percent correct and often having bad timing.[40]

Some of the publicity the AAEJ generated indirectly did have a positive impact. For example, a public relations representative of the AAEJ succeeded in getting articles in the *New York Times, Washington Post* and *Wall Street Journal*. Editorials in major newspapers were a new development, Shapiro noted. "There was a real concern then because it meant that the prestige of the press was coming to bear on the morality of letting an ancient Jewish community die."[41] This was true, but the media ultimately began to pay attention to Ethiopia and the Sudan for reasons having nothing to do with the Beta Israel.

FAMINE

As the Israelis and Americans took Ethiopian Jews out of the Sudan, word began to filter back to Ethiopia that escape to Israel was possible if one could get to the refugee camps. Ethiopian Jews who reached Israel wrote to their relatives in Ethiopia and told them how they had been rescued and encouraged them to leave. The Israelis were sending people into Ethiopia directly and via the Sudan to encourage the Jews to come to the Sudan. Glenn Stein, Associate Director of the UAHC Religious Action Center, said that when he was in Ethiopia in February 1984, on a mission for the Union of American Hebrew Congregations (UAHC), his group encouraged people to leave and gave them money to help them make the trip.[42] In addition, young men began to move to escape conscription, which had been instigated to build up the Ethiopian army for its fight with the Eritrean rebels and, specifically, by Major Melaku Teferra, governor of the Gondar region, to prevent young Jews from leaving Gondar. The primary reason that most Ethiopians left the country for the Sudan, though it was a much less common reason for the Beta Israel to leave, was the increasingly deteriorating economic conditions and the famine.

The last drops of rain fell in Ethiopia in August 1982, and Ethiopian officials reported that five million people were suffering from the drought and three million had been displaced by war, drought, and famine. Although the Ethiopian Jews were not reported to be starving, they were living in the regions most affected by the drought. By the autumn of 1984, the Joint Distribution Committee (JDC) said that half a million people in Gondar faced starvation. In some cases, peasants who fled from the drought-stricken areas of northern Ethiopia drove the Beta Israel from their land or took over land left behind by Jews who had gone to the Sudan.

The situation became increasingly grave for the Jews who remained in Ethiopia as their houses and synagogues were burned down and their cattle and land stolen. The government did nothing to protect them, so it became clear that it would be best for them to leave. "The famine, the wars, and the years of oppression played a part [in why they left]. But perhaps the most important factor was the sense that their community had come to the end of the road and that their existence and ultimate 'redemption,' political and religious, could only be assured by going as a community to the promised land."[43] Not only did more and more Ethiopian Jews want to leave, but it became easier for them to succeed in 1983 when Major Melaku was ousted as governor of Gondar and his successor removed restrictions on travel.[44]

DEADLY CAMPS

Unfortunately, the Mossad operation could not accommodate the ensuing flood of refugees. After rescuing more than 2,000 in 1983, bringing the total in Israel to approximately 5,600, it became impossible to evacuate them as fast as they were coming into the country. Ben-Porat had told the NJCRAC plenary session in February that the camps were virtually empty, but two months later, 3,000 more arrived.[45] According to figures obtained by Parfitt, the Falashas came to the camp at Umm Rakuba at the following rate in 1984: 1,113 in March; 2,523 in April; 2,125 in May; 1,627 in June; 2,500 in July; and 2,012 in August.[46]

Because of the increased numbers, some of the Ethiopian Jews were forced to live in the camps for months and, in some cases, years before their turn to leave came. In the interim, the squalid conditions in the camps led to an alarming rate of disease and deaths. During the period 1980–1984, anywhere from two to five thousand Ethiopian Jews died in the camps. The worst period, according to Rapoport, began in June 1984, after the Mossad ceased its airlift from the secret desert airstrip.[47] Hundreds of Ethiopian Jews became sick, and many died from contaminated drinking water despite the medical teams that the Mossad regularly sent into the camps. An informed source told Rapoport:

> The Israelis conducted a first-class operation, built up a tremendous infrastructure and used only the very best people. But what could a surgeon do when the water remained contaminated and there was not enough food? Or when the patient stopped drinking entirely? The people who died couldn't have been saved. The only way to save them was to get them out of the camps. The Israelis spent masses of money and there was total commitment. The goal of the mission was to bring people out. Nothing was done that could have jeopardized that aim. The Mossad was not in a position to dismantle the camp and disperse the refugees.[48]

One of the nurses at Umm Rekuba reported the deteriorating conditions in the camps to the UN office and the refugee affairs coordinator at the U.S. embassy in Khartoum. The UNHCR sent an investigator who apparently never visited the camps, relying instead on secondary sources, and told his superiors that conditions were not serious. He said there were no shortages of food or medicine and the death rate was "normal." The UNHCR repeated this throughout the year even though there was a preponderance of evidence to the contrary.

The American official, Jerry Weaver, refugee affairs coordinator at the U.S. embassy in Khartoum, carried out his own investigation of conditions and found them appalling. He visited a clinic that did not have any medicine and discovered that people were not eating. The Ethiopian Jews, sometimes as many as fifteen to a hut, stayed inside and would not even go outside to go to the bathroom; consequently, the sanitary conditions were extremely unhealthy.[49] Weaver informed Washington of the situation and officials there began to take a more active interest in the Israeli rescue efforts. According to State Department refugee official Richard Krieger, there were contra-dictions between what Weaver was saying about the numbers of refugees dying in the Sudan and what other people, notably the AAEJ, were reporting. Krieger found out later that Weaver, who has been portrayed as the hero of the subsequent airlifts, deliberately underestimated the number of Ethiopian Jews dying in the camps because, Weaver told Krieger, "he didn't think that it would do any good."[50]

The AAEJ had known about the conditions in the camps for a long time and had been demanding that Israel take quick action. To dramatize the situ-ation, the AAEJ took out ads in Jewish newspapers with lists of Ethiopian Jews who had died. On one hand, the ads had the intended effect of illus-trating that people were dying in large numbers; on the other hand, the Israelis saw them as generating unwanted publicity. In addition, the fact that some of the names on the AAEJ lists were not dead or had died in some way unrelated to the camps in the Sudan further undermined the organization's credibility. The AAEJ responded that it did not matter if a handful of the names were wrong because most were accurate and demon-strated the seriousness of the situation. This was true, but, in America, where the Jewish establishment insisted upon accuracy, even a few mistakes were seen as undermining the whole community's credibility. In addition, the AAEJ had "cried wolf" about the plight of the Beta Israel for so long that its claims were automatically discounted.

A NEW SENSE OF URGENCY

One of the other arguments that the Israelis frequently used with regard to the AAEJ's efforts was that they were unnecessary. Israel was aware of the situation and was doing everything possible to rescue the Ethiopian Jews. They did not have to be told that people were dying in the camps, they knew, and it was this knowledge that persuaded them that a larger-scale rescue would be necessary.

The Mossad planned to accelerate its airlift from the desert airfield and fly four planeloads of Ethiopian Jews out twice a week, but they had to aban-don this plan after it became clear that the airlift had become too risky and jeopardized the entire operation. The reason the danger had increased was that Bedouins had spotted planes taking off and had reported it to the au-thorities. Although the Sudanese officials took no action, the capital was rife with rumors regarding efforts to help the Ethiopian Jews. When a plane landed on May 4, 1984, the Ethiopian Jews driven to the landing site by Mossad drivers panicked and ran off. After several hours, the Mossad agents managed to round up most of the refugees, but some were later arrested, and there was concern that they might give away the operation. Conse-quently, the Israelis decided to suspend the airlift indefinitely. They sent in two more planes and took out all the children they could find and then the operation stopped.[51] Soon after, however, the Israelis began to build a new airstrip, but it would take time to complete.[52]

By the beginning of 1984, all of the Ethiopian Jews from Tigre and Wolkait had reached Israel. It had been much easier for them to get out of Ethiopia because they did not have General Melaku as an impediment. There were still large numbers of Jews stuck, however, in Gondar, the main population center of the Ethiopian Jews. The Mossad operation succeeded in almost completely cleaning out the camps, but the wave of refugees that began to flood the camps in the middle of the year made it clear that the Israelis would need help if they were to complete the rescue. The stage was now set for the dramatic rescues of Operations Moses and Sheba.

NOTES

1. Tudor Parfitt, *Operation Moses: The Untold Story of the Secret Exodus of the Falasha Jews from Ethiopia* (NY: Stein & Day, 1986), p. 54.

2. Nate Shapiro, interview with author.

3. Graenum Berger, meeting with Naphtalie Lavie, head of New York Israeli consulate, January 28, 1982.

4. Louis Rapoport, *Redemption Song: The Story of Operation Moses* (CA: Harcourt Brace Javanovich, 1986), pp. 83–84; confidential interview.

5. General Ephraim Poran, interview with author; Rachamim Elazar, interview with author; Rapoport, *Redemption Song*, pp. 84–85.

6. Poran, interview.

7. Shlomo Hillel, interview with author.

8. Graenum Berger, letter to Edith and Henry Everett, March 19, 1982.

9. Shapiro, interview.

10. Temesgen Report 1982; "Reasons for the Temporary Suspension," 1982–83.

11. Ferede, interview with author.

12. Ibid.

13. Shapiro, interview.

14. Ibid.

15. Confidential interview.

16. Galambos report, Summary of activities in Africa for AAEJ, April 9, 1985.

17. Parfitt, *Operation Moses*, pp. 45–46, 57.

18. Confidential interview.

19. Shapiro, interview.

20. Rapoport, *Redemption Song*, pp. 89, 92.

21. Shapiro, interview.

22. Ibid.

23. Marilyn Diamond and Lisa Freund, report to AAEJ Executive Board, March 6, 1984.

24. Poran, interview.

25. Confidential interview.

26. Yehuda Dominitz, interview with author.

27. Nate Shapiro, "Setting the Record Straight," *Sentinel*, December 26, 1985: p. 13.

28. Shapiro, interview.

29. Haim Halachmy, interview with author.

30. Rapoport, *Redemption Song*, pp. 89–90; Parfitt, *Operation Moses*, p. 60.

31. Adon Taft, "$10 Million Drive on Boards to Save Ethiopia's Black Jews," *Miami Herald*, November 6, 1981.

32. Yehuda Dominitz, letter to Howard Lenhoff, November 13, 1981.

33. Henry Parnes, letter to Yehuda Dominitz, December 8, 1981.

34. Richard Hall, "Black Jews' Escape," *The Observer*, June 19, 1983; Parfitt, *Operation Moses*, p. 60; Rapoport, *Redemption Song*, pp. 89–90.

35. Confidential interview.

36. "Statement by Ethiopian Jewish Leaders on Rescue Operations and Publicity," distributed at NSLRAC plenum, January 26, 1983 (February 1983).

37. Taft, "$10 Million Drive."

38. Rapoport, *Redemption Song*, p. 90.

39. Ibid.

40. Halachmy, interview.

41. Shapiro, interview.

42. Glenn Stein, interview with author.

43. Parfitt, *Operation Moses*, pp. 67–70; Allen Cowell, "Old Troubles Grip the New Ethiopia," *New York Times*, June 26, 1983; Erica Oyserman, "Too Little, Too Late?" *Newsview*, May 24, 1983, p. 14.

44. Rapoport, *Redemption Song*, p. 94.

45. Abe Bayer, memo to NJCRAC and Council of Jewish Federation executives, April 2, 1984.

46. Parfitt, *Operation Moses*, pp. 78–87.

47. Rapoport, *Redemption Song*, p. 107.

48. Ibid., p. 110.

49. Ibid., pp. 111–113.

50. Richard Krieger, interview with author.

51. Rapoport, *Redemption Song*, pp. 86–87; Shapiro, interview.

52. Confidential interview.

CHAPTER 8

Operation Moses

I n the summer of 1984, Israeli agents radioed Jerusalem from the Sudan to inform the government that the number of Ethiopian Jews dying in the refugee camps was increasing. The Mossad and top government officials did not know how to rescue the Ethiopian Jews who remained in the camps. In the past three and a half years, Israel had already brought more than five thousand Ethiopian Jews to Israel, but as many as ten thousand were still believed to be stuck in the squalid camps where contaminated water and lack of food was threatening the entire refugee population with disease and starvation. Between 1983 and 1984, an estimated three to five thousand Beta Israel died during the escape from Ethiopia or because of the privations of the Sudanese camps. Jews were dying every day.

A group of Mossad agents had recommended to the operations chief that Israel initiate an airlift and evacuate everyone in one week, but the Mossad chief was unwilling to risk such an operation until the United States had been given an opportunity to approach Sudanese president Gaafar el-Numeiry.[1] Numeiry had been looking the other way while Israel carried out its rescue efforts for the past four years, but he had become increasingly reticent as his own internal problems mounted and the probability of public disclosure of his cooperation became greater. Since the Sudan was technically at war with Israel and had no diplomatic relations, Israeli leaders knew they had no leverage with the president.

ENCOURAGING NUMEIRY

The United States enjoyed very good relations with the Sudanese and had been providing Numeiry with economic and military aid for a number of years. By approaching the United States for help, the Israelis hoped to avoid undermining the intelligence operations they had carefully cultivated in the Sudan. In fact, Israel had carried out its prior operations with the full support of the U.S. government. At one point, for example, Israel had wanted to trade agricultural tools for Ethiopian Jews still in Ethiopia, and the United States had pledged its support. The Ethiopian government, however, rejected the deal.[2]

There is some controversy as to who initiated the contacts in 1984 regarding an operation to clean out the refugee camps in the Sudan. American officials claim they raised the idea with the Israelis, but the Israelis say that they approached the Americans first. General Ephraim Poran, the man in charge of the rescue operation said that "it was our problem. All ideas came from us." A U.S. State Department source disputes this:

> The Israelis were secondary. . . . This was a U.S. operation. The Israelis got into it pretty late in the day . . . well after the project was conceived and well after it had begun to be discussed. I don't think that it moved into any implementation phase until the Israelis came and asked for our help, but the asking was, how shall I put it, in effect *post facto*. They came and asked us to do something that we were already planning.[3]

When asked if the Americans could have carried out the operation without the Israelis, the official replied: "No, we couldn't have. But when the Israelis became aware just how far this thing had gone and how much momentum there was behind it they thought, 'My God. . . .' " He speculated that the Israelis were swept into action because of all the activity that was taking place and all of the pressure being generated on Capitol Hill.

According to Louis Rapoport, the contacts were initiated at a higher level and were first made in the spring after Prime Minister Yitzhak Shamir told Ambassador Meir Rosenne to ask the Americans to approach Numeiry.[4] In addition, one Ethiopian Jew in Israel said the Mossad was already planning an operation and had begun to build a new secret airstrip in the desert. An entirely different version was offered by Israel's former ambassador to Ethiopia, Chanan Aynor, who said that it was Numeiry who was the "father of Operation Moses." Numeiry wanted to solve the refugee problem once and for all and desperately needed U.S. aid so that he could divert the funds to the army. Numeiry raised the issue with the United States knowing the Americans would pass the word to the Israelis.[5]

The United States had nothing to gain from helping the Israelis rescue thousands of African refugees and a great deal to lose. Numeiry was a best friend to the United States in the strategically important Horn of Africa.

Numeiry was also courted because he was considered a "moderate" Arab leader who could exercise a restraining influence within the Arab League. He had, in fact, been the only Arab leader besides Morocco's King Hassan to give support to Anwar Sadat's peace initiative toward Israel, although later, under pressure from the other Arab states, he joined in condemning the Israel-Egypt peace treaty. Nevertheless, Numeiry remained a friend of Egypt. In addition, Numeiry represented a pro-Western counter to the pro-Soviet Ethiopians.

TIME BECOMES CRUCIAL

By the middle of 1984, American diplomats feared Numeiry's days were numbered as opposition to his regime stimulated increasing unrest. The Sudan was threatened externally by Libya and, more immediately, internally by antigovernment rebels in the south of the Sudan. In January 1984, *Africa Confidential* reported that the army was becoming frustrated with the southern campaign, that many officers were prepared to stage a coup, and that the security forces could not be counted on to be loyal to Numeiry.[6] It was in this context that Israel approached the United States and asked the Americans to put their interests in the Horn of Africa at risk for what could not be considered anything but a humanitarian gesture. In one of the rare instances where humanitarian concerns have been placed ahead of other U.S. interests, the Americans agreed to help.

In early June, Numeiry sent an official to Washington to solicit additional economic and military aid to deal with the shortage of food, the swelling refugee population, and the rebellion in southern Sudan. The envoy met with State Department refugee official Richard Krieger and his boss Ambassador Eugene Douglas. After consulting Douglas, Krieger decided to see if he could play on the Sudanese official's anti-Semitism and willingness to believe in the all-powerful American Jewish community. He told the official that to get the approval of Congress for additional aid to the Sudan it was necessary to obtain the support of the Jewish lobby. The Sudan could help by allowing the United States to take the Ethiopian Jews out of the refugee camps. There was no reason for the Sudan not to help, Krieger suggested, since the hundreds of thousands of refugees were already a burden on the Sudan. Wouldn't it help to lessen that burden by a few thousand at least? In addition, he asked if the Sudan wanted a lot of Jews in the country where they might pose a threat. The official found this line of argument appealing, and although no specific agreement was reached, it was made clear that future aid to the Sudan would be forthcoming if Numeiry cooperated with the Americans in their plans to rescue the Ethiopian Jews.

On July 5, Krieger flew to Israel to inform the Israelis that an understanding had been reached with the Sudanese and to plan an operation. The Israelis wanted to meet directly with the Sudanese official, but Krieger informed them that the Sudanese refused. Consequently, Krieger made the arrangements with the Israelis and then flew to Geneva to finalize the plan with the Sudanese official. Krieger's involvement in these early contacts is the reason American sources believe the United States was responsible for initiating the operation to rescue the Ethiopian Jews remaining in the Sudan.

The chronology of events is a little different according to *Los Angeles Times* correspondent Charles Powers, who was in the Sudan. In his version, the U.S. refugee coordinator in Khartoum, Jerry Weaver, approached a mid-level official in the Sudanese government whom he knew to be "a Muslim and a humanist" and asked him what was preventing the Ethiopian Jews from leaving and was told they lacked travel documents from state security. Weaver asked the official to talk to the Sudanese vice-president and chief of the secret police, Omar Tayeb, to try to set up a meeting. Within twenty-four hours, a meeting was set up between the U.S. ambassador, Hume Horan, Weaver, and Tayeb. Weaver told Tayeb the Ethiopian Jews were dying in large numbers and this was becoming an international problem. Moreover, various clandestine efforts to get the Ethiopian Jews out of the Sudan were taking place and there would no doubt be more as that refugee population grew. The Americans suggested that it would be in the Sudan's interest to allow the United States to airlift the Ethiopian Jews out of the country. Tayeb agreed, with the proviso that the operation be carried out secretly by the CIA. That day, September 21, a cable was sent to the State Department saying a breakthrough on the Ethiopian Jewry issue may have been reached.[7]

Writer Robert Kaplan offers a slightly different story about Weaver's involvement. According to Kaplan, Weaver saw the whole issue as a "political hot potato" and had hoped the Jews would all be taken to Israel by the Israelis so there would be no more "loudmouthed American-Jewish and Canadian-Jewish amateurs, who kept turning up in town to try their hand at Falasha rescue work, getting caught by the Sudanese security forces in the process." Weaver's heart apparently softened during the height of the famine when a Swedish relief worker burst into his office crying, "They're dying; it's terrible; you've got to do something about Um Raquba." According to Kaplan, Operation Moses "might be said to have been born that moment."[8]

The CIA vetoed the idea of its involvement, but the State Department agreed to take on the assignment and struck a compromise whereby the CIA agreed to deputize Weaver. The CIA was still unhappy because the agreement meant "the CIA would have no control, but all the blame" if things went wrong.[9] The CIA station chief in Khartoum told Tayeb that Weaver would be the American in charge of any operation. In October 1984, Weaver, the Mossad, and the Sudanese secret police devised the plan that would take all ten thousand Ethiopian Jews out of the refugee camps. Weaver wanted to drive the Jews from Umm Rakuba fifty miles north to Tuwawa, a place near Gedaref, which would be designated Falashaville. From there, they would be transferred to the airport. Weaver flew to Geneva and presented the plan to representatives of the Jewish Agency, the Israeli government, and the United States, all of whom gave it their approval. The Israelis gave Weaver a suitcase with $250,000 in hundred-dollar bills to buy everything needed for the operation in the Sudan.[10]

ON WINGS OF EAGLES

The easiest way to take ten thousand refugees to Israel would have been by ship from Port Sudan, but that route had been used earlier and had to be abandoned after one group of Ethiopian Jews was caught and a shootout between the Mossad and the Sudanese police had occurred. In addition, Numeiry feared that a massive sealift would be too visible and cause him embarrassment. The Sudanese also rejected the idea of a large airlift from the desert by Israeli military or civilian planes because an earlier Mossad operation using this method had been spotted by Bedouins and had stimulated rumors in the capital. The plan they finally settled upon involved one of the routes the Mossad had used in the past, which the Sudanese had known about but found to be sufficiently low key to be acceptable. The Ethiopian Jews were to be driven to a meeting place outside Tuwawa and then taken on a five-hour trip to the airport in Khartoum. There they would be flown in small groups by chartered jets to Europe, since the Sudanese would not agree to let them fly directly to Israel, with whom they were officially at war. Once in Europe, the Jews would be allowed to fly to Tel Aviv.

The charter company chosen for the mission was Trans European Airlines (TEA), a Belgian company owned by Georges Gutelman, a fifty-one-year-old Orthodox Jew and a close friend of Israel, who reportedly was often used by the Mossad and who also had good relations with the Sudan. Since TEA had routinely flown Muslim pilgrims from the Sudan to Saudi Arabia, the sight of TEA planes flying in and out of Khartoum was not expected to arouse suspicion. Why did Gutelman agree to put his company's lucrative business in the Muslim world at risk? Reportedly he quoted Maimonides, a Jewish philospher: "There is no greater obligation than the redemption of captives."[11] In addition, Israel agreed to compensate him if disclosure of his company's involvement led to a loss of business in the Arab world. Gutelman's participation also had to be approved by the Belgian government, which was reluctant to risk its relations with the Arab and Muslim world. Gutelman succeeded in reassuring the government that the operation could be kept secret and, with the help of his friend Jean Gol, the Belgian minister of justice and a Jew, he secured Prime Minister Wilfried Martens's approval.[12] In Israel, word was spread that everything was set and that Ethiopian Jews were needed to act as translators in absorption centers. Volunteers were taken to seminars without knowing why they were going. One Ethiopian Jew, who could identify the Ethiopian Jewish population, was sent to the Sudan in October, about three weeks before the operation, to serve as the contact between the Mossad and the Ethiopian Jews in the camps.[13]

In preparation for the operation, the Sudanese removed refugee camp officials who were not considered trustworthy and replaced them with people who would cooperate with the plan. The biggest difficulty was rounding up all the Ethiopian Jews. Although most were located in Umm Rakuba, Tuwawa, and Wad el Heluw camps, large numbers were also scattered about the region in other camps. Beta Israel were sent from Israel to the camps to pass the word that the time of their deliverance was at hand and to bring them to Tuwawa. It was difficult to find them because most were masquerading as Christians to avoid being harassed by the other refugees. After two postponements, the first group of refugees was picked up after dark on November 21, 1984, and driven by bus nearly 250 miles along the Gedaref-Khartoum highway to the capital. Weaver elaborated on the initial chaos:

> By about 6:30 we have packed no-one-knows how many people aboard the buses, and we try to leave. People are running after us, total pandemonium. In the confusion, we take the wrong road. We are driving on a dirt track parallel to the Gedaref-Khartoum highway, but we can't seem to get to it. So we stop the caravan, turn the whole damn thing around and go back toward the camp and get on the highway.[14]

They eventually found the correct highway and, after a brief run-in with the police along the way, were met at a checkpoint not far from the airport by Sudanese security officers who informed them the plane was late. The plan had been to drive directly to the stairs of the TEA Boeing 707s, but now Weaver and more than two hundred Jews huddled in a dark corner of the airport. "They were like sheep, absolutely quiet. The kids weren't even crying. . . . These people were starving and sick. And we were bringing out the frailest and oldest and youngest ones first."[15]

At 4 A.M. on November 22, the first 707 landed, and the Jews were loaded on the plane. On board, the Beta Israel were accompanied by Ethiopian Jews from Israel as well as medical teams to care for those in need of treatment. The pilot did not want to take off because at least 250 people had embarked and there were only enough oxygen masks for 220. He said, "It's against the law. Sorry, we can't do it." The Israelis had sent a Frenchman named René to make sure the planes took off without any hitches, and he went up to the pilot and told him that if he did not take off, he would find someone else to fly the plane.[16] It took off shortly thereafter.

The planes received permission to overfly Egypt and travel on to Brussels, where they made a two-hour stopover for refueling and service at a distant part of the airport far from the terminals before continuing on to Tel Aviv. When the planes arrived in Tel Aviv, ambulances took away those who needed immediate medical attention, about one out of every five refugees, and the rest were taken to transit centers and given new clothes.[17]

Every night, except on the Sabbath, buses would pick up groups of about fifty-five Ethiopian Jews and bring them back to Khartoum. Initially, flights carrying approximately 220 passengers left every forty-eight hours. After about three weeks (December 23), the flights left every twenty-four hours. Two shifts of bus drivers and airline crews spent one night in Khartoum between each flight. Altogether, thirty-six flights took 7,800 Ethiopian Jews from the Sudan to Israel over the course of forty-seven days.

The operation was code named *Gur Aryeh Yehuda*, "The Lion of Judah's Cub," but that name was only used by those most intimately involved. To the rest of the world it was "Operation Moses," coined by the United Jewish Appeal to capture the image of the Israelites returning to their homeland when it launched a special fundraising campaign in the United States. According to General Poran, Israel had not originally intended to have such a big operation. "Operation Moses started as some planes going to Europe from time to time," he said, "and then we decided to push."[18] Meanwhile, the Mossad continued to rescue small numbers of Ethiopian Jews, forty-three one time and thirty-six another, by its original route from Khartoum to Israel via Athens.[19]

Operation Moses went off remarkably smoothly, but it was not entirely without complications. The first group was the most difficult because no one wanted to be left behind. All the Jewish refugees rushed the waiting buses, overwhelming the Ethiopian Jew from Israel who had picked the people out of the camps. Weaver, who was there supervising the operation, had to use a cane to hit people and push them back. Afterward he developed a system whereby the Jews were given cloth ribbons of different colors to identify those scheduled for each flight. In the end, Weaver said, only one death occurred during the operation—an old man who died en route. There were also three births, so, he concluded, "I guess we came out ahead."[20]

SILENCING THE CRITICS

In September, a State Department official with close ties to the American Association for Ethiopian Jews (AAEJ) met with the AAEJ's board in New York and informed the group that an operation was being planned. "I said 'trust me.' My credentials are good where this is concerned. Things are happening." He could not elaborate, partly because he did not know the details himself, but urged the AAEJ to remain silent until the rescue could be carried out. "Howard Lenhoff and Graenum Berger were kind of chomping at the bit to launch an all-out publicity blitz, and I said, '*Chevra* [friend], this is not the time.' I said I know things are horrible and that we want to do something, but I said things were happening that would be very seriously undermined by any effort like that."[21]

Because they had heard this all too often before and believed that in the past they had always been lied to, the AAEJ's leaders were skeptical.

According to the State Department official, they did not understand that there were a lot of variables, such as bribing officials, getting permits, and coordinating the airline flights. "Every time it slipped, people said, 'You told us it was happening next week.' I found myself constantly saying, 'I know it slipped, I know we told you it is going to happen now, but you gotta have faith, it's happening.'" Since this official had long supported the AAEJ and was known to have good connections in the government, he was considered a credible source. The board decided over the "violent objection" of Graenum Berger to remain quiet in the hope that this time Israel was carrying out the rescue that the AAEJ had always believed possible if Israel really wanted to save the Ethiopian Jews. However, after many years of experience in dealing with the Israelis, Berger could not believe an operation was really being contemplated and, according to Rapoport, he went ahead and continued to publicize the Ethiopian Jews' plight.[22]

The AAEJ was frequently criticized by Israeli and American Jewish leaders for its past indiscretions in publicizing information considered harmful to clandestine rescue efforts, but, in this case, with the possible exception of Berger, the organization maintained its silence. In fact, the organization's president, Nate Shapiro, said he had strong indications of what was taking place from another sympathetic State Department official. When Shapiro received calls from the press, he refused to talk to anyone, referring them instead to the official. "I tried to kill the stories," Shapiro says. "Everyone assumes that an activist is involved to make themselves feel good and to get their name in the paper, but we wouldn't talk or be quoted."[23] This was not the case, however, among other Beta Israel activists, notably Simcha Jacobovici, who earlier that year had produced a film that was critical of what he believed was the Israeli government's lack of effort to save the Ethiopian Jews.

Jacobovici wrote an article for the *New York Times* titled "Ethiopian Jews Die, Israel Fiddles" and, just six days before the beginning of Operation Moses, led a group of forty activists in a demonstration at the opening plenary session of the General Assembly of the Council of Jewish Federations in Toronto, Canada. Jacobovici demanded that he be allowed to speak and, holding an Ethiopian child in his arms, called for a minute of silence for the two thousand Jews who he said had died in the refugee camps during the summer but could have been rescued if Israel had wanted to save them. State Department officials had urged Jacobovici to keep quiet because an operation was being planned, but he refused.[24] The consequence of Jacobovici's actions was that the General Assembly was disrupted and the plight of the Ethiopian Jews given a great deal of publicity at the very time that silence was called for. Although the Israelis feared the publicity caused by the demonstration might threaten their operation, it was the indiscretion of Israeli officials and the American Jewish establishment that ultimately brought Operation Moses to a halt.

At the same General Assembly meeting, the chairman of the Jewish Agency, Aryeh Dulzin, told in one of the sessions that "one of the ancient tribes of Israel is due to return to its homeland" and, he added later, "when the true story of the Jews of Ethiopia is told, we will take pride in what we have already achieved in this most difficult and complex rescue operation." This seemingly innocuous statement threatened to blow the lid off the clandestine airlift, but rather than stop the press release of his speech, as he could have, Dulzin chose to let it be issued to help the planned fundraising effort to pay for the absorption of the Ethiopian Jews expected to arrive in Israel and, perhaps, to silence his critics.[25]

USING ETHIOPIAN JEWS TO RAISE MONEY

The fundraising campaign was planned the day the airlift started when a high ranking Israeli official met secretly at the Israeli consulate in New York with the leadership of the United Jewish Appeal (UJA) and told them that Israel needed to raise $60 million. The fundraisers were told "a miracle" was about to take place and that they would take the Ethiopian Jews in regardless of whether they got the money from the States. The next day, the UJA devised a campaign to raise the money and invited the leaders of communities that regularly raised more than $3 million to a special meeting in New York on December 2 to set targets for each city. That campaign exploited images of the Holocaust, telling Jews that contributing to the rescue of Ethiopian Jews was as if they had an opportunity to save Jews from Auschwitz. Advertisements were placed in all of the Jewish newspapers in the United States and Canada saying that $6,000 could save a Jewish life.[26] A typical example appeared in the Los Angeles Jewish Federation newspaper on December 27 with the title "You Can Save A Life":

10,000 Ethiopian Jews can be rescued from starvation and persecution. This is an unparalleled movement in history. It is as if we could have saved 10,000 Jews from Auschwitz. We have the historic opportunity to resettle Jews in Israel. Operation Moses has started and will continue until 10,000 Ethiopian Jews are safely in Israel.

Despite its financial crisis, the State of Israel will shoulder the responsibility and many of the costs. Israel cannot rescue those Jews alone. The American Jewish community has responded by committing $60,000,000 to be paid by March 31, 1985. The Los Angeles community has committed to pay $5,000,000 by March 31, 1985.

For each $6,000 one Jewish life will be saved. We have a moral imperative to discharge this obligation. We cannot stand by and watch Jews die especially when we have the means to save them. If the words NEVER AGAIN are to have any meaning, we must respond.

Ironically, the AAEJ had long been criticized for exploiting images of the Holocaust and for claiming in its fundraising appeals that $3,000 was needed to save each life. In addition, the advertisement explicitly stated that the operation was in progress, despite all the warnings that had been given to various individuals and organizations about the possible adverse implications of publicity. The decision to go ahead with the campaign while the airlift was proceeding, and thereby threaten to expose it, became a matter of controversy as some Jewish leaders second-guessed the wisdom of the action.

Apparently, the main reason the UJA went ahead with the campaign was the fear that the appeal for money would be less successful if they waited until after the Ethiopian Jews had reached Israel. UJA Vice President Elton Kerness told Rapoport that the Israelis never suggested that their fundraising efforts might jeopardize Operation Moses. "If we waited until afterward, until everyone had reached Israel, it would have been much harder to raise the funds. We felt it was better to do it now. Many of us thought there might be a backlash because the Beta Israel are black—but the color question never arose. We needed the drama factor, the message that we are saving lives."[27] There was also the pragmatic reason that people were more likely to contribute before the end of the year to take advantage of tax deductions.

The campaign was very successful. American Jews have always been exceedingly generous, even more so when other Jews are in distress, but the fundraising cause was helped by something that actually had very little to do with the plight of Ethiopian Jews. One of the activists explained:

> The fundraising campaign was probably so successful because of the famine, not because of anything else. We just sort of rode along with the tide of the famine. To this day, people think the Jews got out because of the famine. The famine had nothing to do with anything. It just happened at the same time and it worked to our benefit. If the TV and the press had not covered the famine for four months straight right before the operation, and if there had not been a movement in the communities by people like the AAEJ and myself who were interested in the issue and felt we had to educate people, I don't know how successful it would have been.[28]

The famine generated publicity about the plight of Africans in the Sudan; when Jews were shown to be among those suffering, it was not surprising that American Jewry responded. The concern with Ethiopian Jews probably would not have been as great, however, if it were not for the educational efforts of the activists. As Barbara Gaffin says, they helped lay the groundwork for the UJA.

The UJA campaign was dramatic and effective; however, the money they were raising was not explicitly to save lives, but to pay the costs of resettling the Ethiopian Jews in Israel. The U.S. government was already giving Israel $25 million to resettle refugees (the amount was increased to $50 million after the airlift), which included Ethiopian Jews, but that was not expected to be anywhere near the amount required to absorb thousands of people from an undeveloped country.

UJA leaders subsequently claimed their campaign was carried out quietly, but full page advertisements in Jewish newspapers could hardly be called discrete. The UJA's director of the Rabbinic Cabinet, Richard Davis, said the UJA could not rely on the written word, so they had to communicate through synagogues, but that simply was not the case as can be seen from the previously quoted advertisement. It was true that rabbis, primarily non-Orthodox rabbis, played an important fundraising and information role, but there was at least one example of a rabbi being indiscrete. In that case a Los Angeles rabbi disclosed to his congregation that Israel was airlifting three hundred Ethiopian Jews a day from the Sudan at the time that nation was never supposed to be mentioned.[29]

Although the AAEJ claims that it kept silent during the operation, it too was guilty of indiscretion when it published an advertisement in *Israel Today* on December 14, which said that "2,000 Ethiopian Jews died of starvation and disease in Africa awaiting rescue by world Jewry. Are we going to permit the same gruesome fate for the remaining 14,000?" Rather than reveal that an operation was underway, as the UJA did, the AAEJ ad suggested just the opposite; that is, that efforts still were not being made to rescue the Ethiopian Jews.

THE NEWS GETS OUT

Since the publicity given to the fundraising campaign was kept within the Jewish press, the risk that the operation would be disclosed was relatively low. When Jewish newspapers began to publish details of the airlift, however, the threat to the operation increased. The first report was stimulated by Dulzin's remarks at the General Assembly, which were quoted in the November 23 edition of the *Long Island Jewish Week*, just two days before the operation began. The same article revealed that "a dramatic, mass rescue of thousands of Ethiopian Jews and their transfer to Israel is scheduled to begin soon after January 1." The paper's editor, David Gross, said Jewish newspaper editors had been told after the Toronto Congress not to publish anything about the rescue, but he took the Dulzin press release as "a signal to publish something."[30] Not only was the report irresponsible, but it was also inaccurate, since the airlift had actually begun two days earlier.

Two weeks later, a more serious breach of security occurred when Michael Barenbaum wrote in the December 6 edition of the *Washington Jewish Week* that "the rescue of a substantial number of Ethiopian Jews has begun . . . an operation far more systematic than previous efforts is under way." The editor, Charles Fenyevesi, had been asked by Israeli embassy officials and a State Department official not to publish anything about the rescue, but he ignored the advice because no one "high enough" in the State Department had spoken to him and no one had implied the issue was a matter of life and death.[31]

Why was the American Jewish press unable to keep the operation secret while its counterpart in Israel did? Contrary to the claims of the editors who said that they did not know it was to be kept secret, *Israel Today* revealed in its December 14 issue, after the story had broken, that Israeli sources had warned the paper that premature disclosure of the operation could jeopardize the lives of Ethiopian Jews waiting to be rescued. The editors said they first learned of the operation shortly after Israel made a commitment to the project, but they had decided to respect the government's wishes and withhold publicizing it.

Gary Rosenblatt, editor of the *Baltimore Jewish Times*, blamed Israel for not informing American Jewish editors of the details of the story. "Perhaps if the American Jewish newspapers had been apprised of the details of the rescue beforehand and told of the grave risks involved, the way the Jerusalem government briefed Israeli editors, there would have been a similar agreement to embargo the story."[32] The president of the American Jewish Press Association, Robert Cohn, disagreed. "My clear understanding," he said, "was that the Jewish leadership in the United States had been fully apprised of the urgency of keeping this thing quiet."[33] He explained that he learned of Operation Moses on November 15 during a meeting of the association in Toronto from an off-the-record briefing by Abe Bayer and Barry Weise of the National Jewish Community Relations Advisory Council (NJCRAC). Cohen, who was also editor of the *St. Louis Jewish Light*, believed that all of the Jewish newspaper editors understood the story and should keep it confidential, but that assumption proved erroneous. After the stories appeared, it was decided that some mechanism needed to be established to keep the press association's members informed of the latest developments and the propriety of publishing information related to the airlift.

Although the two reports did not provide any details, and appeared in relatively obscure publications that would not be expected to attract the attention of Sudanese officials or anyone else outside the Jewish community, they were seen as a signal to the secular American press that the story was no longer a secret. A number of American reporters, including Bernard Gwertzmann of the *New York Times* and William Beecher of the *Boston Globe*, already knew about the operation, which one correspondent called "about the worst kept secret around," but had agreed not to publish anything because they understood the risks involved.[34]

The Israeli consul general in New York, Ambassador Naftali Lavi, called the publisher of *Israel Today*, Phil Blazer, and asked him to call Warren Hogue, the foreign editor of the *New York Times*. Lavi hoped Blazer could persuade Hogue to cancel a story on the operation. Hogue agreed. After the Jewish papers published their stories, Lavi asked Blazer to call Hogue one more time. The second time Hogue was unsympathetic: "If Jewish newspapers are going to expose the airlift," he said, "I can't see how the *New York Times* cannot report on this."[35] Consequently, the *Times* ran a front page story on December 11 citing the Barenbaum article and revealing that an airlift was in progress. This was followed the next day by a story in the *Boston Globe*, on December 12, 1984, that disclosed that the United States "acted as an intermediary in getting Sudanese officials and Israeli agents together to set up the complex logistics for the humanitarian mission." Once a story hits page one of the *New York Times*, of course, it is no longer a secret; nevertheless, neither the Sudanese, the Ethiopians, nor any of the Arab states reacted, and it appeared the airlift would continue unabated. This, however, was not to be.

ISRAEL'S DISCLOSURE

The head of the immigration department of the Jewish Agency, Yehuda Dominitz, gave an interview to an obscure West Bank periodical called *Nekuda* in which he was asked how many Ethiopian Jews had immigrated to Israel in the preceding year. Dominitz said that he was not allowed to comment, but then later admitted off the record that "more than half are now in Israel." The publication of this interview was taken as an end to the embargo in Israel where no stories had appeared after the editors of all eight of Israel's daily newspapers agreed not to publish anything about the rescue. Two major Israeli papers, *Ma'ariv* and *Yediot Aharanot* ran front page stories quoting Dominitz on January 3, and these were subsequently picked up by the Associated Press (AP) and Reuters, which added additional details about the airlift and then sent the story to their subscribers around the world. The Israeli censor, who had not seen the *Nekuda* story and failed to stop the subsequent ones in the two other Israeli papers, tried to stop the AP release, but was unable to.[36]

Even the worldwide coverage of the story might not have caused the interruption of the airlift had it not been for the decision of Prime Minister Shimon Peres to confirm the story during a press conference on January 4. After that announcement, the Sudanese abruptly ordered the Israelis to stop the airlift. The last TEA flight left Khartoum on Saturday night, January 5, but a second group of 180 Jews from the Semien Mountains was stranded. It would have required only two more days to finish the job and bring all of the Ethiopian Jews in the Sudan to Israel according to Haim Halachmy, although TEA officials said the airlift was scheduled to continue until around January 20.[37] Instead, hundreds were left behind to an uncertain fate.

There has been a great deal of speculation as to why Peres decided to issue his statement. Long-time critics of Israeli policy on the Beta Israel issue accused Peres of sabotaging the rescue because Israel already had enough blacks and did not want any more. After rescuing thousands and leaving only a few hundred behind, this charge seems unwarranted.

Glenn Stein, with the Union of American Hebrew Congregations (UAHC), was more sympathetic:

> I believe that the Israelis felt it was silly for them to be standing in front of the airport, literally standing at the airport on videotape and saying, "No, Ethiopian Jews are not arriving," when in the background you could see Ethiopian Jews coming off the planes. And they did that for weeks and finally they said, all right, just as in the exodus, world public opinion will not allow this rescue to stop, we'll acknowledge it. They acknowledged it and they were wrong. It was a mistake, a bad mistake. Do I think it was with malicious intent? No, but I think it was a mistake and Jews died because of it.[38]

This explanation, however, also seems unlikely. The Sudanese, after all, had made it clear that secrecy was essential, and it was possible for Numeiry to deny everything in the papers so long as Israel did not confirm the airlift was in progress. Haim Halachmy, director of HIAS, offered another explanation. He said Numeiry had informed Peres beforehand that he was going to stop the airlift, so the prime minister simply chose to announce the operation first. No other sources interviewed for this book would confirm this version. On the contrary, they found this story implausible.

Prime Minister Peres told the Knesset he had approved of the press conference after he had been informed that details had already been published around the world. He said his motive was to "divert attention from delicate aspects and to put the matter in their proper portions."[39] The most likely reason, the one most people interviewed gave for Peres's action, was that he was concerned with domestic politics. On one hand, he wanted to divert attention from a banking scandal that was causing the government embarrassment and, on the other hand, he wanted the opportunity to take credit for the operation before anyone else could.

FALLOUT

"It must be hoped . . . that once the present hue and cry subsides the effort can be resumed and the remaining refugee Jews of Ethiopia reunited with their families here," the *Jerusalem Post* wrote on January 6, 1985. The *Post* reported the following day that the chairperson of the Jewish Agency hoped the worldwide publicity would create pressure on the Sudanese to allow the rescue to continue. The reaction around the world to the revelation of Operation Moses was mixed, with the Arab and Muslim world expressing outrage and the Western nations admiration. Iran, for example, accused the Sudan of collaborating with the United States and Zionism "to exploit the famine in Ethiopia to realize Israel's racist designs," and the Palestine Liberation Organization (PLO) asked the Arab states to intervene to prevent the Sudan from allowing the Jews to leave.

The Sudanese accused the Ethiopians of selling Jews for spare parts and the Ethiopians countered with claims the Sudanese were Zionist sympathizers who had abducted the Beta Israel for money. Ethiopian leader Mengistu Haile Mariam told the Canadian Broadcasting Corporation:

> These people were forced from our territory, from parts of Ethiopia where we do not have tight security. They were almost dragged against their will to go to Israel. The most astounding thing in this context is the fact that this particular case has for the first time prompted the Arabs and the Israelis to join against Ethiopia. This act is illegal and inhuman, and it is an indirect form of slavery. The whole world knows the injustice to which the Jews have been subjected . . . the Jews are now reversing the injustice and committing it against the Ethiopians. The crushing fact is that the Falashas, in order to escape this situation, are now committing suicide simply to get out of the alien situation they have been forced into.[40]

The truth was that a handful of Ethiopian Jews had committed suicide in Israel, but this was related to the difficulty of adapting to their new environment and had nothing to do with being forced to emigrate. All of the Ethiopian Jews who reached Israel had endured great hardship to get there because that is where they wanted to be, where they had dreamed for years of living, not because anyone forced them to go.

Since Israel was still supplying Ethiopia with arms, there was also the suspicion that most of the Mengistu outburst was bluster for internal consumption. After all, Mengistu and his predecessor, Emperor Haile Selassie, had asserted that all Ethiopians were one people and had long discouraged any efforts to recognize minorities as having any special distinction or rights. They were particularly fearful that the perception that one group was receiving preferential treatment of some sort might set a precedent that would create greater turmoil in Ethiopia, especially among the Eritrean secessionists. Nevertheless, just a few days after denouncing the airlift, Ethiopia accepted a $250,000 shipment of food and medicine for famine victims from Israel.[41]

The reaction to Operation Moses in America was jubilant. The American Jewish community hoped the courageous rescue of thousands of blacks who were brought to Israel with little more than the shirts on their backs would once and for all lay to rest the canard that Zionism was racism. Although Operation Moses proved this was the case, it was naive to believe that it would change the minds of those who were convinced otherwise. Thus, for example, rather than receive the unreserved praise of the American black community that Jewish leaders expected and hoped might help mitigate the tensions that had built up between the two communities, most blacks reacted with indifference.

Perhaps American Jews expected too much. They thought that everyone would be impressed by the fact that the small State of Israel would carry out such a daring operation to rescue a few thousand starving African refugees, especially when Israel's actions were contrasted with those of every other nation, which were prepared to leave the remaining four hundred thousand refugees to their fate. Some of Israel's critics turned the humanitarian nature of the operation on its head and accused Israel of singling out people to live while allowing thousands of others to die. To these people, the fact that those chosen to be rescued were Jews only proved Israel's racist character. The negative reactions in the United States were in the minority, however, with most people agreeing with William Safire, who wrote in the *New York Times* that "for the first time in history thousands of black people are being brought into a country not in chains but as citizens."[42]

The operation also had been a victory for the U.S. State Department, which still carried the burden of its failures to rescue European and American Jews during World War II. The U.S. ambassador to the Sudan, Hume Horan, explained his feelings after accompanying Weaver one evening to transfer a group of Jews onto the plane to Israel:

> I felt that at that moment we were really behaving like Americans should. That this was what the Foreign Service was all about. You know, you spend so many years working on this policy and that policy whose affects wither away, and it's rare that you get the opportunity to do a good deed, a sheer *mitzvah*. No matter what was going to happen to these people, you knew they were going to be better off where they were going than where they were.[43]

The reaction in Israel was even more ecstatic and was typified by Yosef Lapid, who wrote in *Ma'ariv*:

> I became a Zionist on the day I fled with my mother from the Budapest ghetto and we had nowhere to hide. They wanted to kill us and in the whole world we had no place to go. We had to return to the ghetto, but since then I have known that there has to be a place somewhere on the face of the earth which can offer haven to a Jewish child whose life is threatened by Nazis or by famine. In brief that is what Zionism is. Welcome, my black brothers. You are helping us to understand what we are doing here.[44]

However, the elation over the rescue of nearly eight thousand Ethiopian Jews in Operation Moses was tempered by the knowledge that hundreds of Ethiopian Jews were left behind in the Sudanese refugee camps. After the suspension of the airlift, Prime Minister Peres pledged: "We shall not rest until our brothers and sisters from Ethiopia will come safely home."[45]

NOTES

1. Louis Rapoport, *Redemption Song* (NY: Harcourt Brace Jovanovich, 1986), pp. 119–120.

2. General Ephraim Poran, interview with author.

3. Confidential interview.

4. Rapoport, *Redemption Song,* pp. 118–121.

5. Chanan Aynor, interview with author.

6. *Africa Confidential,* January 4, 1984.

7. Charles Powers, "Ethiopian Jews: Exodus of a Tribe," *Los Angeles Times,* July 7, 1985; Charles Powers, "A New Life in Israel for Ethiopians," *Los Angeles Times,* July 8, 1985; Charles Powers, "U.S. Evacuates Ethiopian Jews," *Los Angeles Times,* March 23, 1985; Charles Powers, "Ethiopian Rescue: An All-U.S. Operation," *Los Angeles Times,* March 27, 1985.

8. Robert D. Kaplan, *The Arabists* (NY: The Free Press, 1995), pp. 211–212.

9. Ibid., p. 216.

10. Ibid., p. 219; Powers, "Ethiopian Jews."

11. Tudor Parfitt, *Operation Moses* (England: Weidenfeld and Nicholson, 1985), p. 96.

12. Ibid., p. 96.

13. Confidential interview.

14. Powers, "A New Life."

15. Kaplan, *The Arabists,* p. 223.

16. Powers, "A New Life."

17. Powers, "Ethiopian Jews," and "Ethiopian Rescue" (July 7 and March 27, 1985); Rapoport, *Redemption Song,* p. 136.

18. Poran, interview.

19. Rapoport, *Redemption Song,* p. 135.

20. Powers, "Ethiopian Rescue."

21. Confidential interview.

22. Rapoport, *Redemption Song,* p. 90.

23. Shapiro, interview.

24. Rapoport, *Redemption Song,* pp. 139–140; Parfitt, *Operation Moses,* p. 101.

25. Rapoport, *Redemption Song,* p. 141; Parfitt, *Operation Moses,* pp. 102–103.

26. Rapoport, *Redemption Song,* pp. 137–153; Parfitt, *Operation Moses,* p. 103.

27. Rapoport, *Redemption Song,* p. 155.

28. Barbara Gaffin, interview with author.

29. Rapoport, *Redemption Song,* p. 165; Parfitt, *Operation Moses,* p. 103.

30. Rapoport, *Redemption Song,* pp. 141–142.

31. Ibid., p. 142.

32. Ibid., p. 146.

33. Edwin Black, interview with Robert Cohn, editor of *St. Louis Jewish Light* and president of the American Jewish Press Association.

34. Rapoport, *Redemption Song,* p. 138; Wolf Blitzer, "Imperiling Ethiopia's Jews," *Washington Post,* January 20, 1985.

35. "Operation Joshua: How It Unfolded," *Israel Today,* March 29, 1985.

36. Yehuda Dominitz, interview with author; Parfitt, *Operation Moses,* pp. 105–106; Rapoport, *Redemption Song,* pp. 139–150.

37. Haim Halachmy, interview with author; "Peres Vows Israel Will Finish Rescue," *New York Times*, January 8, 1985.

38. Glenn Stein, interview with author.

39. "Peres Says He Ordered Airlift News," *New York Times*, January 9, 1985.

40. Parfitt, *Operation Moses,* p. 114.

41. *Los Angeles Times*, January 10, 1985.

42. William Safire, "Interrupted Exodus," *New York Times*, January 7, 1985.

43. Kaplan, *The Arabists,* p. 225.

44. Rapoport, *Redemption Song,* p. 182.

45. "Peres Vows Israel Will Finish Rescue," *New York Times*, January 8, 1985.

CHAPTER 9

Operations Sheba and Solomon

P ublicly, it did not appear that the disclosures about Operation Moses would prevent the Jews remaining in the Sudan from ultimately making their way to Israel. Sudan president Numeiry told the *New York Times* in January 1985 that the Ethiopian Jews were free to go as long as they did not go directly to Israel. As was so often the case with such statements, however, it was designed primarily for public relations and did not reflect the reality in the Sudan. Meanwhile, the Ethiopian government was no more forthcoming than it had been prior to the operation. This became clear in early February 1985, when senators Paul Tribble and Dennis DeConcini visited Ethiopia and tried unsuccessfully to persuade the Ethiopian government to allow the Jews remaining there to emigrate. In the United States, the American Association for Ethiopian Jews (AAEJ) was mobilizing the network it had developed from its years of lobbying on Capitol Hill. One key aide, Dawn Calabia from Representative Stephen Solarz's office, explained:

> We did briefings, had meetings with U.S. ambassadors in the region, wrote letters to the President and Secretary of State. We were constantly calling and asking questions about what was being done. We met with the United Nations High Commissioner on Refugees, the ICRC, ICA, and made it very clear that this was a priority. We want them out and we wanted them out quickly. There

were no reasons for delays. It doesn't sound like much, but it's like if you're a teacher and you get three letters of complaint and the three letters also go to the principal, something usually happens in the classroom.[1]

"DEAR COLLEAGUE"

Perhaps the most important contribution made by American activists was to enlist Senator Allan Cranston's help to stimulate the U.S. government to act. AAEJ president Nate Shapiro heard that California publisher Phil Blazer wanted to mount a rescue operation, so he decided to fly out to California to meet with him. After a breakfast meeting, the two men, who already knew the senator well, adjourned to Cranston's hotel room and suggested that he circulate a letter to his colleagues calling on the president to use American influence to help rescue the Ethiopian Jews in the Sudan. Cranston agreed, and Shapiro and the AAEJ's Capitol Hill representative, Lisa Freund, wrote the letter.[2]

In about thirty-eight hours, Cranston succeeded in obtaining the signatures of eighty senators; Senator Alfonse D'Amato signed up the remaining twenty. In fact, six senators had been so anxious to sign they did so twice. In the partisan world of Senate politics this was a rare achievement and represented a strong indication of congressional concern on the issue. Cranston also sent a separate letter to his colleagues urging them to keep the issue secret, which they did. "I think it's unprecedented," Cranston said later, "that 100 senators knew something and did something of value without publicizing it."[3] Cranston presented the president with the letter on February 21. The letter said, in part:

> Given the strong ties that exist between our government and the government of Sudan, it is our hope that you can take steps to insure swift resumption of the airlift. On January 21, President Gaafar el-Numeiry stated in the *New York Times* that the Ethiopian Jews and all other refugees now living in Sudanese refugee camps were free to leave the country provided they did not go directly to Israel. We welcome his humanitarian response, and as the procedure for the departure of the 3,000–4,000 Jews already exists, we would urge you to seek President Numeiry's permission for the immediate resumption of the airlift.[4]

Although it was done with less fanfare, sympathetic members of the House circulated a similar letter.

According to Richard Krieger of the State Department, the impact of the letters was primarily to reinforce a decision that had already been made to help the Ethiopian Jews. "We were looking for ways to try to get things moving again."[5] Shapiro disagreed:

> That was absolutely not so. Chester Crocker's bureau at the State Department were not going to do a thing. I was told that by a number of people. They

wanted nothing else to do with it. They were mad that the Israelis had blown the information. There was no American Jewish initiative at all. The Israelis told everyone to do nothing. NJCRAC had a memo saying do nothing, say nothing, take no action. Don't talk to the Israelis, don't talk to your congressmen, don't talk to your federation. It was that blanket because it was a terrible embarrassment. In the meantime, people were stuck there.[6]

Meanwhile, Phil Blazer, who had helped recruit Cranston to circulate the "Dear colleague" letter, met on January 11 with California state senator Alan Robbins. Together, they came up with the idea of chartering a plane to Khartoum and bringing 460 Ethiopian Jews to Los Angeles. On February 22, Blazer met with Princeton Lyman, deputy assistant secretary for Africa, and Krieger at the State Department. They told Blazer it was impossible to move Ethiopian Jews out of the Sudan "at this time." Blazer was not discouraged. He succeeded in getting a mutual friend, Jerry Weintraub, to set up a meeting with vice president George Bush, who he spoke to after the meeting at the State Department. Krieger briefed the Vice President's staff before he arrived, however, and, "naturally, nobody was going to buy his idea," said Krieger. Blazer did raise the issue of a private airlift, but Bush discouraged him and said the United States would take care of the remaining Jews. From that meeting, Krieger conceded, "came the germ of using the Vice President and his upcoming trip to Sudan as a nucleus to get the whole program reinstated on a short-term basis." When Blazer had presented his idea at the State Department, Krieger called it "the most outlandish scheme you could possibly think of." He said that he didn't know whether to laugh or have him locked up. "I decided after long discussion, and telling him how ridiculous it was, that if we were into a short-term thing, the idea of trying to fly large planes in and pull them out, not out of Khartoum, but directly out of the south might not be such a cockeyed stunt."

In fact, despite the craziness of Blazer's idea, Krieger and his colleagues decided to devise a massive airlift along the same lines. As a result, Blazer and the AAEJ would later take credit for the operation. Another State Department official was skeptical:

> They say that's what brought about operation Sheba, the fear of Phil Blazer blazing into the Sudan. I think that's a little silly myself. Blazer is a bit of a cowboy and thinks that he blackmailed the Vice President into doing this with the threat of sending in his own air force to get these people out. That's a little simplistic although there may have been some element of that.[7]

BUSH GOES TO SUDAN

Vice President Bush was scheduled to visit Numeiry in March and was given President Ronald Reagan's permission to raise the issue of another airlift with the Sudanese leader. According to Halachmy, Israel asked Bush to raise the issue with Numeiry.[8] Before Bush left, Blazer gave him a copy of the book *The Abandonment of the Jews*, which tells the story of America's failures during the Holocaust, and said, "Please don't let this happen again."[9] U.S. officials had considered resuming Operation Moses. According to Krieger, the State Department preferred that type of operation, but he, the White House, and Israel all preferred a one-shot deal. He said the Israeli ambassador met with Bush and agreed on this option.

When Bush met with Numeiry on March 3, he found that Numeiry did not want a repeat of the earlier fiasco. Instead, he agreed to a quick, one-shot operation. Numeiry insisted, however, that the plan be secretly carried out by the Americans, not the Israelis, and that the flights not go directly to Israel. Why did Numeiry agree to another airlift? One can only speculate, but it is most likely because the reaction to the disclosure of Operation Moses was not very severe, causing him only moderate embarrassment. This was more than offset, moreover, by the goodwill his cooperation had generated in Washington, and he was in particular need of that sympathy as the economic situation in his country deteriorated and unrest threatened his regime. He was especially in need of the $200 million in foreign aid that Congress was holding up because of dissatisfaction with internal corruption, restrictions placed on relief organizations, and the war in southern Sudan. Dawn Calabia suggested that Numeiry might have also been receptive on humanitarian grounds:

> The Muslim faith says you don't kill people and that you respect the rights of the individual. You may want everyone to practice the same religion, but you don't kill people. You don't push them across the border. You don't not feed the hungry. Numeiry claimed he was a statesman. This was a guy who in the beginning of his regime had been an extremely humane man. There was a coup to assassinate him and the people were brought to trial and sentenced to death and he commuted the sentence and released them on the grounds that the Sudanese had to work for the greater honor and glory of the Sudan and it didn't do him any good or the country any good to kill these obviously very talented guys. So Numeiry had this image of himself as this humane, enlightened type. It was to our advantage to play on that.[10]

If appeals to Numeiry's humane nature failed, there was always the more mundane inducement of financial reward. In fact, the Israelis paid bribes to numerous Sudanese officials. One report, for example, said that $56 million was paid to Numeiry with a large part of that also going to Sudanese vice president Omar Tayeb for Operation Moses.[11] It is also known now that Saudi billionaire Adnan Khashoggi played a role in negotiations with the Sudan on behalf of Israel.[12]

On March 8, the night that he was to leave Khartoum, Bush met with Jerry Weaver and the CIA station chief to discuss how to carry out the president's order to rescue the Ethiopian Jews. To avoid the possibility of disclosure, for the sake both of the Sudan and the United States, President Reagan wanted the operation carried out within three to four days. The following day, Weaver took an embassy plane with two U.S. Air Force pilots to check out the runway of a remote airstrip near Gedaref and found that it would be acceptable for the operation. Within the next week, $15 million in aid for Sudan that had been withheld after the suspension of the airlift was ordered released. The remainder of the $200 million was later sent to Sudan.[13]

On March 28, 1985, the operation, code-named "Sheba" (also known as "Joshua"), began with Ethiopian Jews from Israel working for the Mossad picking out the Ethiopian Jews in the camps and taking them to Tuwawa, two miles north of Gedaref, on a back road that joined with the route to the airstrip. Only two days before, the Ethiopian Jews in Israel had been told to report to an army base and flown to the Sudan. The airstrip itself was eight miles outside of Gedaref, just far enough so that it would be difficult to spot the planes from the town. A total of eighteen planes, set up to hold ninety passengers each, were prepared at the American base near Frankfurt, West Germany. Several planes filled with food, water, and medical supplies were flown from an Israeli military base near Eilat to the airstrip in the Sudan.

The first night, the Ethiopian Jews who had been identified by Beta Israel from Israel were taken by truck to the airstrip where six U.S. Hercules transports painted in desert camouflage landed at twenty-minute intervals to pick up their passengers. Sudanese security officers cordoned off the area to prevent any surprises, but unexpected high winds delayed the operation. Nevertheless, all of the Ethiopian Jews were evacuated by 9:00 A.M. The Beta Israel were given visas for European countries. Rather than go to the intermediate destination, however, the planes flew directly to an Israeli air force base outside Eilat where they landed at half-hour intervals and were greeted by Prime Minister Peres. The organizers had originally believed as many as 2,000 Ethiopian Jews were in the camps, but they found only 494, so three planes returned from the Sudan empty. In addition to those flown directly to Israel, another 140 Jews were taken out a few days later by a different route.[14]

A REAL SECRET

Unlike the previous operation, this airlift had been kept secret from all but a handful of State Department and administration officials in the United States and the top officials in Israel. The AAEJ's contact in the State Department did not find out about it until the day before it happened, and he "had been right in the bowels of the problem." Members of Congress most concerned with the issue had an idea that something was up but still did not know when or what was going to happen. American Jewish Press Association (AJPA) president Robert Cohn said that he did not know anything about the operation until he heard a CBS report confirming it, and Blazer only learned of it after the fact, on March 22, when Reagan aide Marshall Breger called him on Bush's behalf to say the operation was a success. The Ethiopian Jew in Israel who was probably best informed on rescue activities also did not know about the operation until it was over.

The American Jewish community was kept in the dark but, despite the earlier experience, continued to carry on a public campaign on behalf of the Ethiopian Jews. In January, Cohn and several other Jewish newspaper editors had met with Abe Bayer of the National Jewish Community Relations Advisory Council (NJCRAC) in New York to discuss how to handle publicity of the Beta Israel issue, and Bayer had promised to keep Cohn informed on a daily basis, hourly if necessary. Even after that, however, there was a wide variation in the degree to which the embargo was observed. Cohn said that he saw an advertisement placed in the *Los Angeles Jewish Community Bulletin*, for example, which published virtually everything the AJPA had said not to publish.[15] In addition, the United Jewish Appeal (UJA) and other organizations continued to place fundraising ads in newspapers, although they had changed their pitch to the need for money to pay for absorption.

NO MORE JEWS?

At the end of Operation Sheba, Israeli officials believed that all of the Ethiopian Jews had been evacuated from the refugee camps in the Sudan. In fact, a handful were left in the camps and anywhere from seven to fifteen thousand were estimated to be still living in Ethiopia. Those remaining behind were believed to be mainly the very old, the sick, the very young, and the women who, for one reason or another, could not make the arduous journey to the Sudan.

On April 4, just a few days after Operation Sheba, while he was out of the country, Numeiry was overthrown. The timing was largely coincidental, since his fall had been expected by U.S. officials for some time. The Sudanese suspected of cooperating with the rescue of the Ethiopian Jews were either imprisoned or executed. Vice President Tayeb was sentenced to two thirty-two-year terms.[16] Anti-American sentiment grew more intense as well, and Weaver found it prudent to leave the country. Although the reaction of the new Sudanese leaders toward the people who had helped in a humanitarian operation was harsh, it was once again an example of an action that was required primarily for domestic purposes. The new leaders needed to demonstrate to their people, and the Arab world, that the Sudan would not tolerate collaborators with the "Zionist enemy."

EXPLAINING AMERICA'S INTEREST

The U.S. role in Operation Sheba was significant in more ways than one. First, the operation was organized and conducted by U.S. State Department, CIA, and Air Force personnel. The CIA, which frequently is criticized for its actions, in this case carried out a humanitarian mission with precision and in the clandestine fashion in which it is set up to operate. The operation was also financed by the United States, which gave the Jewish Agency more than $3 million out of the president's emergency fund for transportation.[17] The entire American government deserves credit for placing its national interests in the region at risk for a purely humanitarian gesture. The U.S. government is constantly criticized for placing security concerns ahead of human ones and yet here was an instance where its leaders did not. Although the U.S. government had nothing to gain from its involvement, the responsible political officials, notably George Bush and Ronald Reagan, stood to reap some political rewards for their actions, at least from the Jewish community, but they surprisingly eschewed the credit they deserved for making the decisions that led to the rescue of hundreds of men, women, and children. Perhaps they felt the Jewish world would learn the truth one way or another and that silence would better serve America's relations with its moderate Arab friends. Regardless, the fact remains that hundreds of Jewish lives were saved through the direct actions of the Reagan administration.

The president and secretary of state approved the plans, but they did not develop them. The men responsible for making this an issue for the U.S. government were primarily lower ranking State Department officials, notably Richard Krieger and Princeton Lyman. These two men took personal interests in the plight of their co-religionists and also happened to be in the right place at the right time. Krieger is given a lot of credit by insiders for his contribution to the rescue. He was the person who helped keep the issue alive and was a source of information for congressional representatives. He also played an important role because his superior, Eugene Douglas, allowed him to do so. Doug Cahn, Representative Barney Frank's legislative assistant, recognized Lyman for his cooperation with Congress: "I think he opened up to a number of congressmen and treated the matter with the same seriousness that the members had on this issue. I give him a lot of credit for moving this along and taking the position that we ought to work with Congress and that Congress might be helpful in certain ways, in securing the monies that might be necessary, securing supplies for the Sudan that were necessary to make arrangements with the Sudanese to allow certain kinds of operations to take place."

Congress also played an important part in stimulating the bureaucracy and the administration to become involved in the issue. Initially, neither Krieger nor Lyman were particularly enthusiastic about becoming involved, but they came around after being prodded by Congress. "I don't think there would

have been the incentive for our government to become as involved as it ultimately did without the pressure from Congress," according to Doug Cahn.
"I don't think they would have found the issue to be on the level of priority that it became." He added, "ultimately, many members of Congress were
surprised at their success. I think the Executive Branch exceeded the
expectations of many members of Congress in their level of involvement. The
Vice President on a trip to Africa taking a personal hand in the operations
end. That was extraordinary," Cahn said reverentially. A State Department
official also acknowledged Congress for stimulating it to act on behalf of the
Ethiopian Jews.

> The fact is that this building [the State Department] gets its money from the
> U.S. Congress and it depends on good relations with the Congress for its sur-
> vival and it's vastly more responsive to suggestions and pressure from Congress
> than it ever is to the public. That's something most people don't understand.
> You write a letter to the President or the Secretary of State, forget it, write a
> letter to your congressman. Don't bother writing to the Secretary of State, he
> doesn't get elected by the people, he doesn't get money from the people. When
> he gets a letter from Senator Cranston or from Senator Lugar then, by god,
> he's going to listen. And the State Department was getting a hell of a lot of
> that from the Hill.[18]

Congress could have taken a different position. As Shapiro noted, the
Senate Foreign Relations Committee could have told the State Department,
"Hey, you are going to run the risk of ruining our relations with the Sudan"
and pressured the department *not* to act. Shapiro gives the committee chairman, Charles Percy, and his staff director, Scott Cohen, a lot of credit for
supporting the AAEJ on the issue. Ironically, Percy was defeated for re-
election largely because of opposition from Jews who believed the Chicago
senator had not been supportive enough of Israel (as evidenced by his vote
for the sale of AWACS radar planes to Saudi Arabia). Shapiro said regret-
fully, "Everyone thinks that Percy wasn't our [American Jews'] friend, but
he was on this."[19]

Why was Congress so concerned with the plight of the Ethiopian Jews?
Primarily because constituents made it clear to their representatives they were
concerned about them. Those constituents were for the most part mobilized
by the AAEJ. It was also a result of the effective lobbying by the AAEJ's
representatives in Washington, first Marilyn Diamond, then David Feltman,
and, finally, Lisa Freund. As Freund pointed out, when one hundred senators signed the letter to the president, it did not happen in a vacuum. Most
of them had been getting cards, letters, and phone calls for years from the
AAEJ's members on the issue. Although some of the Jewish establishment
organizations became more involved as the issue attracted greater publicity,
the spadework to develop a constituency among the grassroots and on

Capitol Hill was largely a product of the information campaign of the AAEJ
and a few other small organizations and individuals.

SHARING CREDIT

The AAEJ unquestionably deserves credit for putting the issue on the
agendas of the American Jewish community and the U.S. government. "The
AAEJ exposed the issue and kept it hot," according to the Anti-Defamation
League's (ADL) Roberta Fahn. "They wouldn't let it die down and that was
important, especially in view of the apathy and hostility of the American
Jewish community." She added, however, that the problem was that the
AAEJ did not let go when Israel began to do the job.[20] A State Department
official also gave the organization credit: "The AAEJ people suffered from
overzealousness, but the airlift would not have happened without them."[21]
This is perhaps an overstatement, but there is no doubt that the U.S. willingness to contribute was a function of years of spadework on Capitol Hill
and efforts to enlist the support of congressional representatives who, in turn,
pressured the State Department. Richard Krieger, for example, readily admits
that "it was the political pressure from the Hill that got State interested."[22]

While the AAEJ merits recognition for its educational efforts, it probably
also deserves criticism for the intemperate nature of its propaganda and its
indiscretion. The organization also does not deserve as much of the credit
as it claims for forcing Israel to act. The planning and implementation of
rescues were not as simple as Graenum Berger implied, and it is the height
of cynicism to believe, as many members of the AAEJ did, that Israel timed
its operations so that Ethiopian Jews would be rescued at the time of large
meetings of American Jewish organizations just so that they could discredit
the AAEJ. "You have to believe that the commander is correctly weighing
the risks and costs," Yehuda Dominitz said. "The AAEJ was naive to say that
Israel saved Jews according to the calendar of Jewish conventions. It's a vi-
cious approach."[23] According to Chanan Aynor, "The pressure groups were
important in keeping the problem alive and confronting the establishment,
but they were wrong in their understanding of Israeli motivations."[24] Speaker
of the Knesset, Shlomo Hillel, who also was the head of the pro-Falasha committee in Israel, added that when American activists came to see him, he
could not convince them that he was no less concerned than they were.
"Their views were absurd," he said. As far as Israel rescuing the Ethiopian
Jews in response to pressure, Hillel concluded: "The United States had no
impact on Israel."[25]

In addition, the AAEJ and its supporters, such as Simcha Jacobovici,
tended to engage in specious reasoning to "prove" their influence. For example, Jacobovici cited the fact that less than one thousand Ethiopian Jews
were rescued during thirty-three years of quiet diplomacy, but fourteen

thousand were saved from 1981 to 1985 when there was a public campaign. Therefore, he concluded, this constituted "a simple statistical correlation that proves that if advocacy did not help save thousands of Ethiopian Jews, it certainly did not hurt."[26]

Other factors unrelated to public advocacy or AAEJ actions could have been and, to a large extent, were responsible for the increase in the numbers of Ethiopian Jews who were rescued. For example, one of the major reasons the number of Ethiopian Jews that reached Israel increased from 1981 to 1985 was that they had escaped to the Sudan and that it was much easier (though still very difficult) to rescue them from that country than from Ethiopia. In addition, the fact that a large number was rescued in the latter period does not necessarily prove that advocacy did not hurt operations because it may have been possible to save more or do so more quickly if not for publicity that forced the abandonment of particular rescue routes or compromised operations.

The evidence suggests that the public campaign was very important in putting the issue on the agenda and keeping it there. It was also important in stimulating the involvement of U.S. officials. It was far less helpful, however, in pressuring Israel to rescue the Ethiopian Jews because at a certain point pressure was unnecessary (if indeed it ever was needed). Menachem Begin had clearly made a commitment to the rescue, and once the Ethiopian Jews had begun to reach the Sudan in large numbers, it became a matter of logistics rather than will, and though there are few specific instances that officials were willing to cite of AAEJ interference, the consensus among Israelis is that the AAEJ private rescue efforts were largely counterproductive.

THE JEWS LEFT BEHIND

At the end of Operation Sheba, a total of roughly fourteen thousand Ethiopian Jews were in Israel. The newcomers from the underdeveloped world had to adjust to their new lives in Israel's highly developed society. The Beta Israel would spend between six months and two years in absorption centers learning Hebrew, being retrained from their primary skills in agriculture and crafts for Israel's industrial society, and learning to live in a modern nation.

Perhaps the most difficult aspect of the transition, however, was psychological. More than 1,600 Jews were separated from their families. A large percentage of the Beta Israel had left behind relatives or were unaware of their fate. Many of the Jews' loved ones had died during the journey to the Sudan or in the refugee camps. The survivors felt guilty because they had lived and also because they had not fulfilled their obligation to bury their dead. The trauma associated with the break-up of the family exacerbated the difficulties of acclimating to a new home and was serious enough to cause a number of Ethiopian Jews to commit suicide. In Ethiopia, the Jews who remained were sending horrific reports of their plight. Rachamim Elazar said 21 Jews were killed by non-Jews in Gondar in 1988 and that women were being kidnaped and raped. Since most of the men, except the young, frail, and elderly, had left the country, the women were left unprotected and most could not do the work in the fields.[27]

More than seventy senators wrote to Ethiopian leader Mengistu in December 1988 thanking him for releasing twenty Ethiopian Jews from jail and asking him to allow family reunification. The Ethiopian Jewry Caucus, which now numbered 112 members, was pushing for an indication that the Mengistu regime would fulfill its obligations under the International Declaration of Human Rights. Members also called on Secretary of State James Baker to make the plight of the Beta Israel a priority.

The continuing support on Capitol Hill was now spearheaded by the the full-time lobbying effort of Will Recant, who was hired to be the AAEJ's director in 1986. Recant strengthened and broadened the organization's contacts with the U.S. government and also successfully improved the AAEJ's relations within the Jewish community. The combination of a change in leadership at several of the establishment organizations and Recant's low-key, positive approach erased most of the animosity that had characterized the establishment's attitude toward the AAEJ. Under Recant and Shapiro, the AAEJ increasingly worked in cooperation with other agencies.

In the five years following Operation Sheba, numerous efforts were made to induce the Ethiopian government to allow the Jews remaining there to immigrate. It was not until 1990, however, that Mengistu agreed to allow the reunification of families. He also pardoned all those Jews who received prison sentences for their attempts to leave the country illegally. The year before, Ethiopia had restored diplomatic relations with Israel and was allowing five hundred Jews to immigrate to Israel each month via Ethiopian Airlines.

In the spring of 1990, U.S. Jews helped broker a deal whereby a rebel-held port would be opened to allow food to be imported to the famine-threatened north of the country. In exchange, Ethiopia agreed to allow three thousand Jews to immigrate to Israel.[28] The flow of immigrants, however, slowed during the summer. Observers speculated that the Ethiopians were trying to pressure Israel to provide more weapons in exchange for the Jews, or they were trying to avoid the embarrassment of having the issue raised while hosting the annual meeting of the Organization of African Unity. The Ethiopians publicly maintained they were simply trying to ensure that non-Jews were not trying to slip in with the Beta Israel going to Israel.[29]

By the end of 1990, thousands of Ethiopian Jews were now converging on Addis Ababa in the hope of receiving exit visas and to escape the fighting and chaos in the north. When they arrived, they found inadequate housing, a shortage of food, and the threat of disease. They also had given up their livelihoods and lands, so they had no income and no place to return to. Many of the Jews were cared for in a compound set up by the AAEJ. The organization was once again making the Israelis uncomfortable by insisting that the Jews were in danger in their villages and that they would be better off in the capital where they could more easily be processed for immigration. As one of the AAEJ's people on the ground observed:

> Finding housing for 20,000 people who have no friends or resources is more than just a challenge, especially when they have come directly from a meager rural existence to a large city. Keeping them occupied when all they know how to do is farm, and keeping them away from liquor and prostitution kept us constantly on the alert. Determining if persons claiming to be Jewish were really eligible to go to Israel under the Law of Return was equally demanding, when at the same time we were doing everything possible to reinforce their Judaism.[30]

The refugee population had reached twenty thousand and the AAEJ was unable to meet their needs. Starting in June 1990, the Joint Distrubtion Committee (JDC) and the Jewish Agency had begun to assume greater responsibility for the Jews. Although it created hardships for the Ethiopian Jews, forced the aid organizations back into action, aggravated the Israeli government, and strained Israeli-Ethiopian relations, evacuating the remaining population would have been impossible if the Beta Israel had remained in their homes.

OPERATION SOLOMON

The worsening internal political situation in Ethiopia heightened the anxiety of the Jews in Israel and prompted government officials to once again make rescue a high priority. When Eritrean and Tigrean rebels began to defeat the Ethiopian government forces for the first time since the civil war began in 1975, the fall of the Mengistu regime became inevitable. Mengistu first tried to use the Jews as a bargaining chip to obtain arms, but the United States persuaded Israel not to give in. Meanwhile, President George Bush sent a letter to Mengistu asking him to permit Israel to take unusual measures to evacuate the Jews in exchange for U.S. support for a cease-fire and peace conference. It is worth noting that this occurred amidst U.S.-Israel tensions over the Mideast peace process and Bush's apparent antipathy toward Israeli prime minister Yitzhak Shamir. One Israeli newspaper editorialized later, "When the real test of Zionism arrived, the United States and President Bush did not disappoint."[31]

On May 21, 1991, Mengistu fled the country. Bush renewed his request in a letter to Mengistu's successor, Tesfaye Kidane, who granted the request. The rebels were less than one hundred miles from Addis Ababa. As the rebels advanced on the Ethiopian capital, fears increased that the Jews would be trapped, and it was uncertain what fate would await them when a new government was formed. Israel also feared retribution for their past support of the Mengistu regime.

Prime Minister Shamir, himself a veteran of the pre-state underground and the Mossad, decided all of the Ethiopian Jews would be airlifted to Israel. The top defense officials warned against an Entebbe-style operation, that too many civilians were involved to be rescued safely. Instead, Shamir accepted the recommendation to obtain the Ethiopian government's approval to take all the Jews to Israel. Israel subsequently agreed to pay the military government $35 million (the Ethiopians had asked for $100 million) to allow the Jews to immigrate.[32] The United States, meanwhile, persuaded the rebels not to attack the capital or airport until after the Jews were evacuated.[33] On the ground, all of the Jews were told to report to the Israeli embassy with only the clothes on their back. They were given either a blue or a yellow decal to put on their clothing, which allowed them to board a bus to the airport. A force of more than two hundred elite commandos dressed in civilian clothes came from Israel to provide security for the operation.

On Friday, May 24, thirty-four Hercules C-130s and jumbo jets—whose seats had been removed to increase their capacity and with Israeli markings covered—began a continuous twenty-six-hour airlift of Jews from Addis. Shamir ordered the Israeli airline, El Al, to violate its normal prohibition of flying on the Sabbath. At one point, twenty-five aircraft were in flight simultaneously, and one El Al 747 set a world record by transporting 1,087 passengers, more than double the normal capacity. Some of the planes were on the ground for as little as thirty-six minutes before taking off loaded with refugees. The operation was named after King Solomon, the man who some believed the Beta Israel had descended from.

When it ended, Operation Solomon had rescued 14,324 Jews. No one died in the operation, but ten babies were born. When the refugees arrived at Ben-Gurion Airport, three hundred buses transported the newcomers to forty-five hotels, guest houses, and mobile homes throughout the country. Prime Minister Shamir welcomed the first arrivals. The *Washington Post* observed after the airlift:

> There is a magical, even a magic-carpet quality to the airlift by which Israel over the weekend plucked the remaining 14,500 or so Jews from the collapsing Ethiopian scene. For Israel it was the latest fulfillment of the mandate of rescue and haven which is the Jewish state's defining purpose. For the poor and desperate Jews themselves, it was the opportunity to begin building new lives in the one place in the world ready to take them in. They are moving from one country and continent to another and from one culture and age to another— truly an epic journey.[34]

The Jews were in Israel by Sunday and the rebels captured Addis Ababa on Monday.

NOTES

1. Dawn Calabia, interview with author.

2. Lisa Freund, interview with author; Nate Shapiro, interview with author.

3. "Cranston Led 100 Senators in Urging Reagan to Rescue Falashas," *Los Angeles Times*, March 26, 1985.

4. Letter to President Ronald Reagan from 100 Senators, January 21, 1985.

5. Richard Krieger, interview with author.

6. Shapiro, interview.

7. Confidential interview.

8. Haim Halachmy, interview with author.

9. Lisa Freund, interview with author.

10. Calabia, interview.

11. Richard Hall, "Massive Bribe for Operation Moses," *London Observer*, April 21, 1985; General Ephraim Poran, interview with author.

12. Louis Rapoport, interview with author.

13. Charles Powers, "U.S. Evacuates Ethiopian Jews," *Los Angeles Times*, March 23, 1985; Charles Powers, "Ethiopian Rescue: An All-U.S. Operation," *Los Angeles Times*, March 27, 1985; Charles Powers, "A New Life in Israel for Ethiopians," *Los Angeles Times*, July 8, 1985; Louis Rapoport, *Redemption Song: The Story of Operation Moses* (CA: Harcourt Brace Javanovich, 1986), pp. 186–187.

14. Rapoport, *Redemption Song,* pp. 187–189, p. 119; Powers, "U.S. Evacuates;" Powers, "Ethiopian Rescue;" Powers, "A New Life."

15. Edwin Black, interview with Robert Cohn.

16. Teshome Wagaw, *For Our Soul: Ethiopian Jews in Israel* (MI: Wayne State University Press, 1993), p. 70.

17. Krieger, interview.

18. Confidential interview.

19. Shapiro, interview.

20. Roberta Fahn, interview with author.

21. Rapoport, *Redemption Song,* p. 91.

22. Krieger, interview.

23. Yehuda Dominitz, interview with author.

24. Chanan Aynor, interview with author.

25. Shlomo Hillel, interview with author.

26. Simcha Jacobovici, letter to the editor, *Moment*, January–February 1986.

27. "Ethiopian Jews Need Help," *Near East Report*, March 6, 1989.

28. "U.S. Jews Get Ethiopia to Open Port for Food Aid," *Washington Times*, May 17, 1990, p. A7.

29. Flow of Ethiopian Jews to Israel is Back to Normal," *New York Times*, July 27, 1990, p. A3.

30. Graenum Berger, *Rescue the Ethiopian Jews!* (NY: John Washburn Bleeker Hampton Publishing Co., 1996), p. 200.

31. *Hadashot*, May 28, 1991.

32. Durrenda Nash Onolemhemhen and Kebede Gessesse, *The Black Jews of Ethiopia* (MD: Scarecrow Press, 1998), pp. 35–36; Graenum Berger, *Rescue the Ethiopian Jews!* (NY: John Washburn Bleeker Hampton Publishing Co., 1996), p. 210.

33. "Israel Completes Ethioia Airlift," *Washington Post*, May 26, 1991, p. A1.

34. "Airlift editorial," *Washington Post*, May 28, 1991, p. A18.

Chapter 10

The Holocaust Analogy

There is a widespread belief that the Holocaust was a unique event in human history that was characterized by a systematic program for the extermination of an entire people. I do not wish to challenge this view here; however, certain analogies can be drawn between the plight of the Ethiopian Jews and that cataclysm, particularly with regard to the behavior of the American Jewish community.

One of the reasons that the Ethiopian Jewry issue did not become a top priority in the American Jewish community was that a great deal of time and energy was devoted to arguing over the question of whether or not a holocaust was taking place in Ethiopia. Given the sensitivity about the use of the word *holocaust*, it should not have been surprising that an uproar would be caused by references to an Ethiopian holocaust by the American Association for Ethiopian Jews (AAEJ). Rather than wanting to provoke controversy, the AAEJ expected to stimulate sympathy for a Jewish community in peril by calling their plight a holocaust; moreover, the organization believed that while the method and magnitude of the Ethiopian Jews' suffering might be different, the result was ultimately the same; that is, the destruction of the community. The AAEJ's dilemma over the description of the Ethiopian Jews was summarized by one individual who admitted the sensitivity about the use of the word Holocaust, which he believed should be used sparingly because it belonged to the Jews murdered by the Germans while the world looked on. The Ethiopian Jews' situation was also terrible, he noted. "Death through hunger, cultural decimation, persons losing their lives while trying to gain access to other countries for the sole purpose of getting to Eretz Israel is all the same—death and destruction while the world looks on."[1]

The accuracy of the descriptions concerning the conditions in Ethiopia was important because the priority of the rescue depended to some extent on the severity of their situation. If, in fact, there was a holocaust, then Israel could not justify failing to act, but if the conditions were something short of that, albeit grave, then Israel could argue that rescuing the Ethiopian Jews was not the government's highest priority.

HOW BAD IS BAD?

The plight of the Jews in Ethiopia varied from time to time after the revolution in 1974, but it was never good. According to Rabbi Yosef Adane, for example, before they began to escape, the Jews in Ethiopia were not treated differently by the government, but they did have problems with their neighbors. In Gondar, the Ethiopian Jews received land and got along well, but the Christians persecuted the Jews in areas outside the towns. After people began to escape from Tigre, an Ethiopian province, however, things deteriorated. Jews were not permitted to move from village to village, and the study of Hebrew and religion in schools was prohibited.[2]

During the chaotic revolutionary period of the mid-1970s, the Ethiopian Jews were sometimes caught in the crossfire between government and rebel forces and that continued up until the time they were rescued. Amnesty International reported that people were being tortured in Ethiopia and in its 1983 report said that three Jewish teachers had been arrested and were allegedly tortured. Amnesty also reported that thirty Jews were in jail for trying to escape, a crime that was categorized as "betraying the revolution" and was punishable by imprisonment—and even death—if committed "under grave circumstances."[3]

As the Jews began to escape across the border in greater numbers, those who were caught were indeed tortured. The most common method was to hang the person upside down and beat their feet with a stick until the prisoner was often crippled. This was to ensure that they would not attempt to escape. The imprisonment of the teachers and other Jews occurred relatively late in the rescue effort. The Ethiopian Jews were already suffering terribly before that, and the AAEJ did not believe the Israelis or the American Jewish organizations were doing enough to either publicize their plight or ameliorate it through rescue.

In 1978, Akiva Kohane of the Joint Distribution Committee (JDC) told a meeting of activists that the attitude of the Ethiopian government toward the Jews was "better than at any time in history." However, Kohane was forced to admit that thirty-eight Jews had been killed by the government and rebel forces, eighteen had been sold into slavery, and five hundred families were dispossessed from their land.[4] Rabbi Marc Tannenbaum of the American Jewish Committee issued a report in January 1979 with similar findings.[5] The Israeli government reported even more dramatic evidence that a serious threat to the Jews of Ethiopia, if not a holocaust, existed. Citing a government announcement, Dvora Waysman reported for the World Zionist Press Service that two thousand Jews had been killed or wounded by rebels opposing the government, and another seven thousand had been evicted from their lands, sold into slavery or were living as refugees outside Gondar.[6]

In May 1979, an Ethiopian Jew from Israel, Zecharias Yona, came to New York to tell American Jewish and Israeli consular officials about the situation in Ethiopia, but the officials refused to believe that things were as bad as Yona described. Based on a census taken by the ORT and the Hebrew Immigrant Aid Society (HIAS), ORT's Sidney Liewant denied Yona's claim that 10,000 Ethiopian Jews were killed or missing. When Liewant said *only* 3,500 were killed or missing, someone shouted that 3,500 was a significant number too. Another ORT official, Paul Bernick, said *only* 50 had been killed and 2,000 were refugees.[7] Discussions between the establishment officials and the AAEJ frequently degenerated into statistical arguments in which the former tried to discredit the figures of the latter while seeming to ignore the significance of even their own numbers. As the person at the ORT meeting said, 3,500 should have been a large enough number of casualties for the Israelis and the other organizations to be very concerned.

Not even the U.S. State Department could provide reliable information on the situation in Ethiopia because the movements of its embassy staff were restricted following the break in U.S.-Ethiopian relations and no one had visited the Jewish villages. In the department's 1980 report on human rights practices in Ethiopia, the Jews were said to have been "relieved by land reform of their pre-revolutionary status as farm laborers, and are treated fairly by the government." The report added, however, that "there have been numerous reports of official harassment." The following year's report said the conditions of the Ethiopian Jews had improved since the revolution, but that their treatment by the regional administrator in Gondar had been "unusually harsh during the latter part of 1981." A year later, the department reported that since mid-1981 the Jews were worse off in the religious and cultural spheres than other ethnic groups in Gondar.[8] The director of ORT, Jean-Claude Nadjer, also reported in 1981 that discrimination against the Ethiopian Jews had diminished "radically" in the last five years and that the revolution had given them their freedom.[9]

INVESTIGATIONS OR COVERUPS?

The AAEJ continued to maintain that a holocaust was taking place in Ethiopia, however, so the National Jewish Community Relations Advisory Council (NJCRAC) sent a mission to Ethiopia in March 1982 to investigate. That group found that the Ethiopian Jews did "face a threat to the distinctiveness of their life as Jews," but they were not faced with the danger of physical annihilation. "Descriptions of the situation . . . in terms of 'Holocaust' and 'Genocide' are inaccurate and a disservice." Moreover, the group came back convinced that Israel was dedicated to the rescue of the Ethiopian Jews, that independent operations (i.e., the AAEJ's) jeopardized the safety of the Ethiopian Jews, and that publicity would expose them to retribution.[10] Essentially, the group came back with all its opinions reinforced. Other Jewish groups that visited the Ethiopian Jews in 1982–1983 found "no signs of hunger or extreme poverty" nor did they hear any stories of torture or murder. An Israeli delegation led by a Knesset member, Dror Zeigerman, confirmed the plight of the Ethiopian Jews had improved but concluded that they were "definitely discriminated against."[11]

The AAEJ believed such missions were nothing but attempts to cover up Israel's inaction. "Look who went on the missions," said AAEJ president Nate Shapiro. "They were sending the people who wanted to keep the issue quiet. They didn't send objective viewers. . . . The Israelis told them to be quiet. Someone would come from the Mossad and explain why they had to be quiet. Every time there would be an initiative, someone from the Mossad would come over and say everything was being done."[12] Shapiro and others believed the people investigating the issue depended on Israel's goodwill to keep their jobs and were not likely to contradict the government line. Moreover, the AAEJ maintained the missions these Jews took were sanitized to hide the truth. The Ethiopian government would, for example, open synagogues just for the duration of the tour group's visit and then close them again. It was all a part of the Ethiopian government's effort to improve its public image and entice tourists to visit.[13]

Barbara Gaffin disagreed with the AAEJ's theory. In 1981 she went on the first Jewish-sponsored mission to Ethiopia. She pointed out that the trip was not sanctioned by the establishment. This is how she described the experience:

> We had heard that there was a holocaust going on. We saw that there was not a holocaust going on, but we understood why the rumors had grown to that extent. People lived in absolute terror. Absolute terror. They were being thrown into prison. They were being tortured. We met with the three leading Hebrew teachers. One was blind. Another couldn't walk properly. It was just a sense of terror and fear that we kept witnessing. Plus, the people were so committed to Judaism and committed to Israel. It was unlike what we had anticipated. We

had been told that they don't know from Israel and we saw categorically that they wanted to go to Israel.[14]

Three years later, Glenn Stein went to Ethiopia for the Union of American Hebrew Congregations (UAHC), the Reform Movement's governing body, and found that the Ethiopian Jews were confined to the bottom rung of society. Beyond that, however, he said that his group did not find any real discrimination except that Hebrew was not allowed to be taught and that the Ethiopian Jews were poor and had no chance for improvement. When asked if a holocaust was taking place, Stein replied:

> The holocaust is a widely used phrase these days. I'm not sure you would call it a holocaust. I am quite certain, as the AAEJ has said previously, that within our lifetime, to be conservative, there will be no more Jews in Ethiopia. Either they will be saved and brought to Israel or they will die, but there will not be any Jews left in Ethiopia. Do you call that a holocaust? It's a holocaust. There's certainly going to be an end to Ethiopian Jewry as we know it. Is it because of a government pogrom? No, I don't think it is. It's because of the socioeconomic position that they are in that is going to force them to leave or die. So I think that it is very serious.[15]

The issue was that the Ethiopian Jews were suffering and not only needed to be rescued, but wanted to emigrate. This became clouded by AAEJ's insistence on referring to their plight as a holocaust.

THE SILENCE OF AMERICAN JEWRY

The AAEJ's rhetoric was analogous to that of Peter Bergson's controversial Committee for a Jewish Army (CJA) during World War II. Ironically, Bergson, considered a militant right-winger, and AAEJ president Howard Lenhoff, an almost equally militant left-winger, adopted similar strategies of trying to attract attention and support by dramatic and sometimes sensationalist appeals for rescue and money for their organizations. For example, a CJA advertisement published in February 1943 had the headline:

FOR SALE TO HUMANITY

70,000 JEWS

GUARANTEED HUMAN BEINGS AT $50 A PIECE

The ad went on to say that "70,000 Jews Are Waiting Death in Rumanian Concentration Camps. . . . Rumania Offers to Deliver These 70,000 Alive to Palestine. . . . The Doors of Rumania Are Open! Act Now!" The ad said that the CJA had been working to demand that something be done to rescue

Jews and asked for contributions to help the CJA's efforts to save European Jewry.[16] The establishment response to the CJA's ad was similar to that expressed nearly forty years later toward AAEJ ads accusing the United Jewish Appeal (UJA) of misleading the public to believe that a $50 contribution could save an Ethiopian Jew (the AAEJ figure was $3,000) and calling the UJA ads irresponsible and unethical. The Zionist leaders in the 1940s said the Bergsonites "had no mandate or authorization from the Jewish public, their actions were irresponsible and sensationalist and they misused the large funds they solicited."[17] Similar charges were made by Jewish leaders against the AAEJ.

There was one critical difference in the motivation for the attacks on the CJA and that was the establishment organizations' fear that the Bergsonites might become a threat to their own power. This concern was related less to the plight of European Jewry, however, than to the question of Palestine. The fight for a Jewish state was the principal concern of all groups, and the establishment was particularly worried that the CJA, which supported the Irgun's efforts (the Jewish underground) to force the British out of Palestine with terrorism, might gain influence over the more moderate elements in the Jewish community that favored a diplomatic solution.

The rivalry between the CJA and the establishment was also rooted in competition for money. In this regard there is a similarity to the AAEJ's relationship with the establishment. There is only so much money available, and the AAEJ's solicitation efforts hurt the UJA's fundraising ability. The issue became particularly acute when Lenhoff began to call on people to contribute to the AAEJ and then to write to the UJA to say that they were deducting a certain amount of their pledge for the purpose of rescuing Ethiopian Jews since the UJA was not contributing any money toward that end. Still, the UJA was raising more than half a billion dollars at the time, so the AAEJ's campaign had more of a negative public relations impact than a financial one.

The division caused by the CJA in the 1940s undermined the unity of the Zionists and thereby, the mainstream groups believed, seriously damaged their ability to pressure the American government to support the creation of a Jewish state. There were some efforts to bring the CJA into the fold, but they foundered on Bergson's unwillingness to submit to the control of the community's leaders. Similarly, the AAEJ's divisive actions prevented the American Jewish community from presenting the unified front that it had so successfully maintained on other issues. Like the CJA, the AAEJ also tried to mend fences and joined the NJCRAC committee set up to monitor the situation in Ethiopia, but it later withdrew when it became clear that the committee was not prepared to take the action the AAEJ believed necessary to save the Jews. In this case, unity was not as crucial as it was during World War II, since there was much less the United States could do for the Ethiopian Jews than it could for European Jews and on behalf of the Zionists.

Nevertheless, author Henry Feingold's judgment regarding the politics of rescue relating to the Holocaust might be just as aptly applied to the politics of saving the Ethiopian Jews:

> A communal base for unified action simply did not exist. Instead there was fragmentation, lack of coherence in the message projected to policymakers, profound disagreement on what might be done in the face of the crisis, and strife among the leaders of the myriad political and religious factions which constituted the community. It may well be that the assumption of contemporary historians that there existed a single Jewish community held together by a common sense of history and a desire for joint enterprise is the product of a messianic imagination.[18]

Another similarity between the establishment's attitude toward the two gadfly organizations was the effort to discredit them. The mainstream groups went to greater extremes, however, to undermine the CJA than the AAEJ. The Zionists, for example, tried to arrange for Bergson to be drafted or deported. No such action could be taken against Lenhoff or the other members of the AAEJ, but there was a conscious effort to "take the play away from the AAEJ" by condemning sensational publicity and unrealistic rescue proposals as dangerous and counterproductive and by issuing their own propaganda that supported the Israeli line.[19]

THE ORTHODOX POSITION

Another of the surprising differences between the response of American Jews to the Holocaust and that of the plight of Ethiopian Jews was the outspokenness of the Orthodox Jews to the former and their silence with regard to the latter. In 1943, for example, elaborate plans were made to convene a conference of all American Jewish organizations to develop a common program to address the postwar problems of world Jewry. The Union of Orthodox Rabbis and Agudath Israel of America withdrew from the conference because of the failure to place rescue on the conference agenda. The union called on the conference to issue a "powerful outcry over the destruction of the Jewish people and demand immediate means for the rescue of Jewish lives."[20]

In contrast, Orthodox organizations were at best silent and, at worst, hostile toward the rescue of Ethiopian Jewry. Of course, no one questioned the Jewishness of the European Jews, but there remained doubts about the Ethiopian Jews even after the Israeli chief rabbi, Ovadia Yossef, officially acknowledged their authenticity. For example, eight years after Rabbi Yossef's ruling, Rabbi Moshe Sherer, the chairman of Agudath Israel, wrote: "Our organization has a long record of helping troubled people and using every possible conduit to rescue Jews [but] my hands are tied at this present time because of the *halachic* [Jewish law] issues involved concerning the Falashas, which to my regret have not as yet been resolved or clarified for me."[21]

Another rabbi, Shlomo Klass, the publisher of *The Jewish Press* (which is advertised as the "largest independent Anglo-Jewish Weekly in the world"), was even more blunt when he said that the Falashas are not Jews. When a correspondent raised the issue, Klass suggested that he "join a Torah education class or enter a Yeshiva, then you'll begin to understand what our religion is."[22] This patronizing attitude was typical of the Orthodox establishment, more so in the United States than in Israel, and was a persistent impediment to aiding the Ethiopian Jews in the 1970s and 1980s. As we will see in the last chapter, American Orthodox opinions have now changed completely.

Perhaps the most important contribution made by both the CJA and the AAEJ was to keep the rescue issue on the Jewish community's agenda and to stimulate the establishment to act. For example, the CJA's plans for large demonstrations led the American Jewish Congress to schedule its own demonstration.[23] The AAEJ's persistent propaganda helped to stimulate the formation of the NJCRAC committee and eventually forced the establishment to take a more active role in speaking out on the Ethiopian Jewry issue.

During World War II, the American Jewish leadership believed that "quiet diplomacy" was the best tactic to use in the effort to rescue Jews and did not realize until late in the war that their efforts were not having any results.[24] Israel carried out a similar policy of silence with regard to the rescue of Ethiopian Jews and urged American Jews to support that policy, and the leadership did. However, the CJA and AAEJ believed that their respective situations were so desperate that more visible campaigns were necessary to encourage rescue activities. In the postwar period, there was the precedent of the public campaign for the emigration of Soviet Jews; however, both the AAEJ and the establishment eschewed a similar strategy on behalf of Ethiopian Jews because of the perception that the Ethiopian government was unaffected by public criticism, whereas the Soviet Union was very sensitive to American (particularly congressional) opinion. This assumption may have been incorrect.

HELP FROM CONGRESS

One of the strategies the establishment did pursue in the 1940s was to enlist the support of Congress for rescue activities. The Joint Emergency Committee on European Affairs (JEC), like NJCRAC, was an umbrella organization comprising the major Zionist organizations, excluding the CJA. In 1943, the JEC tried to persuade Congress to go on record in support of rescue but had no success because Congress was unwilling to challenge the Roosevelt administration's claims that rescue was either impossible or a hindrance to the war effort, and that everything that could be done was being done.[25]

The NJCRAC committee did not seek assistance from Congress on the Ethiopian Jewry issue, but the AAEJ did and was successful in getting resolutions passed, hearings convened, and pressure exerted on the executive branch despite what it considered NJCRAC's attempt to sabotage its efforts. There was very little, practically, that Congress could do in the case of Ethiopian Jews, but what little it could do, it did. On the other hand, Congress could have pressured the administration to take any number of steps to facilitate the rescue of European Jews during World War II but did nothing except adopt an insignificant resolution condemning Nazi atrocities.

There is also a somewhat paradoxical comparison that can be drawn between the behavior of the presidents during the two periods. Franklin Roosevelt, the architect of the New Deal and a symbol of humanitarianism, failed to act to save the European Jews. One incident is particularly illustrative of Roosevelt's attitude. In 1939, the *S.S. St. Louis*, filled with more than nine hundred Jewish men, women, and children who had escaped from Hitler's Germany, was prevented from landing in Cuba and sailed up and down the coast of the United States in the hope that the Americans would permit them to land and find refuge. Instead, the president sent Coast Guard cutters to prevent the ship from landing or any of its passengers from making their way to shore. By contrast, Ronald Reagan, a man vilified by liberals for his lack of humanitarianism, took decisive action in approving Operation Sheba to save a group of Ethiopian Jews, despite the risk to American security interests.

Historian David Wyman suggests that Roosevelt might have been persuaded to institute a rescue program if the American Zionist Emergency Council (AZEC) had pressured the administration. The AZEC, the precursor to the American Israel Public Affairs Committee (AIPAC), had been founded to serve as a political lobby on behalf of the Zionists and proved to be very effective in obtaining support for their program. Rather than lobby on behalf of rescue, however, the AZEC concentrated its energies on the drive for a Jewish state.[26] In succeeding years, AIPAC has become the most powerful foreign policy lobby in Washington and the dominant force among American Jewish organizations. Had its lobbyists weighed in on behalf of the Ethiopian Jews, the AAEJ's task on Capitol Hill would have certainly been easier; nevertheless, the fact that AIPAC did not join the other establishment organizations in fighting against the AAEJ was seen by Shapiro as a positive act. Even with AIPAC's support, the U.S. government probably could not have done a great deal more to help the Ethiopian Jews; however, the influence that AIPAC's members have with Israeli officials might have been used to press them to take more vigorous action.

WHAT DID THEY KNOW?

In recent years, a great deal of research has been done to try to understand why the Jews of Europe were not saved from Hitler's "final solution." The American Jewish community has been widely criticized for its failure to speak out forcefully on the issue and demand action from the U.S. government and its allies. One of the excuses that was long given for this failure was that American Jews did not know what was happening to their brethren in Europe. In an effort to find out what was known, Deborah Lipstadt conducted an exhaustive review of the press accounts during the Holocaust.[27] She found that journalists may not have known just how bad things were, but they did know that the situation was very grave. The information that was published, even reports of millions of Jews having been killed, was often buried on the inner pages of the newspapers. Coverage in the Jewish press was more complete, however, and American Jewish leaders had access to information that indicated the magnitude of the catastrophe in Europe. The truth is that these leaders did react to the news they received. The argument today, with the benefit of hindsight, is whether they did as much as they could have.

In the case of the American Jewish establishment's attitude toward the Ethiopian Jews, similar questions can be raised as to whether enough was done. The claim cannot be made that they did not know. As far back as the late 1950s, reports were issued detailing the deteriorating condition of the Ethiopian Jewish community, and by the early 1970s, the danger signals were becoming increasingly clear. Louis Rapoport reported in April 1974, for example, that it might be a difficult time to press for *aliyah*, "but it may also be the last chance to save Ethiopia's Jews."[28] A prominent Jewish leader, Israel Goldstein, wrote to Graenum Berger in 1976 that the Ethiopian Jews' plight "is a standing indictment of the sins of omission primarily by the J.D.C. and the Jewish Agency."[29]

The American Jewish organizations did not send missions to Ethiopia until late in the game—in the early 1980s—and those were primarily designed to refute the AAEJ's propaganda. Nevertheless, the people on those trips did come back with information as to the plight of the Ethiopian Jews, and even if they did not accept the characterization of their situation as a holocaust, no one could challenge the fact that the Jewish predicament was serious. The tragedy was that the organizations did not ameliorate their plight and were content to wait for Israel's quiet diplomacy to take its course.

In 1982, NJCRAC chairman Bennett Yanowitz said that the Ethiopian Jewry problem evokes "echoes of the European Holocaust": "Painfully we are reminded of the world's dereliction for not having attacked the problem until recently. Ethiopian Jews languished while the world and the Jewish community paid attention to a host of other urgent issues over the last forty years. No one is immune from this charge of not having called attention to the urgent need to rescue the Falashas."[30] In truth, many people did call attention to the plight of the Ethiopian Jews, but the establishment had no interest until the issue had reached the point where it was being referred to as a holocaust. The tragedy is that it took so long for the mainstream Jewish organizations to listen and take action. Once the issue did become a high priority for Israel, and the conditions for liberation were favorable, the rescue was carried out with efficiency and daring.

NOTES

1. Anonymous, letter to Bernard Levy, May 30, 1982.

2. Rabbi Yosef Adane, interview with author.

3. Human Rights Violations in Ethiopia Amnesty International, London, 1983, p. 32; November 1978 edition, pp. 15–16.

4. Aide memoire of meeting convened by Ralph Goldman, December 12, 1978.

5. Tudor Parfitt, *Operation Moses* (England: Weidenfeld and Nicolson, 1985), pp. 38–39.

6. Dvora Waysman, "The Falashas," World Zionist Press Service, September 1, 1979.

7. Graenum Berger, notes on meeting with representatives from the Israeli consulate and Jewish organizations, May 21, 1979.

8. U.S. Department of State, "U.S. State Department Reports on Human Rights Practices," Washington, D.C., February 2, 1981, p. 89; February 1982, p. 88; December 25, 1983, pp. 104–105.

9. Michael Winn, "Falashas: Doomed to Extinction?" *National Jewish Monthly* (May 1981): p. 10.

10. "Report of NJCRAC Mission to Ethiopia," NJCRAC, March 10–26, 1982.

11. David Kessler, "The Falashas—The Jews of Ethiopia: An Almost Forgotten Community," IJA Research Reports (London: Institute of Jewish Afffairs, February 1983).

12. Nate Shapiro, interview with author.

13. Bert Silver, "Still Shrouded in Controversy: Ethiopian Jewry's Rescue," *Washington Jewish Week,* January 2, 1986. Silver was a member of the AAEJ.

14. Barbara Gaffin, interview with author.

15. Glenn Stein, interview with author.

16. David Wyman, *The Abandonment of the Jews* (NY: Pantheon Books, 1984), pp. 86–87.

17. Ibid., p. 346.

18. Henry Feingold, *The Politics of Rescue* (Holocaust Library, 1970), p. 322.

19. Irving Kessler, letter to members of United Israel Appeal Board of Directors and Trustees, April 16, 1982.

20. Wyman, *Abandonment of the Jews,* p. 162.

21. Rabbi Moshe Sherer, letter to Edith and Henry Everett, December 16, 1981.

22. Rabbi Shlomo Klass, letter to Mr. Klayman, August 27, 1981.

23. Wyman, *Abandonment of the Jews,* p. 87.

24. Seymour Finger, *American Jewry During the Holocaust* (England: Holmes & Meier, 1984), p. 17.

25. Wyman, *Abandonment of the Jews,* pp. 94–95.

26. Ibid., pp. 172, 175.

27. Deborah Lipstadt, *Beyond Belief* (NY: The Free Press, 1986).

28. Louis Rapoport, "The Falashas," *Jerusalem Post Magazine*, April 12, 1974.

29. Israel Goldstein, letter to Graenum Berger, April 12, 1976.

30. Bennett Yanowitz, chairman NJCRAC, address to plenary session, Houston, Texas, January 1982.

CHAPTER 11

The Situation Today

One of the difficult aspects of the entire story of the Ethiopian Jews has been to determine the size of the population. From the beginning, the estimates were no more than guesses, and after each rescue operation, still more Jews were discovered. After Operation Solomon, Israeli officials and most activists believed it had brought all but a handful of the Ethiopian Jews to Israel. They discovered later that roughly six thousand Jews had been stranded in Ethiopia's remote Kwara region. In addition, thousands of Ethiopians whom no one had thought were Jewish suddenly claimed they were Jews and demanded that Israel help them immigrate. Activists soon took up their cause, and just when most thought the fate of the Beta Israel had been resolved, the entire debate began again. As before, at the heart of the conflict was the question of the Jewishness of a group called the Falash Mura.

THE FALASH MURA

As we saw in chapter 1, Ethiopian Jews had been the targets of Christian missionaries for many decades. When the missionary activity intensified at the end of the nineteenth century, large numbers of the Beta Israel community converted to Christianity. From approximately that time until Israel began to actively help the Jews immigrate, members of the Beta Israel community had abandoned their faith. Some did so because they were pressured or persuaded by the missionaries, others responded to social pressure, and some may have viewed conversion as a way to improve their economic condition (for example, they could then own land). These people who had once been Jews, or, more often, whose ancestors had been Jews, are referred to as the Falash Mura.

The origin of the term "Falash Mura" is unclear. A census of converts was conducted in the early 1980s in Ethiopia, and the Jew who helped with the work called them *faras muqra*, an Arabic phrase that literally means "crow horses." Another explanation was that the term came from the Agau and means "someone who changes their faith."[1] The Falash Mura did not refer to themselves as Beta Israel until after the Jews had begun to immigrate to Israel.[2] The Falash Mura were virtually unknown until Operation Solomon, when a number attempted to board the Israeli planes and were turned away. The Falash Mura said they were entitled to immigrate because they were Jews by ancestry, but the Israelis saw them as non-Jews, since most had never practiced Judaism and were not considered by the Beta Israel as part of the community.

THE JEWISH QUESTION

Israel has had a number of famous court cases where the question of "who is a Jew" was adjudicated. The most famous involved Brother Daniel (born Oswald Rufeisen), a Jew who converted to Christianity during the Holocaust and had become a Carmelite monk. During his youth, Rufeisen was active in a Zionist youth movement and fled to Vilna, Lithuania, at the start of World War II. There he worked as a slave laborer and escaped to Mir, where he worked for the police as a translator. Rufeisen took advantage of his position and smuggled arms to his Jewish friends and helped drive the police out from Mir before it was liquidated, saving nearly three hundred Jews. Rufeisen hid in the forest and later a convent, where he decided to convert to Christianity. In 1962, Rufeisen, now Brother Daniel, applied to immigrate to Israel, and after being denied, he appealed to the Israeli Supreme Court. The Supreme Court ruled that despite the fact he was born to a Jewish mother, he had since converted and should not be recognized as a Jew by the State of Israel. Following the Brother Daniel case, a new regulation was adopted stating that individuals registered as Jews for the "nationality" and "religion" section of their identity cards must be Jews according to *halacha*, and they must not practice another religion.

Although the Falash Mura did not seem any more Jewish than Brother Daniel, and maybe less so, Ethiopian Jewry activists, primarily from the North American Conference on Ethiopian Jewry (NACOEJ), saw the situation differently. They maintained that the Falash Mura had been forced to convert or had done so for pragmatic reasons without ever really abandoning their

Jewish faith. NACOEJ began to provide aid to the group in Addis Ababa that had not returned to their homes after being left behind during Operation Solomon. Once food and medical care became available, more Falash Mura left their villages for Addis and soon began to overload the meager resources of NACOEJ. The Joint Distrubtion Committee (JDC) entered the picture and provided additional assistance on a humanitarian basis, without accepting the NACOEJ contention that they were Jews entitled to go to Israel.

As the number of Falash Mura in Addis grew, the Israeli position hardened. The official view was that these people were not Jews and, if they had ever been Jews, it was in the distant past. Most were now practicing Christians who simply wanted to get out of Ethiopia by any means possible and saw an opportunity to escape by claiming to be Jewish and thereby earning the right to immigrate to Israel. The Israelis were convinced this motivation would encourage tens of thousands, perhaps most of the Ethiopian population to claim Jewish heritage. The Israeli government was simply not going to absorb the entire Ethiopian population.

The Israeli government found an unexpected ally in this view in the American Association for Ethiopian Jews (AAEJ). Graenum Berger did not believe the Falash Mura were Jews. He went so far as to say he had evidence they had denied aid to the Ethiopian Jews and reported them to the authorities when they tried to escape to the Sudan. Echoing the Israelis, Berger said, "If one wanted to go back far enough in Ethiopian history and consider the descendants of everyone who had converted (voluntarily or forcibly), you could make a case that the majority of the Ethiopian population was 'Jewish,' and should be allowed to emigrate to Israel." Berger added that support for the Falash Mura should come from members of their families and the Christian community.[3]

AAEJ: MISSION ACCOMPLISHED

In 1993, the AAEJ did something quite remarkable for a Jewish organization (or any other nonprofit agency for that matter) and voted to dissolve itself. The AAEJ's board decided that its mission was to rescue the Jews of Ethiopia and members believed that had been accomplished, so no reason remained for them to continue to exist. Some members thought the organization should shift its focus to helping the Ethiopians in Israel, but this was viewed as a different goal, one that should now be the primary responsibility of the Israeli government and native Israelis. It would also require far greater resources than the AAEJ had ever raised. Several members of the AAEJ, nevertheless, founded a new organization in 1993, the Israel Association for Ethiopian Jews (IAEJ). This Israel-based organization was created "to work toward the full and rapid integration of Ethiopian Jews into mainstream Israeli society, to open new educational opportunities for Ethiopian immigrant children and youth and to prevent the development of a black underclass in Israel."

By contrast, the members of NACOEJ believed the Falash Mura were Jews, so the job of rescue was not yet complete. They were not content to provide the Falash Mura with basic necessities. From their perspective, the Falash Mura were no different from the Marranos of Spain, who practiced Christianity to save themselves from the Inquisition but retained a Jewish identity. The Falash Mura also viewed themselves as Jews who just needed help to reconnect with their faith. Given the opportunity, the activists argued, they would become practicing Jews.

The Israelis also disagreed with the NACOEJ. They maintained the Falash Mura were committed Christian believers who were being coached to behave like Jews for the sole purpose of getting out of the country. After all, if they were interested in returning to Judaism, why did they wait until it became clear this was a way to escape? The official line was that given the opportunity the Falash Mura would abandon any pretense of being Jews as soon as they arrived in Israel. One Israeli diplomat said NACOEJ believes "anyone who is poor and miserable should be helped, but it's wrong to dump them on Israel. We have no responsibility to third or fourth generation Christians."[4] Although the Jewish establishment in the United States accepted the Israeli government's view, the growing numbers of Falash Mura in Addis Ababa became increasingly embarrassing. Activists pointed to thousands of poor, starving, sick people who wished only to go to Israel; hence the argument over their authenticity became secondary to their welfare.

The Israeli government set up a committee in 1992 to resolve the question of the Falash Mura. The committee discovered that two thousand had succeeded in reaching Israel during Operation Solomon. Some of these people had already demonstrated they had at least one Jewish grandparent and therefore qualified under the Law of Return for automatic citizenship. Some Falash Mura were also allowed to immigrate on the basis of family reunification. Thus, for example, if an Ethiopian Jew married a non-Jew, they would be allowed to bring the non-Jewish spouse's parents with them to Israel. Jews from other countries were usually not permitted to do this. The committee, headed by Absorption Minister Yair Tsaban, decided the Falash Mura should not be allowed to enter Israel under the Law of Return but nevertheless recommended that the refugees in Addis be allowed to come on humanitarian grounds.

About the same time, Rabbi Menachem Waldman began providing instruction in Jewish studies to the Falash Mura in the NACOEJ camps. JDC did not support the project because the organization believed Waldman was raising expectations that the Falash Mura would all be allowed to immigrate when that was not necessarily the case. Waldman also was submitting lists of people to Israel whom he believed qualified to make *aliyah*. The process was slow, however, and few of the people on the list reached Israel. Finally, in 1997, a decision was reached by all the organizations involved with the Falash Mura—the Israeli government, JDC, and NACOEJ—that a solution was needed to empty the compounds so no more people would come. The government agreed to a one-time humanitarian gesture to bring to Israel everyone in Addis with some connection to the "seed of Israel." Afterward, the camps were to be closed and future immigration was to be based on the criteria used for immigration from all other countries. The government agreed that the Falash Mura would be allowed to come to Israel.[5]

Israel decided the four thousand Falash Mura then in the capital would be brought to Israel in groups rather than all at once. Although most did not enter under the Law of Return, they received all the benefits of immigrants who did.[6] The only other people who were brought en masse to Israel in such a humanitarian gesture were refugees from Kosovo and the Vietnamese boat people. In 1998, Prime Minister Benjamin Netanyahu declared the evacuation of the Falash Mura complete. From that point on Ethiopians would only be allowed to immigrate on the basis of the Law of Return.

The Israeli government's humanitarian gesture stimulated more Falash Mura to come to Addis in expectation of similar treatment. After an initial estimate of fewer than ten thousand Falash Mura, the number soon ballooned to more than thirty thousand. As more arrived, conditions worsened, the embarrassment intensified, and the activists called for additional humanitarian steps. They also began to accuse the Israeli government of the same callousness and prejudice that the AAEJ had attributed to it in the 1970s and early 1980s. Even the rhetoric had seemed familiar as NACOEJ and others began to describe the situation as a "holocaust."

DOUBLE STANDARDS

Activists questioned why the government was looking so closely at the Jewishness of the Falash Mura while turning a blind eye to the background of immigrants from the former Soviet Union. Reports suggested as many as one-half of those immigrants were not really Jews, but this did not seem to affect their immigration.[7] Some activists even suggested that the difference in treatment had to do with race.[8] This charge rankled Israeli officials even more than in the past. Before they would point to having brought in other dark-skinned peoples from places like Yemen to prove race was irrelevant to their decisions; now they could point to to roughly seventy thousand Jews they had already accepted from Ethiopia.

Ironically, the Israeli public felt much more tolerant and enthusiastic about the Ethiopian Jews than the Russians. Any discomfort that the Israelis have with the Ethiopians has more to do with the cultural chasm than race. This is largely offset by the respect Israelis have for what they see as the genuine Zionist impulse of the Ethiopians. The Beta Israel dreamed of returning to their homeland and that is what motivated them to come to Israel. Paradoxically, it is the Russians that the public views as coming to Israel merely to escape the conditions in their country. Israelis realize that most Russians would have preferred to immigrate to the United States than Israel but were not allowed to because of U.S. quotas and pressure exerted on Americans to force them to go to Israel. The Ethiopian Jews, however, wanted only to go to Israel.

To address the question of their Jewishness, the activists began to educate the Falash Mura in Addis and formally convert them. According to Daniel Friedman, all the Falash Mura could be converted, which would be "the first time in two thousand years of post-biblical history that Judaism would be organizing a process of a mass collective religious conversion of people who, having more or less embraced Christianity, were now returning to Judaism."[9]

PRESSURE BUILDS ON ISRAEL

By June 1998, the Jewish Agency had processed all the original cases dating back to 1991 and brought the eligible Falash Mura to Israel. The JDC closed its compound and considered the issue resolved. At Israel's request, NACOEJ also agreed to end its relief activities. According to Israeli officials, however, activists then sent messages to remaining Falash Mura, encouraging them to hurry to Gondar and Addis before they missed the last plane to Israel. During the summer the number of Falash Mura again swelled, with eight thousand relocating to Addis and seven thousand to Gondar. Michael Schneider, JDC executive vice president, observed:

> They were encouraged to uproot from a self-sufficient agricultural lifestyle and put themselves into an extremely hazardous situation. Now, they're urban slum-dwellers. The activists in Israel and America and relatives helped put these 15,000 lives at risk. They took a gamble. They hoped public opinion would force the Israel government to take them in . . . but really didn't consider the consequences if the Israel Government didn't go along with their plan. And now, those same activists and relatives are turning to the American Jewish community to save the 15,000 lives they themselves helped put at risk.

Despite this conclusion, JDC did provide some emergency aid to the Falash Mura, although activists complained the amount was paltry.

While the Israelis still believed the Falash Mura were seeking an escape from life in Ethiopia and were being encouraged by activists to leave their villages, NACOEJ and others insisted the Falash Mura were being forced to leave their homes by their Christian neighbors. NACOEJ's director Barbara Ribacove and journalist/activist Yossi Abramowitz visited Ethiopia and returned with stories of pogroms. Horrifying tales were recounted of villages where Falash Mura tukuls were burnt to the ground and a six-year-old girl was burned alive by a band of anti-Semites. NACOEJ used these reports to justify reneging on its agreement with Israel and continuing its operations in Ethiopia.

The JDC then sent Ami Bergman to investigate the reports. Bergman returned with an entirely different version of events. He was told, for example, that the little girl who died was killed years earlier by a stray shell during the civil war. Bergman also visited the village where the tukuls were torched and learned the incident had nothing to do with anti-Semitism and really was an act of vengeance by someone who had been cheated in a business transaction involving the sale of the tukuls. Adisu Massala, an Ethiopian Jew and member of the Israeli Knesset who also went on the fact-finding trip, said he found no evidence the Falash Mura were being persecuted as Jews.[10]

Israel also maintained that the Falash Mura and their supporters were engaged in a variety of activities that were creating problems, including submitting fraudulent applications, swapping children from one family to another to broaden direct ties to the Falash Mura already in Israel, paying brokers to arrange for Christians to marry Falash Mura to qualify for immigration and changing their family histories in hopes of satisfying the Law of Return. Reports even surfaced of Falash Mura teenage girls being raped by men who believed having a "Falasha" child would make them eligible to immigrate to Israel.[11]

NO END IN SIGHT

The dilemma surrounding the Falash Mura has persisted into the new millennium, with activists claiming that nearly thirty thousand Falash Mura still hoped to immigrate. As the Israeli officials maintained, the numbers have continued to grow, even after accepting several thousand in the 1990s. "It's not so much a spiritual longing," Israel's ambassador to Ethiopia said in reference to the Falash Mura's interest in immigration, "it's an economic refuge."[12] Ironically, the Orthodox Jewish establishment has come to the defense of the Falash Mura. The Rabbinical Council of America, an umbrella group for American Orthodox Jews, called on Israel "to facilitate the rapid *aliyah* of the entire Falash Mura community."[13] Orthodox Jews, who for so many years said the Beta Israel were not Jews, have now said Jewish law holds that repentant Jews, even those who converted to another faith, should be welcomed back to Judaism.

One of the obstacles Israel put up was to require the Falash Mura to apply for permission to immigrate through a relative already in Israel. Activists challenged the requirement and the Israeli Supreme Court ruled that the Interior Ministry had to take applications directly from the Falash Mura in

Ethiopia. Israel subsequently sent additional people to consider applications, but the process is time-consuming because most of the Falash Mura have no documents, and their eligibility has to be verified by field research.

Tensions between advocates and Israelis heightened in the spring of 2000 when Israeli officials asked American Jewry to contribute $50 million toward the resettlement of the Falash Mura. Yuli Tamir, Israel's minister of absorption, said the government would not accelerate the immigration process without a financial commitment from American Jews. Tamir insisted that without funding from abroad, Israel would be unable to provide for their needs. The response of the Americans was that they were prepared to help but could not begin a serious fundraising effort until Israel expedited the immigration process. Activists also were upset that conditions were being placed on helping the Ethiopians. "American support is not a precondition for anyone coming from the former Soviet Union, and it wasn't a precondition for the Yemenites before them," said Ted Friedman of Americans for Peace Now.[14]

Throughout most of the debate on the Falash Mura, the major American Jewish organizations have done little. Their behavior has been similar to that regarding the Beta Israel before the rescues. It was not until November 2000 that the community's umbrella organization, the United Jewish Communities (UJC), sent a delegation to Ethiopia and issued a report on the Falash Mura. The report took no position on the religious status of the Falash Mura and did not say whether American Jewry should do more to help them. The report suggested conditions in Ethiopia were not as bad as the activists claimed, although the Falash Mura still were "at risk."[15]

Early in the new millenium, then, the Israelis find themselves in a no-win situation. They do not want to simply accept unlimited immigration from Ethiopia. They are convinced that tens of thousands, perhaps hundreds of thousands of Ethiopians will claim Jewish heritage if they do not follow strict procedures for determining eligibility to immigrate. In the meantime, the large numbers of Falash Mura who settled in camps in Gondar and Addis have created a severe humanitarian problem. They need jobs, shelter, and food. These needs cannot be ignored, but at the same time, if better services are provided, it will only attract more Falash Mura to the camps. Although the situation is difficult, the JDC maintains that the death rate among the Falash Mura in the camps is lower than among the general population.[16]

The Falash Mura are also in an impossible situation. While Jews virtually everywhere else in the world stay in their homes until they are given permission to immigrate, the Ethiopians uprooted themselves and have nowhere to go. Their land, cattle, and homes have been bought or confiscated by their neighbors. It no longer matters why they left, whether by force, coercion or encouragement from activists, they are now living as urban slum dwellers. They will either be cared for by humanitarian organizations, allowed to immigrate to Israel, live a subsistence existence, or die.

As of this writing, nearly twenty thousand Falash Mura remain in camps in Gondar and Addis. Approximately eight thousand live in their villages near the camps. A UJC mission found that the nutritional value of their diet was low and hunger existed, but they were not starving. The group also said the Falash Mura's health is better than the average Ethiopian, but characterized the population as at risk. JDC is providing some emergency aid, but NACOEJ remains the principal supplier of relief. Even that group came under attack in December 2000. An Ethiopian Jewish organization in Addis circulated a report accusing NACOEJ of human rights violations, physical and psychological abuse, and labor exploitation. NACOEJ dismissed the report as the work of disgruntled ex-employees.[17] Meanwhile, the Israelis here accelerated their consideration of applications. The first priority is being given to divided families, then those eligible under the Law of Return, and finally humanitarian or rare special cases. About one of three applicants are found to be eligible.[18]

Ethiopian Jews in Israel continue to have mixed feelings about the Falash Mura. Some feel resentment because they maintained their identity despite the pressures and opportunities while the Falash Mura did not. Others have relatives among the Falash Mura and want to be reunited. Meanwhile, Israeli officials say many of the Falash Mura reverted to their Christian ways as soon as they reached Israel, while the activists insist the opposite is true, that most have converted back to Judaism.

JEWS OF KWARA

While the controversy has swirled around the Falash Mura, another group of Ethiopians, whose Jewishness was never in question, also sought help and approval to immigrate to Israel. These were Jews living in the remote Kwara region near the border of the Sudan. The estimated 6,000 Kwara Jews never made the trek to the refugee camps of the Sudan or joined the exodus from Addis Ababa. Since rebels controlled the area in 1991, they were unable to reach Addis in time for Operation Solomon. As a result, they were left behind. A year after Operation Solomon, about 3,500 Jews from Upper Kwara managed to immigrate, but approximately 2,500 in Lower Kwara remained stranded.[19]

Few people knew of the existence of the Kwara Jews until 1998. When their plight became known, activists called on Israel to expeditiously arrange for their immigration. One obstacle was the reluctance of the Kwara Jews to move to areas of Ethiopia, such as Gondar, where organizations such as the JDC and NACOEJ were helping the Falash Mura. One reason for their hesitation was the difficulty; traveling north to Gondar, for example, was a dangerous two hundred mile journey. The Kwara Jews were also afraid that if they went to the camps set up for the Falash Mura they would be identified with that controversial population and be prevented from going to Israel.

Interestingly, while most of the major Jewish organizations were reluctant to invest significant resources to help the Jews and the Falash Mura, non-Jews contributed large amounts of money through the Chicago-based International Fellowship of Christians and Jews. For example, that group pledged $2 million in 1999 to help cover the cost of absorbing the Kwara Jews.

The Jewish Agency brought about five hundred Kwara Jews to Israel in the first half of 1999, but the pace was too slow for activists who, once again, accused the Israelis of dragging their feet. A representative of the Interior Ministry was supposed to expedite the immigration process by conducting interviews and issuing visas, but the ministry claimed in May 1999 that its representatives were unable to reach the region because of fighting with the Eritreans. The advocates countered that the fighting was nowhere near where the Jews lived.[20] In June, the Jewish Agency announced that it was making the Kwara Jews a priority and Foreign Minister Ariel Sharon suggested mounting a new airlift. Sharon's idea were quickly rejected because of a concern with upsetting the Ethiopians, who were sensitive to creating the impression that conditions in their country were so bad people had to be rescued from it. The Ethiopians did indicate they were not opposed to moving the Jews out quietly on regularly scheduled Ethiopian Airlines flights.

Although the number of Jews was small, the plan was to bring them all to Israel over a period of forty weeks with one flight a week. The Jewish Agency began busing Jews from Kwara to Addis to wait for flights to Israel in June 1999. This leisurely pace became more problematic as the number of Jews dying while waiting in Gondar increased, and the war between Ethiopia and Eritrea intensified. The Israeli Ministry of Interior dispatched more agents to Ethiopia and began to accelerate the processing of the remaining Jews. Over the next twenty-two days, they issued permits to 1,135 people. In addition, the number of flights increased to twice a week. Over a period of thirty-seven days, 1,388 Jews were brought to Israel. The handful of remaining members of the Kwara community were ultimately brought to Israel in succeeding months. Although Israeli officials wanted to get credit for their actions, they decided to keep the operation quiet for fear of repeating the mistakes of the past and having publicity provoke the Ethiopians to shut it down. The *Jerusalem Post*, which subsequently detailed the mission, agreed to withhold information so as not to jeopardize the operation.[21]

Even without the controversy over their authenticity, the Kwara Jews also faced roadblocks. After Israel had accepted most of the Kwara Jews, about 170 stayed behind because the Israeli government insisted that they abandon their non-Jewish spouses. Although most of the couples had children, the authorities claimed the marriages were shams undertaken for the purpose of helping Gentiles reach Israel. In some cases, Jewish women were offered as brides to Gentiles in exchange for money needed by starving relatives; in others cases, they were taken by force. The Kwara Jews sometimes had to choose between going to Israel and leaving a spouse or a child behind.[22]

ADJUSTING TO ISRAEL

The Kwara Jews did enjoy some advantages by being the last to arrive from Ethiopia. First, many of them already had relatives in Israel to help them adjust to their new homes. Second, the absorption officials had learned from past mistakes and knew better how to handle the newcomers. Third, Ethiopian Jews who already had adjusted to life in Israel were increasingly involved in the absorption centers.

During the first week in Israel, each of the Kwara Jews was given a bank account, an identity card, and was registered for health insurance. Instead of being put in caravans, as most previous newcomers from Ethiopia had been, the Kwara Jews were given apartments. They also immediately began classes in Hebrew and were given a housing allowance—roughly $100 a month for a four-room apartment—and $5,000 for annual living expenses.[23]

Providing basic necessities only addressed some of the problems of socialization. The approximately seventy thousand Ethiopian Jews now in Israel have always faced great difficulties adjusting to life in their new homes. On the most basic level, they have had to cope with moving from the bottom economic rung of one of the most undeveloped countries in the world to a high-tech, developed country. People who never saw bathrooms or refrigerators or other conveniences suddenly had to receive crash courses in modern city living. According to Steve Kaplan, one of the leading authorities on the Beta Israel, "about 20 percent of the Ethiopian Jews are doing quite well, another 20 percent have dropped off the map and the rest are muddling along. More than half of all households have no one working, many are living on 'welfare.' They lack skills and live in the wrong towns with weak economies."[24] One problem is that Israel had very high unemployment throughout the 1990s, and the Ethiopians did not have the training, education, and Hebrew language proficiency to compete in the already constricted job market.

Education is a key to advancement in any society, but it has been especially difficult for the Ethiopians because of the level of illiteracy and because about half of the population is under 19. Children were falling behind their peers at an alarming rate, in the early 1990s with a dropout rate as high as 20 percent. By the end of the decade, however, the figure had fallen to around 7 percent compared to 3.5% for all Israelis. Similarly, the matriculation rate jumped from 7 percent in 1994 to 30 percent in 2001, but still lags behind the national average of 52 percent.[25] While earlier arrivals had most of their children sent off to boarding schools, more recent immigrants, such as the Kwara Jews, were given other choices, with religious schools still preferred over public, secular schools. An ongoing problem has been the inability of Ethiopian Jews to afford to send younger children to preschool. While 95 percent of Israeli children attend these schools, only 40 percent of Ethiopians do. This puts them at a disadvantage before even entering the educational system.

While children learn quickly, parents generally do not. This has created severe tensions within the patriarchal family structure whereby children have to help their parents more in their daily lives, and the parents and grand-parents are no longer the primary sources of a child's knowledge. The in-ability of the father, especially, to speak Hebrew can be extremely damaging to the family dynamic.

> The inability of the parents to speak Hebrew is not only considered a lack of skill but also denotes a lack of modernity in the eyes of the child. Also, seeing that the father's skills are irrelevant in the new setting and that he has no posi-tion of dominance in the family, many of the children ignore him; at worst, they remind him of his loss in status. . . . One social worker observed that "of all the immigrants, the father has lost the most."[26]

By contrast, the status of women has changed (in Western terms) for the better. Many of the traditional practices, such as the seclusion of women during their menstrual periods were abandoned. Ethiopian women have also assimilated more of Israel's social values, adopting a greater role in running the family and assuming more responsibility and autonomy in their inter-actions with people outside the family.

Housing has also been a difficult issue for the Ethiopian community. When the immigrants first arrived they were put in absorption centers and other temporary housing. They were not supposed to stay in these accommoda-tions for long, but many of the Beta Israel, particularly after the initial res-cues, found themselves in caravans and other nonpermanent housing for years. The government offered gifts and grants and mortgages worth up to $100,000, but it is difficult to find a home for this price in Israel, except in slums and poor neighborhoods. Most of the Beta Israel are now in perma-nent housing, but they are concentrated largely in poorer areas of develop-ment towns despite government efforts to avoid settling too many in economically deprived neighborhoods. Incidentally, contrary to Arab pro-paganda, Israel made no concerted effort to settle Ethiopian Jews (or any other immigrants) in the West Bank. The Ethiopians had no interest in living in the territories, preferred to stay with their extended families and clans, and were usually required to buy apartments in the center of the country.

The most troubling statistic regarding Ethiopian Jews has been a relatively high rate of suicide. The reasons are varied, including unemployment, con-cern for relatives still in Ethiopia, guilt over leaving loved ones behind, ill-ness, difficulty adjusting to life in Israel in general and the army, in particular, and personal problems. Suicide was not a problem in Ethiopia, and no one really knows what might trouble a given individual enough to take their own life. In recent years, however, the number of suicides has declined.

In the 1990s, a new issue emerged when it was discovered that many Ethiopian Jews had been exposed to the HIV virus. A furor erupted when reports disclosed that Israeli health officials were secretly destroying all the blood donated by Ethiopians for fear of its contamination. Thousands of Ethiopian Jews and their supporters turned out for a rally in front of the prime minister's office in January 1996 to protest the policy. The rally turned violent and bitter recriminations followed, resurrecting charges of racism against Israeli officials. David Bar-Ilan, former government spokesman and former editor of *Jerusalem Post*, argued that the policy was patronizing rather than racist:

> That the policy is not racist should be clear: The blood of such "high-risk" groups as homosexuals and drug addicts is also disqualified. And in fact, Ethiopian donations of rare blood types are not discarded but used after having been kept long enough to ascertain their safety. Had there been any prejudice against the donors per se, such donations would have also been disqualified. But the patronizing attitude with which the matter has been handled is clearly racist. Officials at Magen David Adom, the agency responsible for collecting blood donations, sought to avoid hurting Ethiopian donors' feelings. Instead of explaining why the blood in question could not be used, the health authorities told the Ethiopians nothing, while furtively discarding their blood. But this "white lie"—shared by hundreds of nurses and medics—was bound to be discovered, ultimately hurting Ethiopians' feelings far more acutely.[27]

Bar-Ilan said this condescending attitude was not uniquely directed at the Ethiopians; rather, it was a longstanding problem between veteran Israelis and newcomers from less developed countries.

A few months after the disclosure of the blood dumping, a state commission recommended an end to the wholesale dumping of blood donated by the Beta Israel and proposed strict guidelines for screening blood from Ethiopian Jews and other high-risk groups. The Ethiopian Jews were upset that no one was punished for discarding their blood, but the issue died down. One interesting aspect of the episode was the lack of reaction by other Israelis to the threat of AIDS. The public did not panic over the possibility that the disease was being imported from Africa with the Ethiopians.

Issues relating to religion also have remained persistent irritants to the smooth assimilation of Ethiopians into Israeli society. When Ethiopian Jews first arrived in Israel, they were required to undergo a conversion ceremony that included ritual immersion, the acceptance of rabbinic law (the oral tradition that had been unknown to them in Ethiopia) and, in the case of men, symbolic circumcision. Reluctantly, most Ethiopians accepted these demands, but resistance gradually grew. In 1985, a group of Beta Israel camped out in front of the chief rabbinate's headquarters for two months to protest the policy. The Beta Israel believed the requirements were degrading and denied their Jewishness. The demand for circumcision was subsequently dropped.

Israeli rabbis refused to marry couples, however, unless they both agreed to immersion in a ritual bath. In 1989, opposition to this decision ultimately led the Israeli Supreme Court to appoint the Sephardi Chief Rabbi of Netanya, Rabbi David Chelouche, as marriage registrar for all the Beta Israel. He did not require any symbolic conversion and Ethiopians married under his auspices were fully accepted as Jews. Ethiopians who insisted, however, on being married by their own priests found that their ceremonies were not recognized by the state. This highlighted the problem of the recognition of the Ethiopian *kessim*. In Ethiopia, these priests had been among the most influential members of the community and were responsible for all religious observance. Because of their unfamiliarity with rabbinic tradition, the *kessim* were denied the authority by the Israeli rabbinate to perform sacred duties. This caused a sense of alienation for both the priests and their communities. Some Ethiopians have made an effort to study the traditions and earn recognition by the rabbinate. In 1995, the first twelve Ethiopian Jews were ordained as rabbis. Efforts have also been made by the government and rabbinate to include Ethiopian priests on local religious councils.

The good news is that as the years have passed, the immigrants who have been in the country the longest have had increasing success in joining the mainstream of Israeli society. Growing numbers of Ethiopian Jews are entering universities and the first doctors and lawyers have begun to graduate. Ethiopians have reached high ranks in the military (95 percent serve compared to 80 percent of native Israelis[28]), a vital achievement for earning respect and promising future careers in Israel. "The army is a lifesaver by forcing absorption," Israeli diplomat Avi Granot said.[29] While most Israeli women also serve in the military, very few female Ethiopians have served, in part because most attend religious schools where their classmates usually claim exemptions.

In 1996, the first Ethiopian Jew was elected to the Knesset, and another Ethiopian Jew was given a consular appointment in the Israeli consulate in Chicago. By and large, however, the Ethiopians have not been successful in creating a unified political front to press for their interests in the way that the Russian immigrants have. The Beta Israel, said Granot, "came from a 2000-year-old feudal system and they didn't realize they had rights of their own. If you don't stand up for your rights, you can be forgotten."[30] In January 2000, the Israeli government announced a major new project to provide job training, education, and other assistance to the Beta Israel. The International Fellowship for Christians and Jews donated $10 million toward the cost of the project. Rabbi Yechiel Eckstein, director of the group, said: "I do believe deeply that if Israel doesn't make an effort in the coming years to get Ethiopians better integrated into society, then the country will have created a black underclass, prejudice, and racism, and a disaster for the Ethiopian community."[31]

The other side of assimilation is the loss of the distinctive Ethiopian culture. Although Ethiopians still celebrate their holidays (the festival of Siggud is now recognized by the entire state education system) and several Ethiopian synagogues have been constructed, they have been drawn more and more into the mainstream practice of (primarily Orthodox) Judaism. Because they never wrote anything down, their history and tradition are being lost. Efforts have been made to record the oral history from the community elders, but the Beta Israel are being drawn into the melting pot.

CONCLUSION

The final major operation, involving the Kwara Jews, encapsulated much of the story of the politics behind the rescue of the Ethiopian Jews. This small group of Jews had been left behind inadvertently but was largely ignored for at least six years. Not enough people were lobbying on their behalf early on to pressure the Israeli government to act. The government also had good reasons for not doing more: The Eritrean-Ethiopian war created political and logistical problems; the Kwara Jews were in no immediate need of rescue; and the Ethiopians were sensitive about a large group of their citizens leaving the country. Advocates also saw a repetition of many of the familiar artificial obstacles, such as a reluctance to send enough emissaries to provide visas. As in the earlier cases, the government ultimately acted and did so with great efficiency. Unlike the dramatic airlifts, however, the government never received much credit for bringing the Kwara Jews to Israel because the operation was overshadowed by the ongoing controversy surrounding the Falash Mura. In spite of all the criticism, Israel's approach to the Beta Israel has been remarkable. "The absorption of the Ethiopians into Israeli society marks a unique attempt to incorporate a non-white group as equal citizens with full rights as part of the dominant population in a western, predominantly white country. As such it represents an ambitious attempt to deny the significance of race (in the sense of color) and assert the primacy of national identity-religion (specifically Judaism)."[32]

Prejudice and racism have, in fact not been a significant problem for the Ethiopians in Israel. On the contrary, they are quite popular. It is common, especially among the better educated, for Ethiopians to marry other Israelis. In one case where an Ethiopian Jew in the army was turned away from an infirmary, apparently because he was black, he received an apology and a meeting with the prime minister, which sent a strong message that discrimination would not be tolerated.[33] In 2000, journalist Shmuel Schnitzer was awarded the prestigious Israel Prize, but the decision was reversed after an issue was made of a 1994 article he had written in *Ma'ariv* referring to the Falash Mura as being "infested with disease," particularly HIV. To the extent that the Ethiopian Jews are viewed negatively, it is usually because of stereo-typical views held by Israelis about Africans.

The Israeli government has also given the Ethiopians benefits above and beyond those typically given to immigrants or to veteran Israelis. They were accepted into the country despite the fact that they lacked skills and would require extraordinary expenditures to ease their absorption long before the country could hope to economically benefit from their citizenship. This is in stark contrast to many Russians who came highly educated and skilled and capable of making an immediate contribution to society. Israel has neverthe-less believed that in the long run the greatest resource it possesses is its popu-lation and the Ethiopians will ultimately make the country stronger. Still, it is likely to take several generations for the Ethiopian Jews to be fully assimi-lated into Israeli society. At that time, the truly triumphant nature of the return to Judaism and the Jewish homeland of this ancient community will become apparent to all.

NOTES

1. Daniel Friedman, "The Case of the Falas Mura," in Tudor Parfitt and Emanuela Trevisan Semi, eds., *The Beta Israel in Ethiopia and Israel: Studies on Ethio-pian Jews* (Surrey, Great Britain: Curzon Press, 1998), p. 72.

2. Chaim Motzen, "Report on the Felas Mora in Ethiopia," American Joint Distribution Committee, New York, 1999, p. 2.

3. Graenum Berger, *Rescue the Ethiopian Jews!* (NY: John Washburn Bleeker Hampton Publishing, 1996), p. 209.

4. Avi Granot, interview with author.

5. Motzen, "Report on the Felas Mora," p. 7.

6. Friedman, "The Case of the Falas Mura," p. 78.

7. Israeli Interior Ministry study cited in the *Forward*, February 18, 2000, pp. 1–2.

8. Abraham Rabinovich, "Clawing at Israel's Gates," *Moment*, December 1998; Yosef I. Abramowitz, "Zionism, Racism and the Ethiopian Question," *Moment*, August 1999; "'No Jews in Ethiopia,' Envoy Declares," *Forward*, August 18, 2000.

9. Friedman, "The Case of the Falas Mura," p. 79.

10. Motzen, "Report on the Felas Mora," pp. 11–13.

11. See, for example, Micha Odenheimer, "The Next Dilemma," *Jerusalem Report* (July 19, 1999), pp. 33–35.

12. "No Jews in Ethiopia," August 18, 2000.

13. Ibid.

14. Jewish Telegraphic Agency (JTA), March 28, 2000.

15. Julie Wiener, "Amid Tension Over Falash Mura, Israel Says It Needs $50 Million," *Forward*, November 17, 2000.

16. JTA, March 28, 2000.

17. Ethiopian Jews Slam U.S. Groups, *Jerusalem Post*, December 8, 2000.

18. "Ethiopia Report—October," United Jewish Communities, October 27, 2000.

19. As with all the population estimates, these numbers vary among sources. Some estimated the total number of Kwara Jews at 3,500.

20. Micha Odenheimer, "Relatives of Quara Jews Lament Another Lost Life," *Jerusalem Report*, May 10, 1999, p. 8.

21. Eli Wohlgelernter, "Anatomy of a Rescue," *Jerusalem Post*, August 13, 1999, pp. 18–19.

22. Micha Odenheimer, "Leave Your Gentile Spouses or Forget about Coming to Israel," *Jerusalem Report*, September 27, 1999.

23. Avi Machlis, "After Years of Frustration, Kwara Jews Are Euphoric," Jewish Telegraphic Agency, July 1999.

24. Steve Kaplan, interview with author.

25. "Ethiopian Immigrants Struggling, "Jewish Telegraphic Agency, January 3, 2002; Yossi Klein Halevi, "The Ethiopian Revolution," *Jerusalem Report*, September 24, 2001, pp. 13–14; Kaplan, interview; Nate Shapiro, interview with author.

26. Teshome Wagaw, *For Our Soul: Ethiopian Jews in Israel* (MI: Wayne State University Press, 1993), p. 89.

27. David Bar Ilan, "Ethiopian Immigrants Deserve More Than An Apology," *San Francisco Jewish Bulletin*, February 2, 1996.

28. Steven Kaplan and Hagar Salamon, "Ethiopian Immigrants in Israel: Experience and Prospects," Institute for Jewish Policy Research, No. 1, 1998.

29. Granot, interview.

30. Ibid.

31. Tamar Hausman, "U.S. Christians to Fund Ethiopian Aid Program," *Jerusalem Post*, January 28, 2000.

32. Kaplan and Salamon, "Ethiopian Immigrants."

33. Kaplan, interview.

Selected Bibliography

Abir, Mordechai. *Ethiopia and the Red Sea*. England: Frank Cass, 1980.

Ashkenazi, Michael, and Alex Weingrod. *Ethiopian Jews and Israel*. NJ: Transaction Publishing, 1988.

Avraham, Shmuel, and Arlene Kushner. *Treacherous Journey: My Escape from Ethiopia*. NY: Shapolsky, 1986.

Ben-Gurion, David. *Israel: Years of Challenge*. NY: Holt, Rinehart and Winston, 1963.

———. *Memoirs*. NY: World Publishing, 1970.

Berger, Graenum. *Rescue the Ethiopian Jews!* NY: John Washburn Bleeker Hampton Publishing, 1996.

Berman, Colette. *The Beautiful People of the Book: A Tribute to Ethiopian Jews in Israel*. Gefen Books, 1996.

Brecher, Michael. *Decisions in Israel's Foreign Policy*. CT: Yale University Press, 1975.

Farid, Majid Abdel, ed. *The Red Sea: Prospects for Stability*. England: Croom Helm, 1984.

Gruber, Ruth. *Rescue: The Exodus of the Ethiopian Jews*. NY: Atheneum, 1987.

Harris, Brice, Jr. *The United States and the Italo-Ethiopian Crisis*. CA: Stanford University Press, 1964.

Kaplan, Robert D. *The Arabists*. NY: The Free Press, 1995.

Kessler, David. *The Falashas: A Short History of the Ethiopian Jews*. England: Frank Cass & Co., 1996.

———. *The Falashas: The Forgotten Jews of Ethiopia*. NY: Schocken Books, 1985.

Kushner, Arlene. *Falasha No More: An Ethiopian Jewish Child Comes Home*. Xs Books, 1986.

Legum, Colin, ed. *Africa Contemporary Record*. NY: Africana Publishing, 1982.

Onolemhemhen, Durrenda Nash, and Kebede Gessesse. *The Black Jews of Ethiopia*. MD: Scarecrow Press, 1998.

Ostrovsky, Victor. *By Way of Deception*. NY: St. Martin's Press, 1990.

Ottaway, Marina. *Soviet and American Influence in the Horn of Africa*. NY: Praeger, 1981.

Parfitt, Tudor. *Operation Moses: The Untold Story of the Secret Exodus of the Falasha Jews from Ethiopia*. NY: Stein & Day, 1986.

Parfitt, Tudor, and Emanuela Trevisan Semi, eds. *The Beta Israel in Ethiopia and Israel: Studies on Ethiopian Jews*. Great Britain: Curzon Press, 1998.

Pearlman, Moshe. *Ben-Gurion Looks Back*. NY: Simon & Schuster, 1965.

Rafael, Gideon. *Destination Peace*. NY: Stein & Day, 1981.

Rapoport, Louis. *The Lost Jews: Last of the Ethiopian Falashas*. NY: Stein & Day, 1980.

———. *Redemption Song: The Story of Operation Moses*. CA: Harcourt Brace Javanovich, 1986.

Selassie, Bereket Habte. *Conflict and Intervention in the Horn of Africa*. NY: Monthly Review Press, 1980.

Stern, Henry. *Wanderings among the Falashas in Abyssinia*. NY: Frank Cass, 1968.

Syrkin, Marie, ed. *A Land of Our Own*. NY: G. P. Putnam's Sons, 1973.

Wagaw, Teshome. *For Our Soul: Ethiopian Jews in Israel*. MI: Wayne State University Press, 1993.

Westheimer, Ruth, and Steven Kaplan. *Surviving Salvation: The Ethiopian Jewish Family in Transition*. NY: New York University Press, 1993.

Yilma, Shmuel. *From Falasha to Freedom: An Ethiopian Jew's Journey to Jerusalem*. Jerusalem: Gefen Books, 1996.

Index

Abileah, Benjamin, 94–96
Abraham, Jed, 42
Abramowitz, Yossi, 194
Absorption (*klitah*), 118, 151, 153, 166, 199–200, 203–204
Abyssinia, 2, 5–6, 10, 41
Ackerman, Gary, 113
Adane, Rabbi Yosef, 178
Adane, Robell, 130–133
Addis Ababa, 10–11, 15, 17, 31–33, 39, 52, 60, 73, 78, 112, 171–174, 192–194, 196–198
Africa Confidential, 145
Africa(ns), 25–29, 31, 34, 36, 48, 83, 112, 116, 122, 152–153, 168, 201, 204
Agau, 2
Agudath Israel of America, 183
AIDS, 201
Akilu, Habta-Wald, 32
Aksum, 2
Aliyah, 18–19, 42, 44–48, 50–53, 63, 65–66, 69, 71, 77, 79, 117–118,
121, 135, 186, 192. *See also* Immigration
Alpert, Bernie, 105–107
Altneuland, 25
Ambober, 13, 44, 78
Amda Siyon, 5
American Association for Ethiopian Jews (AAEJ), 42, 50, 52–54, 59–74, 76–77, 79, 83–86, 88–101, 105, 107–110, 113–114, 116, 118–123, 125–137, 140, 149, 153, 161–162, 165, 168–172, 177, 179–186, 191, 193
American Israel Public Affairs Committee (AIPAC), 122, 185
American Jewish Committee, 48, 76, 179
American Jewish Congress, 184
American Jewish Press Association, 154, 166
American Joint Distribution Committee (AJDC), 8, 14, 39. *See also* Joint Distribution Committee

American Pro-Falasha Committee, 42
Americans for Peace Now, 196
American Zionist Emergency Council
    (AZEC), 185
Amharas, 15, 44, 73
Amharic, 3, 11
Amnesty International, 178
Andargeh Tegabeh, 14
Anti-Defamation League (ADL), 119,
    169
Anya-Aya rebels, 32
Arabia, 2
Arab League, 28, 30, 36, 145
Arab(s), 26–27, 29–35, 43, 51, 59, 99,
    135, 145, 147, 156–157, 166–167
Ark of the Covenant, 2
Asael, Tsfi, 12
Asmara, 10, 12, 30–31, 35, 51
Asrate Kassa, 32
Associated Press (AP), 155
Association of Ethiopian Jews in Israel,
    74, 93
Athens, 85, 87–89, 149
Auschwitz, 151
Avner, Yehuda, 77, 125
Avni, Dan, 26
Aynor, Chanan, 9, 15–16, 18, 33, 46–
    47, 64, 95, 97, 125, 144, 169

Baeda Maryam, 5
Baker, James, 171
Baltimore Jewish Times, 154
Bamaaracha, 69
Bandung Conference, 27–28
Barenbaum, Michael, 153, 155
Bar-Ilan, David, 201
Bar-Yehuda, Moshe, 11–12, 15
Bayer, Abe, 118, 154, 166
Beecher, William, 154
Beeri, Samuel, 11
Beersheva, 43
Begin, Menachem, 19, 35, 51, 59–60,
    62, 64, 67, 70–72, 75, 77, 84, 86,
    99, 121, 125, 135, 170
Belgium, 147–148
Ben-Gurion, David, 19, 28–30
Ben-Porat, Mordechai, 117, 134, 139
Bentwich, Norman, 13–15, 18, 39

Ben-Zvi, Yitzhak, 9, 15
Berger, Graenum, 10, 16, 41–43, 46,
    50–53, 60–61, 66–67, 72, 77, 83,
    87–88, 90, 92, 94–95, 106–108,
    111–112, 125, 127, 136–137, 149–
    150, 169, 186, 191
Bergman, Ami, 195
Bergson, Peter, 181–183
Berhani, Zimna, 72
Bernick, Paul, 179
Blazer, Phil, 154, 162–164, 166
Blumberg, Herschel, 119
Bogale, Yona, 11, 14, 16, 44, 74, 76,
    91
Bonker, Don, 112
Boschwitz, Rudy, 93, 113
Boston Globe, 154–155
Brazil, 31
Brecher, Michael, 27
Breger, Marshall, 166
British OSE Society, 15
Brother Daniel, 190
Bruce, James, 6
Buda, 3
Burg, Yosef, 8, 46–47, 49, 51
Bush, George, 163–164, 167, 172

Cadcaddy, Jack, 131
Cahn, Doug, 107, 109–110, 167–168
Calabia, Dawn, 93, 109, 114–117,
    161, 164
Canada, 40, 45, 136, 151
Canadian Association for Ethiopian Jews,
    74
Canadian Broadcasting Corporation, 157
Carter, Jimmy, 34–35, 62, 86
Castro, Fidel, 76
Central African Republic, 29
Central Conference of American Rabbis,
    8
Chanukah, 4
Chelouche, Rabbi David, 202
Chernin, Albert, 117
Christians, 2, 5, 9, 13–14, 17, 29, 39,
    44, 48, 69, 77, 84, 86, 89, 95, 148,
    178, 191–192, 194–195, 197;
    missionaries, 5–7, 16, 40, 44, 189–
    190

Church of England Mission to the Jews, 13
CIA, 51, 78, 146, 164, 167
Cohen, Scott, 168
Cohn, Robert, 154
Committee for a Jewish Army (CJA), 181–184
Committee for Assistance to the Falasha Population of Ethiopia, 15
Congo, 28
Congress Bi-Weekly, 42
Council of Jewish Federations, 70, 150
Cranston, Alan, 113, 162–163
Crocker, Chester, 116, 162
Cuba, 76
Cush, 2

Dacko, David, 29
D'Amato, Alfonse, 113, 162
Dan, tribe of, 2, 20
Davis, Richard, 153
Dayan, Moshe, 34, 63–64, 70
DeConcini, Dennis, 161
Demonstrations by Ethiopian Jews in Israel, 70–75, 125, 201
Dervishes, 5
Diamond, Marilyn, 116, 168
Dietary laws (*kashrut*), 2, 4, 64
Diredawa, 8
Divorce, 4
Dominitz, Yehuda, 10, 45–47, 51–52, 61, 63–64, 66, 68–69, 76, 83–84, 86–87, 90–91, 93, 95, 120, 134–136, 155, 169
Douglas, Eugene, 145, 167
Dulles, John Foster, 29–30
Dulzin, Aryeh, 71, 90, 93, 151, 153

Eban, Abba, 18–19, 60
Eckstein, Rabbi Yechiel, 202
Egged, 31
Egypt, 27–30, 34, 90, 148; peace treaty with Israel, 27, 72, 76, 99, 145
Eilat, 48, 136, 165
Eisenhower, Dwight D., 29–30
El Al, 88, 129, 173
Elazar, Rachamim, 70–71, 95–96, 171

el-Numeiry, Gaafar, 37, 68, 99, 143–145, 147, 156, 161–164, 166
Eritrean Liberation Front (ELF), 32
Eritrean People's Liberation Front (EPLF), 32, 36
Eritrea(ns), 31–35, 52, 72, 94, 96, 99, 111, 138, 157, 172, 198, 203
Ethiopia: civil war, 32, 59, 79, 83, 172; Dergue, 33, 35–36, 43, 64, 78; human rights, 34–35; relations with Israel, 29–33, 36, 48, 61, 64, 69, 171–172; revolution, 33, 43, 61, 178; schools, 7–13, 15, 17, 44–45, 47, 53, 65–66, 73, 78–79, 111, 113. *See also under individual cities and provinces*
Ethiopian Church, 2, 76
Ethiopian Democratic Union (EDU), 72–73, 84, 90
Ethiopian Jewry Caucus, 109, 171
Everett, Edith, 77, 90, 93

Fahn, Roberta, 119, 169
Faitlovitch, Jacques, 7–8, 10, 16, 20, 41–42
Falash Mura, 189–198, 203
Falasha Welfare Association (FWA), 39–40, 44, 50, 73, 77
Famine, 1, 40, 43, 79, 138, 146, 152, 156–157, 171
Feingold, Henry, 183
Feltman, David, 116, 168
Fenyevesi, Charles, 153
Ferede, 85–92, 100–101, 128–129, 134
Fishman, Hertzel, 137
France, 7, 135
Frank, Barney, 107, 113, 167
Freund, Lisa, 115–116, 162, 168
Freund, Miriam, 46
Friedenburg, Daniel, 10
Friedman, Daniel, 194
Friedman, Ted, 196
Friends of the Beta Israel (Falasha) Community in Ethiopia, The, 42

Gaffin, Barbara, 68, 109, 121, 152, 180

Galambos, Gabe, 129–133
Gaon, Nissim, 91–92
Gavariyahu, Rabbi Chaim, 11–12
Gedaref, 87, 89–91, 100, 128–31,
   133, 146, 165
Geez, 3–4
Germany, 7, 40, 46, 95, 135, 185;
   Frankfurt, 92, 94–95, 134, 165
Ghana, 28
Gilbert, Robin, 13–14, 66
Ginsberg, Ed, 40
Gol, Jean, 147
Goldstein, Israel, 18, 186
Gondar, 5, 8, 13, 15, 17, 40, 44, 59–
   60, 62, 65, 73, 76, 78–79, 87, 111,
   116, 122, 138, 141, 171, 178–179,
   194, 196–198
Goodman, Hirsh, 119
Goren, Rabbi Shlomo, 21, 43
Gotthold, Rabbi Zeev, 19
Granot, Avi, 202
Greenberg, Rabbi Irving, 120
Gross, David, 153
Gulf of Aqaba, 29
Gutelman, Georges, 147
Gwertzmann, Bernard, 154

Ha'aretz, 18, 63
Ha-Dani, Eldad, 2
Hadassah, 41, 46
Haifa, 31
Haile Selassie, 2, 13–15, 18–19, 30–
   33, 35, 43, 52, 73, 111, 157
Halacha(ic) (Jewish law), 15, 19–20,
   48, 183, 190
Halachmy, Haim, 42, 60, 62–63, 66,
   83, 85, 88, 91, 95–97, 106–107,
   137, 155–156, 163
Halevy, Joseph, 7
Halpern, Bill, 88–93
Harel, Dan, 16
Hebrew, 3, 10–11, 43–44, 47, 60, 65,
   72–73, 77–78, 114, 170, 178, 181,
   199–200
Hebrew Immigrant Aid Society
   (HIAS), 42, 45, 62–63, 70, 83, 88–
   90, 93–95, 156, 179

Hebrew University, 47, 61
Herzl, Theodor, 25
Herzog, Rabbi Yitzhak, 12
Hildesheimer, Rabbi Azriel, 6, 19
Hillel, Shlomo, 49, 51, 64, 72, 86, 90,
   96–98, 127, 169
Histadrut, 28
Hitler, Adolf, 185–186
Hogue, Warren, 154
Holland, 40
Holocaust, 25, 69, 72, 112, 115, 119,
   151–152, 164, 177–181, 183, 186–
   187, 190, 193
Horan, Hume, 146, 158
Horn of Africa, 29, 32, 34, 36, 97,
   118, 144–145
Houphouet-Boigny, Felix, 28
Human rights, 110, 116, 179
Hyman, Shari, 66

Immigration, 21, 36, 48, 60, 63, 75,
   85, 90, 111, 117, 120, 155, 157,
   161, 171, 173, 181, 189–198, 202,
   204. See also Aliyah
Institute of Applied Social Research, 47
International Fellowship of Christians
   and Jews, 198, 202
International Red Cross (IRC), 89, 161
Iran, 29–30, 68, 71, 97, 156
Iraq, 8, 71, 90, 97
Irgun, 182
Isaiah, 2
Israel: aid to Africa, 28–29, 31;
   Foreign Ministry, 14, 16–18, 26,
   75–76, 85, 95; Interior Ministry, 87,
   198; Interministerial Commission,
   21; Knesset, 28, 71, 74–75, 117,
   156, 180, 195, 202; Law of Return,
   20, 46–50, 172, 192–193, 195, 197;
   military aid to Ethiopia, 34, 36, 51–
   52, 60–61, 63, 157, 172; Ministry of
   Absorption, 47, 50; Ministry of
   Health, 16; Ministry of Religion, 19;
   peace treaty with Egypt, 27, 72, 76,
   99, 145; relations with Ethiopia, 9,
   18–19, 30–33, 48, 61, 64, 69, 171;
   relations with the United States, 60;
   Supreme Court, 195, 202

Israel Association for Ethiopian Jews (IAEJ), 191
Israel Today, 54, 153–154
Italy, 7–8, 14, 30–31

Jacobovici, Simcha, 150, 169
Jacobson, Gaynor, 89
Jeroboam, 2
Jerusalem, 2, 4, 6–7, 12, 30–31, 41, 62, 65, 68, 74, 143
Jerusalem Post, 44, 50, 61, 74, 84, 119, 133, 156, 198, 201
Jesus, 2
Jewish Agency, 9–15, 18, 20, 43–48, 52–53, 61–63, 66–67, 71, 74–76, 85, 87–90, 92, 95, 110, 118, 120, 135–137, 147, 151, 155–156, 167, 172, 186, 194, 198
Jewish Chronicle, 39
Jewish Colonization Association (JCA), 15, 17–18, 42, 71
Jewish Horizon, The, 9, 54
Jewishness of Ethiopians, 15, 18–20, 47, 49, 71, 117, 184, 189, 193–194, 197, 202; circumcision, 2, 20, 201–202; conversion ("renewal"), 18, 20–21, 46, 201–202
Jewish Post and Opinion, 45
Jewish Press, The, 184
Jewish Student Press Service, 95
Jews, 90; Ashkenazic, 21; Indian, 19; Sephardic, 21, 54; Syrian, 118; Yemenite, 8–10, 54, 193, 196
Joint Distribution Committee (JDC), 40, 45, 48, 50, 65–66, 70, 72, 77, 95, 138, 172, 179, 186, 191–197; American Joint Distribution Committee (AJDC), 8, 14, 39
Joint Emergency Committee on European Affairs (JEC), 184
Judaism, 2–4, 6–7, 10–11, 21, 111, 172, 180, 190, 192, 194–195, 197, 203–204; Conservative, 3, 20; Orthodox, 3–4, 20, 47, 75, 183–184, 195, 203; Reform, 3, 20, 122
Judith, Queen, 4–5

Kaplan, Robert, 146

Kaplan, Steve, 199
Karaites, 20
Kavy, A.H., 42
Kay, Julian, 39–40, 44–45, 50–51
Kenya (also Nairobi), 51, 83, 89, 110, 128–131, 133–134, 136
Kerness, Elton, 152
Kes Debetra Gothe Assress, 14
Kessler, David, 18, 39, 50, 77
Khartoum, 84–5, 87–90, 92, 95, 99–100, 126, 128–132, 134, 136, 139, 146–149, 155, 163–164
Khashoggi, 164
Kfar Batya, 10, 12–13, 20, 41
Kidane, Tesfaye, 172
Kimche, David, 90
King Hassan, 145
King Solomon, 2, 41, 173
Kirkpatrick, Jeanne, 43
Klass, Shlomo, 184
Kohane, Akiva, 72, 179
Kook, Rabbi Isaac, 12
Koor, 50
Krieger, Richard, 140, 145–146, 162–164, 167, 169
Kwara, 11, 189; Jews, 197–199, 203

Labor Party, 49
L'Alliance Israélite Universelle (AIU), 7
Lantos, Tom, 109, 113
Lapid, Yosef, 158
Lastah massacre, 44–45
Lavi, Naftali, 154
Lebanon, 30, 36, 68, 90, 128
Leeder, Sandy, 129
Lehman, Chanan, 71
LeLand, Mickey, 113–114
Lenhoff, Howard, 43, 53–54, 60, 64–67, 69–71, 83–85, 91, 94–96, 105, 107–8, 115, 118, 135, 137, 149–150, 181, 183
Levy, David, 71
Levy, Gershon, 40, 65–66
Levy, H.G., 17
Libya, 32, 145
Liel, Alon, 85
Liewant, Sidney, 179

Lipstadt, Deborah, 186
Litvek, Yosef, 47–48, 54
London Observer, 136
London Society for Promoting
    Christianity, 6
Longet, Daniel, 85, 87–90, 92, 100–
    101, 128
Long Island Jewish World, 153
Los Angeles Times, 52–53, 146
Lourie, Arthur, 18
Lyman, Princeton, 163, 167

Ma'ariv, 48, 155, 158
Maimonides, 147
Marriage, 4
Martens, Wilfried, 147
Massala, Adisu, 195
McGovern, George, 76
Meir, Golda, 19, 25–26, 28
Melaku Teferra, 78–79, 111, 138, 141
Menelik, 2, 5
Mengistu, Haile-Mariam, 34–36, 43,
    51, 60, 62, 114, 171–173
Miami Herald, 135–137
Morocco, 8, 145
Moses, 3, 20
Mossad, 31, 34, 36–37, 52, 60–61, 72,
    75, 84–87, 93, 97–98, 100, 126–
    130, 133–134, 138–140, 143–144,
    146–149, 165, 173, 180
Muslim(s), 5, 7–8, 13, 27, 29, 32–33,
    35–36, 84, 114, 146–147, 156, 164

Nadjer, Jean-Claude, 179
Nairobi Standard, 133, 136
Narkiss, Uzi, 43, 53
Nasser, Gamal, 27, 30–31
Nathan, Abie, 122
National Council of Jewish Women, 8
National Jewish Community Relations
    Advisory Council (NJCRAC), 93,
    112–113, 117–119, 121, 136, 139,
    154, 163, 166, 180, 182, 184–186
National Religious Party, 46, 75
Negus Claudius, 5
Negus Ishak, 5
Negus Susenyos, 5
Nekuda, 155

Netanyahu, Benjamin, 193
Newman, Aryeh, 11
New Republic, The, 73
New Testament, 2–3
New York Times, 90, 105, 136–137,
    150, 154–155, 158, 161–162
Niles Safari, 131
Nissim, Moshe, 75
Nissim, Yitzhak, 12
Nixon, Richard, 33
Nkrumah, Kwame, 28
North, Oliver, 68
North Africa, 54, 119
North American Conference on
    Ethiopian Jewry (NACOEJ), 121,
    190–195, 197
North American Jewish Student
    Network, 59, 74

Oil, 29
Olympic Airways, 88
Operation Magic Carpet, 95
Operation Moses, 42, 69, 97–98, 109–
    110, 113, 129, 137, 141, 143–144,
    146, 149–152, 154, 156–158, 161,
    164
Operation Sheba ("Joshua"), 109, 141,
    163, 165–167, 170–171, 185
Operation Solomon, 172–173, 189–
    192, 197
Oral Law, 3, 20
Organization for Rehabilitation and
    Training (ORT), 13, 40–41, 65–66,
    70, 73, 76, 78–79, 87, 95, 97, 113,
    179
Organization of African Unity (OAU),
    27, 32–33, 171
O'Rourke, Thomas, 129–133
Ottaway, David, 51
Ovadia, Hezi, 19, 42, 46

Palestine, 30, 41, 182
Palestine Liberation Organization
    (PLO), 32, 36, 156
Pan-Arabism, 27, 32
Paran, Mordecai, 42, 52
Parfitt, Tudor, 65, 97, 133, 135–136
Parnes, Henry, 135–136

Passover, 4, 11
Percy, Charles, 110, 133, 168
Peres, Shimon, 155–156, 158, 165
Poran, Ephraim, 19, 51, 61, 68, 75, 84, 91, 97–98, 126–127, 134, 144, 149
Port Sudan, 88, 90, 100, 126, 147
Powers, Charles, 146
Priests (*kes, kessim, kohanim*), 3–4, 10–11, 16, 44–45, 202
Pritzker, A.N., 106, 108

Queen of Sheba, 2, 41

Rabbinical Council of America, 195
Rabin, Yitzhak, 50, 60, 62
Racism, 46–47, 53–54, 120, 158, 193, 201, 203
Rafael, Gideon, 64
Ramati, Shaul, 75, 95
Rapoport, Louis, 16, 19, 40, 44–46, 49–50, 61, 73, 84–85, 100, 109, 133–137, 139, 144, 150, 152, 186
Raymist, Malkah, 9, 12, 54
Reagan, Ronald, 163, 165–167, 185
Realpolitik, 26
Recant, Will, 171
Red Sea, 29, 33, 48, 83, 129, 136
Rehoboam, 2
Rescue, 41–43, 45–46, 50–51, 53, 59–60, 62–64, 67–70, 74–76, 79, 83–97, 109, 120, 122, 126, 128, 134–136, 146, 151, 153, 156, 158, 170, 178, 180–184, 187, 189, 191, 196; airlift, 62, 98, 126–127, 139–141, 143–144, 146–150, 153–154, 157, 162–167, 169, 172–173, 198; arms for Jews, 34, 51, 61–63, 68, 171; Frankfurt operation, 92, 94–95, 134; Juba affair, 129–134, 136; publicity, 50, 73–74, 135–137, 140, 149–156, 161, 170, 180, 183–184; sea route, 126, 136, 147. *See also* Operation Moses; Operation Sheba; and Operation Solomon
Resnikoff, Bernard, 48
Reuters, 155
Rhodesia (now Zimbabwe), 27

Ribacove, Barbara, 121, 194
Robbins, Alan, 163
Rockowitz, Eli, 118
Roebel, Mahariya, 78–79
Roosevelt, Franklin, 185
Rosenberg, Henry, 111–112, 115–116, 128–131, 133–134
Rosenblatt, Gary, 154
Rosenfeld, Alexander, 9
Rosenne, Meir, 114, 144
Russia, 26, 108

Sabbath (*Shabbat*), 2, 4, 6, 8, 64–65, 73, 111, 149, 173
Sabi, Uthman Salih, 32
Sadat, Anwar, 27, 62, 145
Safire, William, 158
Sapir, Pinchas, 53, 63
Saudi Arabia, 29, 33–35, 147, 168
Say, Peggy, 68
Schneider, Michael, 194
Sebag, Gabi, 49
Seko, Mobutu Sese, 28
Seyoum, David, 77–78
Shamir, Yitzhak, 144, 172–173
Shapiro, Nate, 65, 76, 83, 86, 90–91, 94–98, 105–108, 116, 122, 125, 128–130, 133–134, 137, 150, 162, 168, 171, 180, 185
Sharon, Ariel, 198
Sherer, Moshe, 183
Sh'ma, 54
Shultz, George, 117
Siggud, 44, 203
Simon Wiesenthal Center, 74
Sivan, Yehuda, 10, 12
Slave Trade, 26–27, 72–73, 179
Solarz, Stephen, 93, 109, 113–114, 116, 161
Somalia, 29, 31, 33, 35, 62, 110–111
South Africa, 27
Soviet (Russian) Jews, 36, 43, 53, 69, 74–75, 110, 115, 118, 184, 193–194, 202, 204
Soviet Union, 30, 34–36, 43, 53, 59–60, 62, 64, 69, 85, 110, 115, 118, 184, 193, 196; Russia, 26, 108
S.S. St. Louis, 185

Standing Conference of Organizations
  Interested in the Welfare of the
  Falashas, 39
Stein, Glenn, 122, 138, 156, 181
Stern, Henry, 6
St. Louis Jewish Light, 154
Straits of Tiran, 29
Sudan, 1, 7, 19, 32, 36–37, 67, 78–79,
  83–93, 95–99, 101, 109–110, 113–
  114, 116, 126–128, 132–138, 143,
  145–149, 152–158, 161, 163–168,
  170, 191, 197. *See also under*
  individual cities
Suez War, 29, 31
Suicide, 170, 200–201
Sweden, 75
Switzerland, 7, 40, 91–92, 135, 146–
  147
Synagogue, 4–5
Syria, 30, 50, 59, 71, 90
Szold, Henrietta, 41

Talmud, 3
Tamir, Yuli, 196
Tannenbaum, Rabbi Marc, 179
Tarfon, Rafi, 40
Tartakower, Aryeh, 42, 46, 49–52, 61–
  63, 66, 85
Tayeb, Omar, 146, 164, 166
Technion, 31
Tegegne, Baruch, 84, 89–90, 92, 94
Tel Aviv, 28, 63, 71, 89, 101, 106, 148
Temeskin, Haile, 94, 128
Tigre, 3, 5, 77, 111, 141, 172, 178
Togo, 26
Trans European Airlines (TEA), 147–
  148, 155
Tribble, Paul, 161
Tsaban, Yair, 192
Tubman, William, 28
Tukul(s), 3, 12, 195
Tunney, John, 115
Turgeman, Eli, 76, 78, 83–84
Turkey, 29–30
Tuwawa, 126, 146–148, 165

Uganda, 128
Ullendorf, Edward, 15

Umm Rekuba, 126, 139, 146, 148
Union of American Hebrew Congregations
  (UAHC), 122, 138, 156, 181
Union of Orthodox Rabbis, 183
United Jewish Appeal (UJA), 75, 106,
  119, 149, 151–153, 166, 182
United Jewish Communities (UJC),
  196–197
United Nations, 27, 31, 34; General
  Assembly, 26; High Commissioner
  for Refugees (UNHCR), 85, 90,
  132–133, 139, 161; Zionism is
  "racism" resolution, 33, 54
United States, 26, 29–36, 40, 43, 50,
  62, 73–74, 83, 94, 96, 99, 110,
  114–115, 127, 134–136, 145–147,
  151, 154, 156, 161, 173, 182, 184,
  194; Agency for International
  Development (USAID), 77, 132–
  133; Congress, 107, 109–110, 114,
  116–117, 122, 133, 145, 162, 164–
  165, 167–168, 184–185; relations
  with Ethiopia, 108–109, 116–118,
  179; relations with Israel, 60, 152,
  169, 172; relations with the Sudan,
  37, 68, 143–145, 155, 162, 164–
  165, 167; State Department, 31, 35,
  60, 62, 73, 109, 112, 115–116, 120,
  133, 137, 140, 144, 146, 149–150,
  153–154, 158, 162–165, 167–169,
  179
United Synagogue of America, 8
Uria, Gedalia, 60

Waldman, Rabbi Menachem, 192
Wall Street Journal, 137
Washington Jewish Week, 153
Washington Post, 51, 136–137, 173
Waysman, Dvora, 179
Weaver, Jerry, 139, 146–149, 158, 164–
  166
Weintraub, Jerry, 163
Weise, Barry, 154
Weiss, Ted, 109
Weizman, Ezer, 59
Winston, Diane, 8
Wolkait, 7, 141
Wolpe, Tom, 113, 116

World Jewish Congress (WJC), 14–15, 39, 75
World Zionist Organization, 9
World Zionist Press Service, 179
Written Law (Torah), 3, 16, 20
Wuzuba, 12
Wyman, David, 185

Yakob, Zarra, 5
Yanowitz, Bennett, 119–120, 186
Yediot Aharanot, 155
Yerday, Avraham, 74
Yeshayahu, Yisrael, 9
Yitzhak, Rachamim, 77–79, 110, 115

Yom Kippur War, 53
Yona, Zacharias, 72, 74, 94, 179
Yosef, Rabbi Ovadia, 20–21, 46, 49, 53, 183
Youth Aliyah, 42, 46

Zaire, 132–133
Zeigerman, Dror, 180
Zimra, David ben Solomon ibn Avi (Radbaz), 19
Zionism (Zionists), 21, 25, 32, 54, 59, 69, 73, 77–78, 99, 156–158, 166, 172, 182–184, 190, 193
Zohar, David, 54

About the Author

MITCHELL G. BARD is the Executive Director of the nonprofit American-Israeli Cooperative Enterprise (AICE) and a foreign policy analyst who lectures frequently on U.S.-Middle East Policy.